Debatable Diversity

Critical Perspectives Series
General Editor: Donaldo Macedo
A book series dedicated to Paulo Freire

Debatable Diversity: Critical Dialogues on Change in American Universities
by Raymond V. Padilla and Miguel Montiel

Forthcoming:

Pedagogy of Freedom
by Paulo Freire
Ideology Matters
by Paulo Freire and Donaldo Macedo
Cuba's Economic Crisis
by Elisa Facio
Latinos Unidos: Ethnic Solidarity in Linguistic, Cultural, and Social Diversity
by Enrique Trueba

Debatable Diversity

Critical Dialogues on Change in American Universities

Raymond V. Padilla
and
Miguel Montiel

ROWMAN & LITTLEFIELD PUBLISHERS, INC.
Lanham • Boulder • New York • Oxford

ROWMAN & LITTLEFIELD PUBLISHERS, INC.

Published in the United States of America
by Rowman & Littlefield Publishers, Inc.
4720 Boston Way, Lanham, Maryland 20706

12 Hid's Copse Road
Cumnor Hill, Oxford OX2 9JJ, England

*The views expressed in this book represent the professional ideas, experiences,
opinions, perceptions, and understandings of the authors alone, with the sole
purpose of assessing and improving the American system of higher education.*

British Library Cataloguing in Publication Information Available

Library of Congress Cataloging-in-Publication Data

Padilla, Raymond V.
   Debatable diversity : critical dialogues on change in American
universities / Raymond V. Padilla and Miguel Montiel.
      p.   cm.
   Includes bibliographical references and index.
   ISBN 0-8476-8730-9 (cloth : alk. paper). — ISBN 0-8476-8731-7
(pbk. : alk. paper)
   1. Education, Higher–Aims and objections—United States.
   2. Minorities—Education (Higher)—United States. 3. Hispanic
Americans—Education (Higher)   4. Universities and colleges—United
States—Sociological aspects.   5. Higher education and state—United
States.   6. Educational change—United States.   I. Montiel, Miguel.
II. Title.
LA227.4.P33   1998
378.73—DC21   97-4397 CIP

ISBN 0-8476-8730-9 (cloth : alk. paper)
ISBN 0-8476-8731-7 (pbk. : alk. paper)

Printed in the United States of America
⊗™ The paper used in this publication meets the minimum requirements of American
National Standard for Information Sciences—Permanence of Paper for Printed Library
Materials, ANSI Z39.48–1984.

To Paulo Freire,
who reminded us that the ontological vocation
of humans
is to become more human
and that to know
is to know through critical dialogue

.

Contents

Foreword[1]

Rubén Martinez

Universities have served different interests since their beginnings in religious orders several centuries ago. American colleges emerged from established religious, political, and social conventions and served "special interests" through the end of the nineteenth century (Jencks & Riesman, 1969). The rise of land grant universities and graduate programs in the 1860s transformed established curricula by including new disciplines and subjects, and through the promotion of "electives" and "academic freedom." Departments became the basic academic units, and traditional authority was replaced by bureaucratic authority. By the 1960s, when Chicana/os and other ethnic minority groups entered American universities in "substantial" numbers, the American university had been for a number of years a central part of the military–industrial complex that resulted from the cold war (Aguirre & Martinez, 1993; Nieburg, 1970; Wright, 1993).

The entry of Chicana/os and other previously excluded ethnic minority groups into the academy occurred in the context of rapid social and institutional changes. Like many other institutions, colleges and universities were greatly impacted by the civil rights movement and by the political and industrial shifts that characterized the period (Wright, 1993). Since that decade, societal changes have accelerated and expanded. Today's colleges and universities face immense challenges at the level of objective societal changes (cultural, demographic, economic, global, and technological) and at the level of institutional and political responses to such changes (including public accountability[2] and relative declines in state funding).

It is in this context that ethnic minorities in general, and Chicana/os in particular, begin the daunting task of engaging in collective self-reflection about their lives in the academy.[3] Every step explores new ground, both institutionally and intellectually. A Chicana/o intelligentsia did not exist within the academy until very recently, and only now can the systematic analysis of this intelligentsia begin.[4] The first major generation of Chicana/os scholars is today part of the senior academic ranks (albeit small in terms of overall representation), and collective reflection on Minority and Chicana/o life in the academy (that is, the workplace) is not only possible but the logical next step in the evolution of this particular intelligentsia. How have ethnic minorities, such as Chicana/os, adapted to life in the academy, not as students but as faculty and as academic administrators?

Workplace issues such as relations with colleagues, promotions, roles and responsibilities, programmatic initiatives and program development come quickly to mind (see Aguirre, Martinez & Hernández, 1993; Martinez, Hernández & Aguirre, 1993/94; Aguirre, Hernández & Martinez, 1994). In the present context of widespread restructuring of higher education and the establishment of "new generation" and "responsive" institutions, all faculty are impacted (Newson, 1994). But Chicana/os, as representatives of an ethnic minority group, are experiencing the academy as a "new frontier" whereas American faculty are experiencing it as a changing institution.

The cultures of Chicana/o and American faculty often clash as the former group's members learn the norms and processes of their new environment, and the members of the latter group struggle to retain control in the face of perceived internal and external threats. The internal threats are presented not only by Chicana/os, but by the broader category of faculty of color — African Americans, Native Americans, and Asian Americans — and by American women, who tend to pursue parallel agendas of access and social justice (however these groups define these concepts). The external threats stem from a rapidly changing environment, hostile legislators, and publics critical of access, costs, quality, and productivity.

The cold war institution that Chicana/os entered in the 1960s was one that emphasized teaching, research, and service. This was a period of both unparalleled wealth and paranoia about communism. The embeddedness of higher education in cold war activities had several significant effects: 1) the growth of universities, 2) the idea of higher education as an entitlement and as a necessary aspect of national defense, 3) the sanctity and secrecy of "research," 4) the fragmentation of knowledge, 5) the concept of "peer review" as the main yardstick of validity, 6) the creation of a national marketplace for professors, 7) a sense of commitment to the profession and nation rather than to the state or the institution, 8) the development of research sites and facilities supportive of the military–industrial complex (that is, the development of secret weapons), 9) the victory in the cold war, 10) and present–day questions about the parts of the cold war machinery that should be retained, along with questions about their costs and purposes (Juhasz & Martinez, 1996).

Today's academy is greatly impacted by the continuing conversion from a military–industrial to a post–military–industrial society. Indeed, the role of today's university has become ambiguous given the loss of purpose that came with success in the cold war. Public expectations of faculty are changing and, consequently, the roles of faculty are beginning to change—there is more emphasis on teaching and mentoring. Toward this end, reward structures are being changed, albeit slowly, to further promote changes in faculty roles. In this context, Raymond Padilla and Miguel Montiel, both senior faculty members at Arizona State University, have set in motion a critical dialogue on change in the academy. This dialogue is part of the context of change impacting the academy, and should concern all segments of higher education because it brings forth viewpoints based on marginal social positions, which—as George Simmel and Karl Marx pointed out a hundred years ago— afford profound insights into social reality.

The dialogue is a necessary feature in the evolution of the Chicana/o intelligentsia. The subject of Padilla and Montiel's reflexivity is primarily their experiences as Chicano faculty members at Arizona State University (ASU) over the past fifteen or so years. The dialogue is frank and insightful—the latter being a function of the former. *Debatable Diversity* not only establishes a new plane of discourse for Chicana/os, it presents a rhetorical approach in the framework of the late Paulo Freire (1970a, 1970b, 1973, 1985). Padilla and Montiel approach their subject as creative beings who problematize their existential situations at ASU and bring the full force of their knowledge about the world to bear on those situations. Their aim is to deepen their understanding of the workings of the institution and of the range of behavioral, cultural, and attitudinal adaptations among Chicana/o faculty.

With broad experiences as faculty members and as administrators, Padilla and Montiel examine the successes and failures of their efforts to promote initiatives in universities that they believed would benefit Chicana/os, minorities, and the campus in general. Because Chicana/o faculty and administrators in particular, and minorities in general, are dispersed across many colleges and universities, they often feel isolated and relatively powerless. The dialogue initiated by Padilla and Montiel should help many to overcome the isolation by linking them to a conversation about common experiences among them.

To be sure, Padilla and Montiel are explorers in a frontier that is new to them as Chicana/os, as members of an oppressed ethnic minority group that, for all intents and purposes, had been completely excluded from the academy through processes of institutional racism (Aguirre & Martinez, 1993). Ironically, the academy is at the same time somewhat known by Chicana/os, as it is the *situs* of the Chicano Student Movement, which was a core component of *El Movimiento* of the 1960s. So, now the talk has started about the workplace experiences of Chicana/o scholars, and the collective discourse will inevitably yield new understandings of their experiences and those of other ethnic minorities. At another level, that of the production of knowledge, the dialogue will establish more firmly "Chicana/o life in the academy" as the subject matter for systematic research and study.

As the dialogue in this book demonstrates, much light is shed on the workings of the academy through the discursive approach. While the insights are not the result of formal, more systematic approaches, they are insights nonetheless — and formal study can begin with the rich soil uncovered by Padilla and Montiel.

There is a dialectical interplay between academic culture and individual behaviors. As Tierney (1997) has correctly pointed out, an institution of higher education does not have a unitary culture that assimilates members of the academy. To be sure, there are behavioral expectations relative to teaching, research, and service, but expectations differ across disciplines and colleges (Tierney, 1988). Moreover, it is certainly the case that individuals impact institutional cultures. There is an interplay between the two levels whereby individuals are socialized sufficiently into the institutional culture to be acceptable, at the same time the individual interprets, negotiates, promotes and/or resists, and modifies the prevailing culture.

Aronowitz and Giroux (1991) would cast the dialogue by Padilla and Montiel as part of the postmodern dynamics of the academy wherein the voices of the excluded reject the unitarian culture promoted by Americans (mostly American males) in favor of a more radical democracy. Whether or not such casting is appropriate remains to be seen; however, what is clear from the Padilla–Montiel dialogue is that the academy is rife with power politics — struggles among individuals and groups to promote their interests and values within the academy.

Chicana/o faculty (that is, those who are self avowedly Chicana/os as opposed to calling themselves Hispanics or some other label that is palatable to Americans) frequently pursue a Chicana/o agenda — one that most often seeks to increase access to educational and employment opportunities, and to improve retention of Chicana/os at all levels of the academy by changing the institutions themselves. Such changes are reducible to the politics of the reallocation of resources in a context of value frameworks in which American–controlled units pay homage to diversity but do not elevate it to a funding priority of consequence.

In the pursuit of a Chicana/o agenda, Chicana/o faculty struggle to maintain a safe distance from the dominant culture that threatens to coopt them. The dominant culture of the academy seeks to assimilate them into individual roles that emphasize American–centered norms, conformity, acceptance, and service. To be a critical Chicana/o scholar requires the constant pursuit of social justice, as Padilla so eloquently states in the early stages of the "conversation." It is this constant pursuit of social justice that clashes with the culture of the academy. This clash occurs at many levels, including those of interaction norms, standards of excellence, and resource allocation. The academy, like the broader American society, values social justice as an abstraction but tends to ignore it in the pursuit of other values (e.g., success, excellence, efficiency, etc.), all of which are framed in western terms.

Academic politics, we often hear, are the worst type among the many types of politics — meaning they are the most difficult for survival. The veracity of this view is not altogether clear, but the idea of highly intelligent individuals does not, in and of itself, exclude intense passions and pathological personalities. The passions and intellectual capacities combine shared governance structures to produce highly engaging and, in my view, neurotic politics.

Certainly the structure of the workplace minimizes hierarchies under the values of openness and collegiality, but selected "interest groups" among faculty and administrators shape priorities and the allocation of funds across units and programs within the parameters of the overall interests of specific institutions. Formal and informal hierarchies are created, maintained, and changed by strong personalities and interest groups.

Not only is there a continual clash between the priorities of ethnic minorities and their Euro-American counterparts, but there are divisions among minority groups and within and among Chicana/os themselves that constitute the context in which Chicana/o initiatives are promoted. For instance, there are Chicana/os who are willingly used by Americans against other Chicana/os. Whether in pursuit of their own personal interests or for other reasons, some Chicana/os become willing pawns in American efforts to resist minority–initiated institutional changes. Power politics makes clear the need for Chicana/o, and other ethnic minority, scholars to pay attention to egos when pursuing initiatives in the academy — after all, academic egos often express their pathologies as political agendas.

One of the most illuminating features of the Padilla–Montiel dialogue has to do with the internal workings of the academy. These Chicana/o argonauts are greatly interested in learning more about the terrain they traverse and, like ethnic minority faculty in general, are interested in learning the ways of the academy. They reflect upon Chicana/o initiatives and how the latter are moved through the institution. They pay close attention to the positions of other minority groups vis-à-vis Chicana/o-driven initiatives. They consider the shared governance context and its conditioning of the general process. They discuss the strategies employed by faculty and administrators in relation to specific initiatives.

Padilla and Montiel examine events and activities in order to make political sense of what happened — ultimately, for the purpose of shaping the political contexts of their future initiatives. In a sense, this reflexive exercise functions, on one level, as a type of "tactical debriefing." Knowing the factors that impinge upon and shape administrative decisions can enhance the likelihood of realizing specific goals. The pursuit of administrative careers, for example, is circumscribed by decision-making pitfalls that quickly shorten seemingly outstanding careers. In such contexts, certain decisions are not probable though possible. In other words, decisions may be made on the basis of perceived political consequences and not on the basis of what is best for the institution. It may be, as Padilla argues, that senior- and middle-level administrative leadership has been subordinated to the achievement of the next promotion.

Today, there is a loud call from many quarters for new leadership in higher education. The new leadership is expected to be visionary and bold — one that does not place career interests first, but which places institutional achievements and excellence first. Of course, where there is a cacophony of voices there also is a multiplicity of visions. "New leadership," from a Chicana/o perspective, ensures that Chicana/o agendas are part of the institution's vision. Like Padilla and Montiel, I do not mean the augmentation of the dominant agenda with an additional program for Hispanics, but one that incorporates the objective interests and educational needs of Chicana/os and other oppressed groups as part of the pursuit of a real educational democracy — one devoid of racial practices.

Is the academy truly a beacon of light in society?[5] Can it be such in one marked by multiple tensions and conflicts that threaten to break it apart? What are the qualities of such an institution? The values of academic freedom, collegiality, and excellence are essential to such a role. In practice, however, "academic politics" undermine these values. Conflicts over theoretical paradigms, academic programs, resources, and new hires often result in long-term animosities among "colleagues," and both winners and losers bide their time — waiting for years for the opportunity to "punish their enemies." Montiel speaks of such an instance in the very first page when he points out that an "enemy" of his sought to get "revenge" for an earlier "run-in" by trying to derail the establishment of the Hispanic Research Center. Admittedly, this is a perception on the part of Montiel, but every seasoned academician knows that this is the "stuff" of academic politics. The question that arises regarding such a situation is this, "Can academicians rise above their local politics to serve the higher ideals of the academy?"

Not only is new administrative leadership needed, new faculty leadership also is greatly needed. In a post–cold war context, many faculty have retrenched and are dragging their feet relative to the changing role of the university, especially in the publicly funded ones. The research university model remains in their minds prominent and attractive, but it may be obsolete in a post–military–industrial context. Moreover, faculty members sometimes hold personal values dearly even if they are in conflict with institutional values. For instance, an institution may value diversity, but individual faculty members may not—indeed, they may oppose diversity—and they undermine institutional achievement in this area by pressuring administrators to pursue other priorities. These pressures may be worked through external networks that link them to legislators and other influential members of the community. Can this conflict of values be framed as a conflict of interest between personal and institutional values? Should there be room for bigots and racists in the academy? These are some of the issues faculty must consider when clarifying expectations relative to professional deportment. How else can the academy serve as a beacon of democracy in society?

Padilla and Montiel raise many profound issues in this "talking book." As with all conversations, the discussion takes many twists and turns, but these meanderings yield many panoramic insights for us to enjoy and ponder. The authors are brutally honest in their discussions. Issues are brought out in the open that often only are heard in whispered conversations in offices with closed doors. "Off the record" conversations are presented here to reveal the real workings of the academy, at least within the sectors familiar to Padilla and Montiel.

Should these private conversations be made public? Yes. Absolutely they must! One of the great travesties of American democracy is that those in power structure "public" choices to give the appearance of democratic practices, yet rarely do the needs and concerns of a "diverse public" structure the choices. Padilla and Montiel rip away the veil shrouding the power politics of the academy to reveal aspects of its actual practices. Within the institution there are interest groups that include administrators, faculty, staff, and students. Each of these categories is subdivisible along many dimensions of special interests, each situated differently on hierarchies of status, power, and class. These subcategories are differentially linked to external networks of influence and interests that impact the operation of the academy. Of course, the institution maintains such links as a routine matter of operation.

Despite the value of autonomy, the academy is not insulated from the broader political struggles in the locality where it is situated, nor from those at regional or national levels. Recent conservative cultural movements, for instance, under the leadership of William Bennett and others, have sought to reaffirm and, where deemed necessary, reinstate the canon of Western civilization. In general, students are expected to adapt to the precepts of society, while the gap between democratic principles and practices continues to widen. This "talking book" is significant even if all that it does is ask us to consider the gaps in democracy that exist in our institutions of higher education. This is a particularly timely subject given the need for universities to convert to a post–military–industrial order.

One of the primary emphases in the conversion or restructuring discourse of the academy is "responsiveness." Universities are expected to address the needs of their service areas by reinventing themselves so that the elements of the traditional triad of teaching, research, and service stand as equals in terms of institutional responsibilities. In this model, faculty are called upon to meet the needs of increasingly diverse student populations, to conduct locally relevant research, and to demonstrate loyalty and commitment to the institution (as opposed to being loyal to their disciplines and being oriented toward national markets).

The traditional model (that is, the research university) called upon faculty to serve American democracy by helping protect it from communism. Excellence was achieved by maximizing opportunities for individual talent to move about in a national marketplace that brought talent and research resources together. In contrast, the "responsive institution" model seeks to bring the expertise and knowledge of the faculty to bear on local and regional issues as a means of helping the nation address problems of economic and community development, domestic violence, gang violence, poverty, educational mediocrity, and so on.

More generally, however, the nation is wracked by culture wars (i.e., identity politics) that threaten to bring into existence either a higher order of democracy or a retrograde order that refuses to transcend the institutionalized "isms" that gave rise to the culture wars in the first place. These culture wars are more than the expessions of anomie that attend epochal social changes. The "twilight of common dreams" is real in that the unitarian culture promoted through militant anti–communism, laissez–faire economics, and traditional social conventions is collapsing, more as a result of epochal social change than from a deliberate strategy by a group or category of people (dare I mention American liberals?).

It is difficult to predict how members of the dominant group will receive this book—that is, if they actually take the time to read it. Certainly the authors are forthright about their views and perceptions: they are Chicanos and their expressions embody their passions, interests, and experiences as ethnic minority males. Will their insights resonate with the view of American faculty members? Probably not, as the latter often don't (and the majority don't attempt to) understand these issues from perspectives outside the Americentric frameworks they hold. As is the case with well-written novels, there are many levels to this book—Chicana/o scholars are its first audience, and the members of this group will be attracted by the praxis-oriented discussion.

Faculty and scholars of color are its next audience, and there are so many commonalities across ethnic minority groups that the conversation will likely resonate with them. American faculty and scholars also are primary audiences, and it is their engagement in, and willingness to join, the conversation that is crucial to shaping the collective vision and role of tomorrow's academy. Without American faculty stepping forth to direct the academy's adjustment to the post–military–industrial context its anomic condition will persist.

Hopefully, the higher concerns of the authors will not be lost in acts of naming players in the power politics arena. Surely the power politics context of the academy will give rise to voices denouncing this new style of book writing. There will be those who will be greatly offended by the violations of academic norms, especially that of casting aspersions toward colleagues, or any appearance of such. The book, however, is neither formal study nor journalism—its primary aim is collective self–reflection, and, as such, intends to clarify rather than to blame or denigrate. We live in a time of great challenges and great opportunities. Let us join the conversation in the hope that through it we can overwhelm the former and perceive the latter.

Notes

1. I want to thank William Takamatsu Thompson for his critical comments throughout the writing of this Foreword. His insightful criticisms made it much more understandable than as originally written.

2. Politicians tend to overgeneralize the complaints they hear from concerned citizens. For a good overview of public support for higher education, see Harvey and Immerwahr (1995).

3. African Americans have been positioned to examine the ideas, theoretical views, and status of black scholars since the establishment of black colleges and universities in the postbellum period. Examination of the black intelligentsia was well established by the 1930s, when Charles Johnson, W. E. B. Du Bois, and others were doing it. Asian Americans,

Native Americans, and Chicana/os have had to wait until a critical mass of scholars came into existence. For an example of some of the challenges faced by a segment of African American scholars, see Ross and McMurray (1996).

4. Mario T. García (1989) has begun this very important work by focusing on the lives and works of Carlos E. Castañeda, George I. Sánchez, and Arthur L. Campa.

5. I do not mean to imply here that the university has as its primary purpose to serve as a beacon of democracy to the rest of society. Clearly the production of knowledge and the dissemination of that knowledge are its twin purposes. But I believe that the academy in a so-called democratic society pursues and reflects the highest ideals of humankind, and should therefore embody the practices corresponding to those ideals—particularly those of democracy.

Preface

Have contemporary colleges and universities, the traditional seats of higher learning in western culture, turned into academic factories for the production of technical knowledge on an industrial scale? Have these institutions become the boot camps for training the vast armies of bureaucrats and technicians who are required to run the bureaucracies of the military, the corporate state, and the multinational corporations? Has there been a collapse of epistemological space in our universities, so that knowing is restricted to a single dimension of technical, objective knowledge, relentlessly pursued in the service of a hedonistic, consumer society in the throes of launching the "information age"? These are some of the questions and themes that we problematize in this "talking book," which uses the "ethnic moment" to generate what Freire calls "epistemological curiosity" (Freire & Macedo, 1995) and to critique contemporary American higher education. Unquestionably, this book encompasses an ethnic, and particularly a Chicano, angle of vision, but the problems, issues, contradictions, dilemmas, and possibilities discussed in this book implicate everyone. In the brave new postmodern society that we are creating from the ashes and industrial waste of modernity (Fox & Miller, 1995; García Canclini, 1995; Olalquiaga, 1992; Turner, 1990), we all feel the weight of oppression and alienation as we see ourselves floating in an ocean of sound bites and Internet bits, drifting ever farther from each other. This book says that spiritually impoverished life in our universities need not be so. Or at least that we should think and talk about it and include many voices as we look for alternatives.

This book examines the nature of university life in the United States during the last third of the twentieth century. In writing this book we were keenly aware of the fact that we are not the only ones concerned about the state of American higher education, as is evident from the spate of publications that has emerged during recent years to chastise, uphold, or reform the practices of the academy (Bok, 1982, 1986; Bloom, 1987; Huber, 1992; Solomon & Solomon, 1993). Ours is not yet another book on higher education management (Chaffee & Sherr, 1992; Keller, 1983), practical as these might be; nor is it still another conservative attack on the presumed corruption of higher education through the avowed loss of standards inherent to the diversification of colleges and universities. We hope that those involved in the current higher education debates (Newfield & Strickland, 1995) find useful ideas in our work, but we want to locate our book within a much larger historical framework, one that encompasses at least two centuries of developments in higher education. It is worthwhile to review several of the important critiques of higher education during this period.

During the mid part of the nineteenth century, John Henry Newman (1976) provided a thoughtful and inspired vision of western universities as they transitioned, following the German model, from their traditional focus on theology, law, and the humanities to the empiricist and positivist world of modern science. What Cardinal Newman pointed out to those who were busily redirecting the concerns of higher education toward the compartmentalized natural and social sciences was that universal knowledge (the proper goal of higher education) could not be so absent religious knowledge, that secular and religious knowledge rightfully conceived supported each other, and therefore that religious knowledge should not be banished from the campus. He imbued universities with a magisterial mission that emphasized the dissemination and extension of knowledge rather than the generation of new knowledge as an end in itself. Newman's discourses on higher education were highly influential in shaping our understanding of the modern university (Pelikan, 1992), even though he was not very successful in turning back, or even blunting, the onslaught of positivist science, which was undoubtedly the main impetus for his work.

Fifty years or so later, Thorstein Veblen (1957) provided an equally inspired critique of American universities, only this time the critique was aimed at protecting the privilege of positivist science from the presumably grubbier profit-centered interests of the business community now intent on wielding influence over higher education. The remarkable success of the land grant colleges and universities in harnessing science to agricultural production and engineering, thus accelerating the development of both agribusiness and industry, caught the eye of businesspeople who decided that perhaps higher education also could be used to promote corporate and business interests. As this corporate presence began to be felt ever more strongly on campus, Veblen mocked it through his "Memorandum on the Conduct of Universities by Business Men," which is the subtitle of his famous book.

Veblen charged that business influences on campus would result in a transformation of academia, and not necessarily for the better. The most likely effect of the introduction of business principles into the academy, Veblen argued, would be the businesslike administration of academic affairs. This he felt would lead inevitably to a bureaucratic form of organization and to a system of "scholastic accountancy." This business model was in sharp contrast to the more decentralized and autonomous community of scholars involved in expanding the frontiers of knowledge that Veblen favored. What is remarkable today is that the business influence in universities is so pervasive that we can hardly imagine a time when someone should be alarmed at the prospects of businesspeople running universities.

In a sense, Veblen's battle was waged in the interest of maintaining the autonomy of positivist science in the academy because scientific inquiry was threatened by the dominance of business interests and the leisure class. His solution to avoid the devaluation of the academy was quite simple: Remove undergraduate instruction from the universities, along with the professional schools, such as law and business administration, which were driven mostly by vocational interests. This amputation was supposed to cleanse the campus of undergraduates from the leisure class who were majoring in gentility as well as from the graduate students in the professional schools whose interests did not properly fit in the academy.

Veblen's work is remarkable not only because of its astonishingly prescient view of what was to come in academia under the sway of businesspeople, but also because he provided a stark, if somewhat satirical, account of life in American universities at the turn of the century. As an insider who was at the same time an outsider in academia, he poked fun at the pretensions of both faculty and university administrators. The university presidents, whom he refers to as "captains of erudition," were seen as extremely malleable to the interests of businesspeople as long as the presidents were regaled with attention and celebrity. Faculty, on the other hand, had surrendered their trust to maintain and enlarge knowledge in exchange for academic entrepreneurship and its attendant privileges. As with Newman before him who saw the influx of positivist science into the academy, Veblen saw the coming tide of bureaucracy and entrepreneurship that would engulf higher education, but neither was able to persuade the universities to change their course to a significant degree.

What Veblen could not imagine is how thoroughly the universities would become saturated by the business model. A new element, not yet visible during the preparation of his book, needed to appear on the scene before the professoriat would leap headlong and irremediably into the business model. That element was the federal government and the exigencies of war. For it was during World War II that academic brain power was first harnessed to the national defense in response to both patriotism and the lure of megabucks that were made available to prosecute the war and were funneled to academics. The best and the brightest in academia were enlisted to run projects, centers, and laboratories geared exclusively to the war effort, which is to say to the production of improved military technology under contract. Over the years, this led to the rise of the professor as academic entrepreneur in a way that would have startled even the far-seeing Veblen. So rapid and dramatic was the influence of federal grants and contracts on universities, that Clark Kerr (1963), once president of the University of California, felt compelled to write a book on the uses of the university as a means to warn the academy about the perils of the "federal grant university." Taken together with Dwight Eisenhower's warning about the "military-industrial complex," Kerr's volume could be taken as a warning against the dangers to academia and society in the "academic-military-industrial" complex that coalesced during the cold war.

As Kerr rightly pointed out, one important effect of federal grants was to liberate the individual faculty member from dependency on his or her academic department for salary, influence, and prestige. Once a faculty member could plug into independent sources of funding outside the department, indeed outside the university, there was little incentive for the faculty member to assume responsibility for the needs of the local department, campus, or community. Professors could now become academic entrepreneurs. This had tremendous negative implications for maintaining whatever was left of the community of disinterested scholars defended by Veblen (but see also Goodman, 1964), and could only result in the further fragmentation of the university into fiefdoms of varying sizes that were created and kept afloat by academic entrepreneurs who now held sway on campus.

By the 1960s faculty had gone over completely to the business model, but perhaps in ways hardly expected by the businesspeople to whom Veblen wrote his famous memorandum. Beyond running the university on business principles, which businesspeople favored and Veblen feared, the university became an enterprise zone with faculty as the new impresarios simultaneously bragging and worrying about the payroll they needed to meet in order to keep their ventures afloat. At the same time, university administrators transformed themselves from captains of erudition to the lieutenants of academic entrepreneurship. They eagerly supported the interests of the entrepreneurial and well-heeled faculty (who worked under the protection of tenure), and perpetually yearned to move up to the next level of bureaucratic administration or to advance to the next layer of prestige in the institutional pecking order of higher education.

Little wonder that the conservative business class, still nominally in charge of academia during the 1980s and 1990s, became restive with this arrangement. What is the use of leading an academic institution consisting of a virtual army of professorial entrepreneurs operating under the privileges of tenure and thus for all practical purposes uncontrollable? So it became increasingly clear to everyone that the businesspeople, who were supposed to be at the helms of colleges and universities, had lost control of these institutions to the academic entrepreneurs and their administrative lieutenants. What was not clear to everyone was that the academic entrepreneur was the result of largesse by the federal government as it responded to the grip of the military industrial complex on American institutions during the cold war.

It was during this period of the entrepreneurial academy that Chicanos first gained entrance in significant numbers to colleges and universities in the United States. Propelled by rapidly changing demographics, a new social awareness and support for civil rights, plus the youthful rebellion of the baby boom generation (Reich, 1970), particularly against an unpopular war in Vietnam but more generally against established cultural conventions (Roszak, 1969), Chicano students found themselves isolated, invisible, and excluded within predominantly White and European-centered colleges and universities (Olivas, 1986). Confronting stereotypes, discrimination, and invisibility even in academia, Chicano students sought to forge a new positive identity and to establish an intellectual presence on campuses (Chicano Coordinating Council on Higher Education, 1969). They meant to pursue justice for themselves and for the larger Chicano community outside the universities. In doing so, they actively challenged the academy to live up to its lofty ideals, which had long since been made hollow by the business turn in American higher education.

Chicanos also challenged academia to open new epistemological spaces where we could get to know and see ourselves and others. This book is an expression of that epistemological challenge. As the reader will see, dialogue, not as mere conversation but as an approach to critique and self-reflection (Freire & Macedo, 1995), is the method that we use in this book to create a new epistemological space that is inclusive of a Chicana/o voice and presence. Through dialogue (Maranhão, 1990), we have problematized our lives as Chicano academics struggling to create presence and an intellectual life within American colleges and universities. Through dialogue we attempt to distance ourselves from our own actions in order to understand better who we are and who we want to be. Also we want to understand how our personal lives are shaped by the institutions around us and how we can empower ourselves to create utopian visions for those same institutions based on our critically examined values, ideals, history, and imagined futures.

Ours is a pragmatic epistemology, born out of the struggle and suffering that results from living in a society that is extraordinarily conscious of difference — ethnic, racial, gender, and sexual — and that uses difference as a means to maintain and promote exclusion as well as to define privileged enclosure. The pragmatism of our epistemology stems from our need to survive in American society, and especially in the inner sanctum of the privileged social space known as the university. To survive we need to know critically the nature of the universities that we inhabit and their connections to the larger society that sustains them. It is within that larger society that our Chicano community is, so far, precariously attached.

The sheer precariousness of our existence, however, encased as it is in a shroud of ethnicity, gives rise to an ethnic moment that opens up pragmatic epistemological space. Now we are simultaneously insiders and outsiders, participants and observers, subjects and objects, foreigners gone native, who examine our social institutions with the studied gaze of the traditional academic and the fascination of the newly arrived. Situated in the pragmatic epistemological space created by the ethnic moment, we are able to scrutinize and learn about the society around us and the institutions that give it life and character. The ethnic moment thus empowers us to understand institutional life in a relevant context and to change it if we so desire.

But the pragmatic epistemological space that we have created gives rise to even greater and richer possibilities. The space is large and comfortable enough to give us the freedom to perform an epistemological somersault that turns our critical, analytical gaze away from the exclusively social and toward the self, or perhaps better stated, to the social in the self and vice versa. Through this epistemological somersault, we are able finally to critically examine ourselves and our circumstances and to discern alternative horizons of possibilities emanating from distinctive histories that we can claim and pointing to alternative futures that are there for us to construct. This is truly risky business, but also full of possibilities and hope for Chicanos and for society as a whole.

This book recounts and problematizes the struggle to create a Chicano presence in academia. The issues discussed encompass a vast terrain that covers ethnic concerns, to be sure, but that also seamlessly expands to include larger concerns beyond the problems of any particular group or personal interest. Through our dialogues, we ponder the future of American higher education in the postmodern era of multivocality and diversity. We wonder whether the ever-increasing multiplicity of special interests will serve only to further fragment academic life and to distance it from the local communities that nurture it. We wrestle with questions such as: How can the idealism and utopian vision brought by Chicanos to academia be reconciled with the entrepreneurial university of the cold war period? Who controls the universities and how is their autonomy to be maintained in order to promote disciplined inquiry? Will the presence of new ethnic, racial, and other specifically self-defined groups simply add further fragmentation to an academic enterprise already too fragmented by the entrepreneurial faculty and the rigid compartmentalization of knowledge? Why do universities appear to be drifting at a time when they need to be ever more attentive and responsible to the needs of a changing society? Why is it that leaders can't lead (Bennis, 1989)? How does the social disease of racism distort the functioning of the academy so that both majorities and minorities, men and women, become trapped in ideological squabbles or in the struggle to control jobs and bureaucratic power? How can we make our democracy work better? How can we critique ourselves? Can we imagine a better future for academia and society and work to bring it about? For those who are interested in these and similar questions, read on. The dialogue is wide open. Your participation is essential. There is room for everyone. Expand the circle and join in.

Acknowledgments

We acknowledge the generosity, and, we dare to believe, the astuteness, of the taxpayers who provided us the opportunity to devote our lives to academic interests. We hope to give something in return through this book, however small.

We appreciate the contributions of so many individuals and organizations who provided us the opportunity to learn about universities and about ourselves. We wish to castigate no one and thank all those who taught us lessons, both positive and negative.

Thanks especially to the readers who gave us critical feedback, to the anonymous reviewers, to the publisher, and to the editorial staff.

Hats off to Maritza Montiel who transcribed the tapes. Likewise to her dad, the good sport, who lost the toss and thus became the second author.

Series Editor's Foreword

Raymond Padilla and Miguel Montiel's book, *Debatable Diversity*, not only is timely but also sheds important light in understanding the increasing cultural, gender, ethnic, and racial unrest across university and college campuses in the United States that reflects our society's intensified xenophobia. On some campuses, the division along race, ethnic, and gender lines is so serious that Christina Hoff Sommers, a philosophy professor at Clark University, says: "It's a little like Bosnia out there right now."[1] In response to the racial unrest at the University of North Carolina at Chapel Hill, Associate Chancellor Edith Wiggins remarked, "It has been brutal. . . . There is blood all over campus."[2] Even on more progressive campuses where curriculum diversity has been more or less embraced, the diversity, in most cases, has given rise to the creation of centers, institutes, and programs that, according to Professor Sommers, are "now organized into race/class/gender centers where you can nurse and nurture your anger. . . . I think you're going to have very active groups, mobs in some cases, outraged and making a variety of demands."[3]

Raymond Padilla and Miguel Montiel are correct in pointing out that diversity on university and college campuses is, at best, debatable and, at worst, a figment of our imagination. The Western cultural commissars' reactionary position against campus diversity fails to recognize a more fundamental question: Why are groups divided along race, class, and gender lines angry and, in some cases, outraged? Partly, the response would have to point to the elitist Western cultural hegemony that has dominated university life. One might also point to the white patriarchy that has, in the past, relegated the "other" as cultural subjects to the margins of university life and, in some cases, to a culture of silence. Even in cases where centers, institutes, and programs for disadvantaged groups—such as women's studies programs—are created, these units remain at the margins of university life. My colleague and friend Ramon Flecha from the University of Barcelona, Spain, calls this diversity for inequality. In other words, instead of making diversity the core of university life, these centers, institutes, and programs are often relegated to the periphery. What conservative educators fail to acknowledge is that the present racial and cultural unrest on campuses is the enactment of history, although manifested in different forms. For instance, what is the difference between the recent incident in which an African American student at the University of Massachusetts—Amherst was beaten up by a white visitor and the incident on December 10, 1850, when Harvard students demanded the dismissal of blacks from the classroom, stating that "the intermixing of white and black races in the lecture rooms . . . was distasteful to a large portion of the class, and injurious to the interest of the school . . ."[4] If conservative educators were to make historical linkages between these two episodes, they would soon learn about the truth inherent in the popular adage "The more things change, the more they stay the same."

The tirade against diversity in higher education is not, unfortunately, limited to conservative educators. Even liberal educators such as Arthur Schlesinger, Jr., become concerned that a "cult of ethnicity has arisen both among non-Anglo whites and minorities to denounce the idea of a melting pot, to challenge the concept of 'one people' and to protect, promote, and perpetuate separate ethnic and racial communities."[5] Schlesinger's position not only is dishonest but also serves to alarm the population regarding what he refers to as the "multiethnic dogma [that] abandons historic purposes, replacing assimilation by fragmentation, integration by separatism. It belittles Unum and glorifies Pluribus."[6] A more honest account of history would highlight the fact that African Americans did not create laws so they could be enslaved; they did not promulgate legislation that made it a crime for them to be educated; nor did they create redlining policies that sentenced them to ghettos and segregated neighborhoods. Unless Arthur Schlesinger is willing to confront the historical truth, his concern for the disuniting of America is yet another veil to mask white male supremacist values that place the discriminatory policies in the United States beyond analysis—thus, beyond scrutiny. What Schlesinger fails to recognize is that there was never a "common culture" in which people of all races and cultures equally participated. The United States was founded on a cultural hegemony that led to the genocide of Indians and privileged the white patriarchy to control and relegate other racial, cultural, and gender groups to a silenced culture.

Debatable Diversity makes it abundantly clear that one of the major challenges facing elite institutions of higher education, particularly self-proclaimed "liberal" institutions such as Harvard, is the liberals' para-

doxical posture with respect to race issues. On the one hand, liberals pro-
gressively idealize "principles of liberty, equality, and fraternity [while
insisting] upon the moral irrelevance of race. Race is irrelevant, but all is
race."[7] On the other hand, some liberals accept the notion of difference
and call for ways in which difference is tolerated. For example, there is a
rapid growth of courses, seminars, workshops, and textbooks ostensibly
designed to teach racial and multicultural tolerance. But what the tolerance industry does, in fact, is hide the asymmetrical distribution of power
and cultural capital through a form of paternalism that promises the
"other" a dose of tolerance. In other words, since we co-exist and must
find ways to get along, I will tolerate you. Missing from this posture is the
ethical position that calls for mutual respect and even racial and cultural
solidarity. As Susan Mendus argues, tolerance "presupposes that its object is morally repugnant, that it really needs to be reformed, that is, altered."[8] Accordingly, faculty members at liberal institutions would be
immensely happier if multicultural and ethnic courses would moderate
their present emphasis in critical theory. They would prefer that minorities endorse a form of racial and cultural tolerance, practiced by the liberal sectors within U.S. society as part of a management process, in which
the different "other" is permitted to think or, at best, hope that through
this so-called tolerance, the intolerable features that characterize the different "other" will be eliminated or repressed. This obvious contradiction
in a liberal pedagogy of tolerance led Goldberg to point out that

> liberals are moved to overcome the racial differences they tolerate and
> have been so instrumental in fabricating by diluting them, by bleaching
> them out through assimilation or integration. The liberal would assume
> away the difference in otherness, maintaining thereby the dominance of
> a presumed sameness, the universally imposed similarity in identity.
> The paradox is perpetrated: the commitment to tolerance turns only on
> modernity's natural inclination to intolerance; acceptance of otherness
> presupposes as it at once necessitates delegitimization of other.[9]

Tolerance for different racial and ethnic groups as proposed by
some white liberals not only constitutes a veil behind which they hide
their racism but also puts them in a compromising racial position. While
calling for racial tolerance, a paternalistic term, liberals often maintain the
privilege that makes them complicit with the white supremacist ideology.
In other words, the call for tolerance never questions the asymmetrical
power relations that give them privilege. Thus, many white liberals willingly call for and work for cultural tolerance but are reluctant to confront
structural issues of inequality, power, ethics, race, and ethnicity. They

therefore divert our attention from measures that lead to social transformation and that would make our society more democratic, less discriminatory, more humane, less racist, and more just. This form of racism is readily understood by its victims, as observed by Carol Swain, an African American professor at Princeton University: "White liberals are among the most racist people I know; they're so patronizing towards blacks."[10]

This liberal paradox is inherent in the politics of representation characterized by a form of "Benetton color coordination" where multicultural analysis is reduced to a study of the exoticized "other" so as to learn, for example, how Puerto Ricans dance Salsa, how Chicanos celebrate Cinco de Mayo, or why Haitians believe in Voodooism. On the one hand, the superficial analysis of these cultural traits guarantees the white students their "comfort zone" while creating the illusion of a commitment to embrace the racial and cultural "other." On the other hand, a superficial approach to race and cultural analysis fails to prepare us to deal with the tensions and contradictions generated by the coexistence of multicultural groups in a racist society.

Most liberal faculty members feel comfortable with a politics of representation where a "Benetton color coordination" approach is given primacy. But these faculty members would feel extremely uncomfortable with a diversity approach in which students are provided with opportunities to develop tools to critically understand how to make sense of difference in our world. There is no way for students to make meaning out of the material conditions within which they are situated unless the academic world begins to seriously encourage them to engage difference—in terms of not only its representation in the curriculum but also the politics that inform these different representations. This obviously involves different ideologies, different ways of being in the world, different ways of acting, and different ways of thinking. To do otherwise is to deny historicity, thus creating a disarticulation among different bodies of knowledge that inform multiple realities.

Although most liberal faculty members tolerate a politics of representation, they have an almost visceral reaction to a diversity approach that includes the representation of politics, as evidenced in a Harvard professor's comments on Pepi Leistyna's term paper:

> The assumption that ideological sophistication is a sign of cultural progress ignores the fact that many people just don't give a damn about this kind of complex verbalization. They may be temperamentally bent toward building, or singing, or hoeing corn. So the problem for me is to prevent the overinterpretive egghead from claiming a special corner on sacred (significant) knowledge—but still get his or her due. It always

makes me a little wary about the extent to which the critical theorists (Freire, Giroux, etc.) appreciate the great range of talents of people who are not so much deluded by all this professional garbage complex elaboration of language. So they often cannot protect themselves, either from specialized professors of literacy or specialized professors of critical literacy.[11]

One should not be at all surprised by the arrogant dismissal of representation politics by this professor, since he is functioning within the ideological parameters delineated by the prevailing ideology of Harvard. These parameters were made abundantly clear by a former senior administrator at Harvard, who sanctioned diversity at Harvard with the following remark: "I don't mind recruiting minority students so long as they are the right kind of minorities."

The "right kind of minorities" means that one is demonstrably supportive of the dominant ideology or, at least, aspires to be part of the dominant order. Thus, as a society, we can accept Clarence Thomas, with his questionable credentials, as a Supreme Court justice, whereas we do not allow Lani Gunier to be assistant attorney general because she showed signs of independent critical thinking. The "right kind of minorities" is what most white liberal professors prefer to have when they hire "a black person in 'their' department as long as the person thinks and acts like them, shares their values and beliefs, [and] is in no way different."[12] That is why many professors (both liberal and conservative) often prefer to hire a middle- or upper-class foreign professor to fulfill their universities' affirmative action policy rather than a working-class person whose ideology overtly points toward the denouncement of all forms of oppression. Thus, an upper-class professor from Venezuela would be preferred to represent the Latino community over a community member who demonstrably works to transform the oppressive conditions that shape and maintain the existing human misery in many Latino communities. What these professors fail to understand is that speaking the same language, let's say Spanish, does not necessarily translate into real representation of community needs, wishes, goals, aspirations, and dreams. They also fail to understand that the community is not a monolithic entity bereft of contradictions, tensions, and ideologies.

Raymond Padilla and Miguel Montiel go beyond describing the struggles and "deferred" dreams involved in incorporating minority faculty and students into rigid Eurocentric higher education institutions. In their unquiet dialogue they provide readers with a safe pedagogical space to deconstruct the dominant white ideology and to understand how ethnicity and race interpenetrate each other, a concept that Pepi Leistyna refers to as "racenicity, a process through which the ideological construction of race has a significant impact on ethnicity."[13] What becomes clear in *Debatable Diversity* is that difference must be linked to questions of power where racial, cultural, and gender categories, among other characteristics, are treated as political categories that do not exist in a power vacuum. These categories exist in relation to one another, mediated always by asymmetrical power relationships.

In *Debatable Diversity*, Raymond Padilla and Miguel Montiel successfully demonstrate that dialogue as conversation about individuals' lived experiences does not truly constitute dialogue. By always adhering to a critical posture that includes self-criticism and reflection, the authors share with the readers the true pedagogical meaning of dialogue. Epistemological curiosity is never sacrificed and the object of knowledge is never sidestepped to give room to a feel-good process of sharing experiences, in which dialogue is reduced to a form of group therapy that focuses on the psychology of the individual. The authors of *Debatable Diversity* guide the readers through the labyrinth confronting minority faculty and students in higher education institutions in their struggle to "pursue justice for themselves . . . and how [they] can empower [themselves] to create utopian visions for those same institutions based on [their] critically examined values, ideals, history, and imagined futures." Raymond Padilla and Miguel Montiel's *Debatable Diversity* is an indispensable book in that it shows how minority faculty and students in higher education often live in a borrowed cultural existence—an existence that is almost culturally schizophrenic—that is, being present and yet not visible, being visible and yet not present. It is a condition that invariably presents itself to the reality of minority faculty and student life in higher education—the constant juggling of two narratives, two cultures, two discourses, and two ways of being in the world and with the world. It is a process through which we come to know what it means to be at the periphery of the intimate and yet fragile relationship between domination and subordination.

> Donaldo Macedo, Editor
> Critical Perspectives Series
> A book series dedicated to Paulo Freire

References

1. "Court Division for Jeffries Raises a Host of Questions," *Boston Globe*, 16 May 1993, p. 17.
2. Sanolf and Mimerbrook, "Race on Campus," p. 57.
3. "Court Division for Jeffries."

4. Ronald Takaki, *Iron Cages: Race and Culture in 19th Century America* (New York: Oxford University Press, 1990), p. 254.

5. Arthur Schlesinger, Jr., *The Disuniting of America: Reflections on a Multicultural Society* (New York: W. W. Norton & Company, 1992), p. 15.

6. Ibid. p. 17.

7. David T. Goldberg, *Racist Culture* (Oxford, Eng.: Blackwell, 1993), p. 6.

8. Cited in Goldberg, *Racist Culture*, p. 7.

9. Goldberg, *Racist Culture*, p. 7.

10. Peter Applebone, "Goals Unmet, Duke Reveals the Perils in Effort to Increase Black Faculty," *New York Times*, 19 September 1993, p. 1.

11. Pepi Leistyna, "Veritas: The Fortunes of My Miseducation at Harvard," in *Tongue-Tying Multiculturalism at Harvard*, ed. Donaldo Macedo (forthcoming).

12. bell hooks, *Killing Rage: Ending Racism* (New York: Henry Holt and Company, 1995), p. 185.

13. Pepi Leistyna, "Racenicity: Whitewashing Ethnicity," in *Tongue-Tying Multiculturalism at Harvard*, ed. Donaldo Macedo (forthcoming).

Chapter 1

Constructing this Book

RP: As a result of our last conversation, a strategy for writing the book is becoming clearer. Let me show you the progress that we've made in organizing the relevant documents. These items relate to what became the Ad Hoc Committee for Chicano Faculty Development. It was the group that advocated for the creation of the Hispanic Research Center (HRC) dating back to 1982, 1983, and 1984. Here is the first memo that was sent out regarding the HRC. It dates from the time when the vice president for academic affairs had just arrived on campus. We wanted him to support something of interest to us, so we invited him to lunch. That was the purpose of the first memo. You can see how the terminology changed from Chicano to Hispanic and from Chicano studies to faculty development. There were several faculty who participated in the early stages of the project, but for one reason or another dropped out. You were prominent during the critical third phase when the center was actually being approved and launched. Later I became the first permanent director.

You and I took a trip to California to visit Chicano studies programs and centers. There you see the travel request for that trip. Here is the first concept paper where I sketched the rationale for the Hispanic Research Center. I also offered some other possible initiatives for the university. The documentation goes well past ten years.

MM: So as a strategy for analysis we could follow one activity?

RP: We could describe an activity's chronology, the related memos, and implementation strategies. That's one idea about what we might do. The HRC activities go on for over ten years.

MM: It is interesting to note that we got slightly derailed by one of my old enemies in the School of Social Work where I taught during my first ten years at the university, and who tried to stall the process by requesting that we get curriculum vitae from faculty who had indicated an interest in participating in the HRC. She and I had a run-in when the dean of the School of Social Work was hired several years back. I guess she felt it was her turn to get revenge by attacking our effort.

RP: There is an interplay of small agendas with larger ones. Local battles that are fought at the program, department, or college level have implications for larger battles that are fought at the university level or even outside the university. People have to be able to see those kinds of connections as they work with an institution.

MM: You have to go through the whole documentation, otherwise you start analyzing early drafts.

RP: Early drafts allow one to see the chronology, and the kinds of pressures that we were under—what we were responding to in making all those revisions. The number of drafts of the HRC proposal is amazing. I kept the earlier drafts because without them one loses sight of the tremendous struggle that is reflected in those drafts. They are indices of the political process in academia and reflect whatever compromises we made along the way. There is value in looking at those drafts every step along the way. I think that too often Chicanos believe that proposals are done as a one-shot deal. If you want something done, you simply propose it and it gets accepted forthwith. In fact, it's really a drawn out process. It is a test of wills to see who can stand the pressures and who can be creative enough to reposition themselves as necessary to keep things going and at the same time not lose sight of their basic goal. That is the trick that is so hard to teach people. There is subtlety in the approval process that gets people lost. It seems to be designed that way. When engaging academic bureaucracies sometimes it feels like you are inside a great big gizzard full of rocks where you can get ground down right out of existence.

Are We Lost?

MM: We got lost. What I mean is that our original intention was to develop a community of scholars where Chicanos would have the opportunity to explore Chicano issues in a spirit of community, thus building a Chicano body of knowledge. It seems to me that this did not happen, and there are many reasons for it. It can be argued, for example, that many of us did not put the proper effort into the enterprise, that there was a reluctance to follow the leadership that was available, that the center was viewed as a resource that people could exploit without providing anything back in return. For an enterprise to work, there must be something other than individual rewards. The individuals within the group must respect each other and there must be focused effort to sustain the enterprise. What we need to do is analyze why our efforts ended up devoid of the spirit necessary to develop and sustain a community of scholars. This is why I say that we have gotten lost.

RP: I don't think we got lost.

MM: Are you satisfied with the results? This conversation should help us understand better where our efforts have led us, and to figure out where we need to go. The important issue is to find our way without getting derailed by all the nonsense that goes on in the university.

Defining Moments

RP: Going back to constructing this book, we could review the many documents that we have assembled to identify the defining moments or events. This can be done relatively quickly to select the key documents that signify the turning points that we can use to tell the story of how we attempted to change the university.

MM: Let's look at defining moments and turning points for a minute. What do you mean by that as an example?

RP: As an example, we can look at the speech by Alfredo Gutierrez, who at the time was the majority leader of the Arizona State Senate, to the Arizona Association of Chicanos for Higher Education (AACHE) in Flagstaff. From the very beginning, AACHE had politics high on its agenda. AACHE recognized that if we were going to be players at all we had to engage the political system. To be a player you must have some idea as to what your goals are, what you are striving for. And your goals should be lofty. AACHE's initial stance was one of political engagement.

At the Flagstaff AACHE conference, Senator Gutierrez spoke very candidly and very perceptively about *la política* and the Chicano agenda. He made several important contributions. First, he made it clear as to what it might mean to play seriously in the political arena. His message was very straightforward. It is the idea that we have to get away from the notion of the academician as being outside the political process. We must get involved politically; we have to get our hands dirty. It is not only okay for the academician to be involved in the political world, in fact, it is necessary. Gutierrez reinforced the idea that we have to get political by criticizing the academic folks who always maintain that they are nonpolitical.

Second, Gutierrez also provided a rationale for becoming political. He said that the business of America is not business, it is not schooling, it is not health, it is not anything else along those lines. The only business of America is politics. If you recognize that then you have to get involved in the political system.

His third point was that we as Chicanos had to get away from feeling singled out as special, either negatively or positively. That's when he told the little story from one of Samuel Beckett's plays. The protagonist was running around the stage groaning and moaning about his pain and suffering and why it was he who was singled out for such pain. His father popped out of a garbage can and said, "We didn't know it was going to be you!" Gutierrez's point is that everyone has problems and you can't just sit around complaining. It is how you cope with your problems and how you engage them that matters. You cannot really engage the world successfully as a marginalized ethnic person. You have to engage the social system without feeling sorry for yourself or blaming the world for your troubles. The system did not know that it was going to be us!

MM: Peter Skerry, a political science professor at UCLA, has just come out with a new book, *The Mexican Americans, the Ambivalent Minority*. He argues that Mexican Americans are at a political crossroads. We can go one of two ways. The first way is the minority, post-civil rights route that calls for specific strategies and responses from social institutions: It is a victim-oriented strategy where people in control are accused of racism, sexual harassment, and homophobia and that entails an affirmative action response. The second way is to follow the route of the ethnics — the Jews, the Italians, the great hoards of Europe who came to America. This is a more entrepreneurial approach requiring involvement in economic develop-ment in its original meaning. Skerry claims that Mexican Americans have not come to terms with the direction they want to pursue. Given current politics — the reversal of affirmative action policies in California and the move to the right of the Arizona Board of Regents, to name just two examples — that is not a bad suggestion. I think that Gutierrez's point is that the minority, the Black strategy, is really not the direction that we should take.

I think Skerry makes some important points about the direction in which Chicanos or Mexican Americans are headed. However, the problem also lies in our society's sway toward what Ralph Nader calls a corporate mentality as opposed to a civic mentality. Nader argues that the corpora-tions are single minded in their intent. The "bottom line" — the maximiza-tion of sales and profits — is what gives focus to people working for corporations. Civic culture, however, is concerned with broad issues such as health care, education, the environment, and the general quality of life. Yet, we are raised ideologically with a corporate worldview so that we tend to focus on welfare for the poor, primarily minorities, rather than the massive transfers of public wealth that go to corporations and sports franchises; likewise we see crime as caused primarily by minorities rather than by corporate criminals who plunder the environment, the air waves, and the financial system. There are dozens of examples of corporate criminals in Arizona, but our citizens rarely focus on them as a central issue. They choose instead to focus their attention on gang criminals and undocumented immigrants. While understanding gang behavior is important, clearly we also should begin to see the connections between corporate welfare and crime and the poor quality of services and education that are available to our children.

A couple of years ago I had a student in one of my courses in public administration who was adamant in claiming that most of the problems in society were the fault of minorities because they were destroying the free enterprise system. He was a twenty-five-year-old capitalist. I asked him if he owned a house or property or a business. He said no. I wondered how one could be a capitalist and yet not own any capital. Anyhow, it seems that one of the great dangers in our society is the absence of a civic culture, and this impacts not only minorities but everyone else as well. And while I think that Skerry makes a good point, it is this lack of civic culture that should worry us more than his admonition.

RP: Returning to Gutierrez, I think that his speech was a defining moment because as an astute politician he captured the essence of what we were thinking and saying in AACHE and fed it back to us from his own angle of vision as a politician. He basically validated our political stance and tried to set it within a context larger than academia. It is a defining moment because there is clarity in terms of what happened.

Plans, Politics, and Power

MM: I just took part in a panel where there was an exchange between one of our Chicano leaders and a Jewish leader. It was a very honest exchange where the Jewish man told us in no uncertain terms that if we were to ever get anything done we had to get focused on our agenda. The response was that we are part of a diverse community and we should not be expected to have a focused agenda. So the question is: What kind of politics?

RP: That is the question that the Chicano academics should have asked and engaged. That is the theme of the dialogue that should have taken place if the group in fact wanted to continue in a political mode.

MM: Did the group follow through?

RP: The group had a difficult time engaging the political world, and instead moved more toward a rationalist academic model.

MM: Have we moved more toward the politics that Blacks have followed: The politics of victimization, race and racism, and affirmative action? Or ethnic politics?

RP: It was a mixed response. If you look at the AACHE plan it is very clear that the plan is not about a mendicant people coming forward with their hats in their hands. The plan proclaims that Chicanos are partners with others in the state and that we are participants in society. We are going to participate fully in social institutions, and we are going to reshape things. The plan invited the powers that be to work together with Chicanos to reconstruct social institutions, particularly higher education. It was not just a question of asking for a small handout. Unfortunately, the universities interpreted the Chicano initiative precisely as you have indicated, that is, along the minority paradigm. So you might say that we talked past each other. Thus, Anglos fundamentally misconstrued the initiative of the Arizona Association of Chicanos for Higher Education.

Skerry is very astute in saying that Chicanos historically have had the options that you mentioned. The choices made have varied from place to place; some have made choices that look more like the Black minority model and others have chosen more in line with the European ethnic model.

MM: Clearly, the university treats us like it treats all minorities and in some cases women, lesbians, and homosexuals.

RP: When you say "like every other minority" it means automatically the classic paradigm of Whites and Blacks.

MM: Yes, but it includes women, lesbians; it is now talked about as diversity. Do you recall the sociologists of the sixties, including Glazer and Moynihan, who predicted that disenfranchised minorities, like Chicanos and Blacks, if given the opportunity, would eventually integrate into the mainstream? Well, it did not happen, especially for Blacks. I am not sure about Chicanos, but clearly we are lumped together in one pot. Diversity means you cut the pie and let the groups fight over the pieces of the pie. That is diversity.

RP: It is interest-group politics. The underlying paradigm is still one of disenfranchisement — the mentality of the ex-slave coming back to the master. It is a controlled and not truly free bidding for power. There is a bigger group sitting on top of it all that is controlling most of the power. Minorities fight for the little bones and the crumbs. It is not a real bid for power. If it were not so, then you might see some real changes, but none of the bidders for change has been able to make real changes so far. It is a constrained bidding for power within a Black and White paradigm of giving a little bit and holding back a lot.

MM: We cannot assume, however, that all people in official positions always have power, that they dictate the direction of important events. While it can be argued that they often receive or distribute most of the resources that the institution has to offer because of the positions that they hold, they do not necessarily determine the direction of social events any more than other groups. For example, university presidents at our university have not really accomplished the more important goals that they set out. Their strategic plans were not really actualized.

RP: They don't have any plans when you come right down to it.

MM: They do have plans.

RP: They are not very meaningful. We went through a whole strategic planning process at the university some years back. It accomplished little or nothing of substance, and I told the dean so when we were starting the process in the College of Liberal Arts and Sciences. I was the only administrator who had the guts to tell the dean that the process was basically worthless, because the rationalism implied in the model is not a significant factor in the way resources are allocated in the university.

MM: There are plans. Why do they go about squandering all those resources in those plans if they are not serious about them? It is just that they don't have the power to implement them. There has been a continual discussion to improve undergraduate education but, if anything, it has gotten worse, not better. It is the growth of the Valley of the Sun and the politics of the Board of Regents that has determined the direction of change — more cement, more students, more administrators — not the need for improved undergraduate education. There are many other examples of unmet needs, such as improved community service and fundamental changes in how minorities are treated.

RP: Okay, let's talk about power. If you are saying that they don't have power in the sense that a dictator or a king or a general has power, I agree. I don't think the university is that kind of institution. We live in a culture where there is a tremendous fear of power, and the institutions have been designed to promote a balance of power. In theory, no one interest group ever really can monopolize power for very long. It is the old federalist checks and balances system. It is very difficult to get anything approved or changed in the legislature. If you look at the approval process, maybe you get 5 percent of what you originally thought you were going to get. In fact, you may wind up opposing your own legislative bill that turns out to do the opposite of what you intended.

The university, more than other institutions, reflects in the extreme this notion of balance of power. Balance of power is central to the idea of the community of scholars, academic freedom, and so on. There is a strong tradition within the institution that the president, unless there are very unusual circumstances or a very weak faculty, cannot just dictatorially make things happen. The president has to do a great deal of massaging to get things done. The system cannot move unless this kind of massaging is done, which by definition makes for an inefficient system. Efficiency rests somewhere else, say like in Mussolini who made the trains run on time because he did have absolute power.

Academic Fragmentation and Gamesmanship

MM: There are distortions in the way that the university operates. For instance, it is replete with what C. W. Mills called intellectual entrepreneurs; people who are viewed as scholars but are not so. These are individuals who bring in a great deal of money to the university (and, of course, to themselves), who hardly teach, and who ultimately end up serving the interests of those in power. Distortions are also created by the many interest groups and the fragmentation that is new to the university. I remember, for example, that in the midseventies the type of discourse that surrounded the hiring of Ismael Dieppa, the first Hispanic dean at the university, did not reflect the fragmentation we now have. Make no mistake, the attack against his hire by two faculty members and a handful of people from the community was racially motivated. His defenders, however, crossed ethnic lines. They included Hispanics and Anglos, both men and women. It would be difficult to get such a unified response now. Academics have traded a sense of justice for interest-group politics in the university.

RP: I agree. Not only a sense of justice, but intellectual integrity has been diminished. How you get tenured and promoted often does not reflect the true quality of your work, your thinking, or your creativity. It reflects more how you have networked with various interest groups, for example, to get your stuff published in certain journals or to make speeches at particular professional conferences, not to mention interest groups at the department and college levels.

MM: It's not just the type of journals. It is not unusual to find faculty with good performance records denied promotion. There are other factors. You can have a good record and still get attacked.

RP: Because the academic record is always susceptible to critique. One of the great strengths of academia, a critical attitude, is turned on its head and becomes its weakness. Academia is founded on critique, and therefore, people examine tiny little faults. Using the legitimacy of academic critique, people can attack you politically and devalue what you do, essentially reducing your work to rubble. When critique is used in this manner, to gain political advantage and not as a dialogue to advance knowledge, it becomes a grindstone for destroying people.

A Postmodernist Book on Public Policy

RP: Going back to writing this book, we can identify incidents or events in these documents that are interesting in and of themselves and that enfold the organizational dynamics of the university. For example, we can focus on the Dieppa incident, which you have analyzed, and use it as a basis for a critical dialogue. If we look at enough of these incidents in the right sequence, we can examine the institution in its various facets and unfold layers of meaning in organizational behavior.

MM: There are two issues I want to touch on. The first has to do with Senator Gutierrez's AACHE speech. How can it be a defining moment if no one was paying attention? The Gutierrez speech illustrates a dilemma that minorities face in their confrontations and struggles with the universities. Minorities identify what we feel are important and even momentous events that are not viewed as important by those who control academia. So this book will be an attempt to identify events or defining moments that have been ignored by the universities but that we view as important. I suppose that this is what it means to be marginal.

The other issue is whether we should approach these issues inductively. In other words, next time we meet should we approach these issues without any preconceptions? Or do we want to start from a theory? I think that the latter is not too productive.

RP: We could do it either way. I suppose that we could sit down and write the book in a very linear and rational manner. But my intent is to be postmodernist; to use the postmodernist lens to critique institutional change. I want to see if we can capture the actual process of social involvement, which is chaotic and unpredictable. As you take action, you get glimpses of the situation here and there while you try to keep in mind what has gone before and to feed forward information. Things are very tentative and uncertain and I hope to convey this somehow. I also want to insert the authors into the whole process as reflective actors.

It will be a postmodernist book on public policy and the development of institutions. It will no longer assume an essential rationality to things. It will pay attention to the subjective moment and to the expression of one's own agency in the world and to the intrusion of the world in one's intentions and actions.

MM: We want it to be more transcendent. The important thing is not necessarily to say what happened, as in a chronology, but to give insights to people who have gone through the incidents, or similar ones, and have not thought critically about what happened.

Change seems to be the main thesis of this book. We have approached our organizing efforts with the intent to change institutions of higher education in Arizona. You have been at the university for more than a decade and I for two, and it is time to reflect on what has happened. Who participated in this effort? What is the relationship between Chicano organizations and higher education institutions? How have the institutions responded to our efforts and why?

To my mind the purpose of these dialogues is to examine the idea of institutional drift. How and why has academia deviated from its mission and why does it seem to be serving narrow political interests? Why has it neglected to serve more broadly the people who pay its bills?

I want to explore the tremendous gap that exists between what people say and what they do in the actual world of minority-university politics and administration, where lack of consistent policy and administrative continuity, political interference from many constituencies, administrative job hunting, internal minority disputes, divide and conquer tactics among university administrators, dissimulation in the exercise of power, and numerous other seemingly random activities hinder the process of instituting a coherent, rational, and just cultural diversity strategy.

RP: Also to give ourselves and others a chance to understand what happened. However, we will be constructing our understanding of what happened by reconstructing past incidents and events involving ourselves and others. There is nothing there really in those documents that we have assembled, except the opportunity to interpret the past. There is no absolute past that we can glue together from snippets of past incidents that we can garner from those piles of documents. We will be reconstructing the past in and through this book. So you might say that in this case we will be constructing method and content simultaneously for this book.

MM: Let's see where this journey will take us.

Chapter 2

Social Justice and Idealism

MM: You have accused me and other Chicanos of being idealists. Let's talk about what this means. I take it as peer criticism and as a way to learn. Some people go to therapy. I listen to my friends.

RP: Certainly you and I have been talking about fair play (or its absence), diversity, idealism, and hedonism. That's because these ideas form part of the *problemática* Chicana in the context of American universities. As long as the chicanada were outside of the universities, in fact outside of all the mainstream institutions, it did not matter very much whether we were idealists, realists, pragmatists, fatalists, or whatever. But once we got into the universities during the late sixties, our values clashed with those prevalent in the universities. So we have to ask ourselves, exactly what was the nature of this clash?

The Demand for Social Justice

RP: I am suggesting that the clash has to do with a core of idealistic values to which Chicanos subscribe — consciously or unconsciously. Actually, you have to infer the core values from our behavior, i.e., from what we have said and done over the last twenty-five years or so. You also have to look back historically. When you discern this historically rooted idealism then you can see more clearly how it would clash with the hedonism and self-promotion that is characteristic of our society and of American universities at the end of the twentieth century. Perhaps the Chicano idealism would not have clashed so sharply with the type of university that, say, Cardinal Newman envisioned toward the end of the nineteenth century in his famous statement regarding the ideals of the university. In some ways,

Chicanos in the 1970s were more in tune with Cardinal Newman's ideas than with the kind of federal grant university described by Clark Kerr in the 1960s in his well-known statement about the uses of the university.

MM: But what do you mean by this idealism?

RP: It is one view of what Chicanos have been doing in universities, which can be labeled simply as "idealism." Think about it this way. Once the chicanada found themselves in the universities during the late sixties and early seventies, they expected the universities to do certain things: to behave in a certain way, to exhibit and display certain values. Not only did they expect this behavior, they demanded it. For example, the chicanada demanded that the universities behave as if social justice actually mattered. They collectively said something like: "We are not being allowed to participate fully in this institution. That is not just. You must allow us to participate." There was supposed to be no further discussion about the matter.

Such a demand is based on the idea that social justice in and of itself is an abiding value in the society and in the universities, and that social justice must be implemented forthwith. It overlooks the way in which contemporary society and universities really function: There is a constant battle among various interest groups for resources, power, influence, and control. The distribution of resources and influence is always contested and problematic. It is probably the case that when Chicanos first arrived on the campuses, we were not singled out to receive an unjust hand. It is just that nobody automatically receives a just hand. It is easy to see the victims of the universities fall like dead flies all the time, and the fallen include all races, creeds, whatever. There is unending carnage going on in the universities. The ongoing bidding for control and power is largely outside any real concern for social justice. Well, let's say that social justice plays only a very small part, so that things are not completely savage.

Things can become very confused because universities pay a lot of lip service to high ideals, including social justice. If you listen to the rhetoric of the universities, it does indeed resonate with the pure idea of social justice and similar lofty ideals. But if you look at their behavior, their idea of social justice is that whatever you are able to get you should get as long as your behavior is not too foul. In a pragmatic sort of way, it is the boundaries of foul behavior that operationalize the idea of social justice in the universities. If you don't go around acting totally outside the boundaries of decency (and those boundaries are fairly distant), then whatever you are able to get is justly deserved, and whatever you have lost or failed to acquire is justly lost. You have no grounds to complain.

MM: I have observed that there are many Chicanos who are incapable of playing such a game. Chicano idealists are likely casualties in the type of political environment that you describe. I would like to examine a couple of those cases.

The first person who comes to mind is J. J. who is a very creative and bright man—one could describe him as a "pure heart." It did not take me long to realize that he was incapable or perhaps unwilling to put up with the political strife in the university. I recall how he was attacked by militant feminists because of his conservative views on women's issues, and by the faculty who did not think that his work merited credit. He was vilified outside of the classroom. He was never confronted on his ideas on a one-to-one basis. Today these same people would have filed some type of charge against him, and the affirmative action office would have heard it, and he would not have been able to defend himself. He has theories about crime that are innovative, but somehow his talents were not appreciated as I feel they should have been. There exists in universities an inability to contemplate ideas that are outside the accepted political boundaries.

Tomás Atencio, a Chicano activist and scholar of long standing, is another example. He has a long paper trail. He has written extensively in a journal that he himself founded. His work is often cited by scholars, including me. His ideas are routinely appropriated, including the idea that we incorporated into the Community Documentation Program at the Hispanic Research Center, which he freely shared with us. He is a remarkable teacher. He is a long-time activist who early on addressed the concerns of migrants, the water and land rights of the people of New Mexico, environmental issues in the barrios, and most recently networking to connect villages of New Mexico through the Internet. He calls it the electronic *resolana*. He is also a very talented wood-carver.

These are two people who are truly intelligent. We are not talking about people who are negligent in their work. We are talking about people who are serious about their work but it just does not fit the prevailing social construction of reality, that is, submitting papers to journals, and so on. It does not mean that they were not productive scholars. They were productive as scholars. It is just that they did not fit the criteria for productivity that were set up by the universities.

We can also argue the other side of idealism. We can look at idealism as a weakness. When you told me that I was an idealist, I took it as a very critical statement that Padilla was making against me. I'll tell you why. I thought, and still do, that you have a way of criticizing me that kind of stops the world for me a little bit and perhaps it also serves as a corrective mechanism. You can say that an idealist is a person who does not accept reality. In other words, someone who lives in a fantasy world and who is also reluctant to engage the world because he or she is disgusted by it. It is a negative way of operating; you can even call it being a "cry baby." In other words, that you are crying about the existing situation, that you are not satisfied, and that you are not able to accept the world for what it is.

That kind of posture in the world consumes a lot of your energy and might even force some people who dropped out to start participating in the world again. For example, I don't see that my getting away temporarily from the world makes me jaded. I see it as an opportunity to reflect. I'll probably jump back into action because the same thing has happened two or three times in my life already. I jump out of activism for two or three years, then jump back in. But it seems that when I jump back in I am jumping into the same thing and nothing really has changed. This may sound nihilistic or whatever. But it is also important to analyze issues in terms of our own personality as Chicanos.

The Racist Boundary

RP: I don't necessarily see idealism as negative. In using the idealism label to characterize Chicanos as a whole, I am trying to understand why Chicanos do what we do within the universities. Clearly, there are many Chicanos out there who just follow the regular university pattern: They know how to publish in journals, they say the right things, and they position themselves correctly. We usually think of such Chicanos as those who are on an upward career path. They are virtually indistinguishable from any other professor of any other race or religion. They have pretty much the same goals as other professors, except that they also have the option to use Chicano identity and Chicano pressure groups as one more tool to pursue their trajectory to success.

There are plenty of such Chicanos around. They are usually smart, well trained, often ambitious, and normally they are very well liked at the university. The latter is not always true because sometimes they are seen as too ambitious. That can be held against them. In essence, they run afoul of the invisible racist boundary to Chicano career ambitions. In our society it is often the case that good people do racist things so that in the end universities are racist and Chicanos can go only so far. Chicanos are confronted by the racist boundary when they strive for real power and authority in a university. As long as they don't seriously bid for such power and authority, people will be happy to consider them as colleagues.

But the minute that such Chicanos reach for the threshold of power, for example applying for an administrative line position, they get into trouble. At that point, their ethnicity becomes primary, and they have very difficult choices to make. That is why you don't see Chicanos as presidents, vice presidents, and even as full professors. Chicanos may get tenured (and that is tough enough) but they will have a hard time becoming a department chair. If they do become chairs, they will have a very hard time becoming deans and so on up the power hierarchy. As the potential for power escalates, the invisible racist boundary comes into play more and more prominently.

But putting aside for a moment the upwardly mobile Chicanos, there are other Chicanos, like the ones you mentioned, who are equally bright and well trained, but who do not accept as given the way that the universities function—in the contentious and racist ways that we talked about earlier. They have a different idea about what universities should be. They truly believe in social justice as real and palpable, and that it should occur in the universities and other social institutions. This is not the kind of social justice that has foul boundaries in a distant horizon. The social justice of which they speak is personal and immediate. It is a code of ethics to live by.

MM: But isn't all this a bit paradoxical? That there would be Chicano idealists when you consider our own background and the type of government that we came from that is hardly just. If you look at the history of Mexico, it is very unjust. I was raised on the Mexican border, but in 1982 I lived in Guadalajara, the second largest city in Mexico. There I witnessed first hand the many problems that Mexico faces—pollution, poverty, political and business corruption, poor schools. Yet, it is undeniable that Mexican people are resilient and have learned to "take it." Mexican people are different from Anglos; they have a tragic, not an epic sense of life, a history of Spanish rule and *mestizaje*, and clearly a less democratic orientation to power. Mexico is hierarchical. It clearly supports a *patrón* system where you lick the boots of the next person and somebody licks your boots. I realize that not all of us come from Mexico, as you and I do. My daughter is fifth-generation Arizonan so that side of our family has been in the United States for a long time, as have many people from New Mexico and Texas. Their situation may be different from more recent immigrants, even though there are still many signs of oppression. Anyhow, there is a rigid hierarchy in the university. So why do we not fit more easily into the university?

Idealism as Resistance

RP: You may be hinting at a good hypothesis there. Yes, it is true. We as a community, and Latin Americans in general, have a history of oppression going all the way back to time immemorial. So the idealism could be a reaction to that very oppression. The idealism is counterposed to the oppression, to the hierarchy, to the boot licking; it is therefore a form of resistance. That is why the idealism has such a stark form. It enfolds a collective historical consciousness that resists outrageous oppression. As Chicanos have experienced centuries of oppression, with little power to overcome it, our sense of social justice has become ever more finely honed, idealized if you will, so that it no longer has any real connection to the pragmatic world around us. Idealized social justice can be maintained without any real hope that it will actually happen. Thus, idealized social justice can function almost like a religion: It gives you power to survive precisely because of its purity. So it becomes important from an ideological standpoint to maintain that because that is what keeps you going in the face of great injustice and oppression.

MM: You cannot imagine the kind of pain that Atencio goes through because of the unjust treatment he receives, particularly from the chicanada at the university. His posture brings him much suffering and it is real — lack of prestige, resources, rank, pay. Atencio's situation should be important to all of us because it highlights what has happened to many Chicano academics. Here you have a man who at the age of sixty is still working as a lecturer. Atencio has been an important player in the history of Chicano and New Mexican thought, and there are multiple ways to document this claim. But this has not been recognized by many of his colleagues at UNM as indicated by their allegations that he has "a degree from a second-rate department." Yet, he is teaching where he got his degree. They also allege that his "publications are limited to regional themes," and that the "faculty's action to deny him a regular position was done to protect him from failure." All this shows a general disregard not only for him as an individual but for Chicano and New Mexican thought in general.

His work in service learning deals with a cutting-edge issue that should be important to the community, but it is disregarded by the university — at least when driven by Chicanos. It is clear, at least to me, that the university is truly outside the interests of a large segment of the population in New Mexico. Regional and local issues are important and should be recognized and rewarded. It seems to me that the U. S. Senate leader and his colleagues should be concerned with local and regional issues. It seems that Speaker Newt Gingrich and Alvin Toffler certainly think these issues are important since they are advocating devolution and decentralization.

I think that what is happening to Atencio is not unique to UNM. It seems to me that at this juncture the university is unwilling to grant him credit when it comes to ideas about change, yet his work is significant. You and I have borrowed his ideas and they have served us well — the *resolana*, the importance of oral history, crypto Judaism, the *academia*, the idea of service learning, and the documentation center to name just a few. University officials and many faculty members caught up in their own narrow professional interests are unwilling to view Chicanos and Indians as agents of change. Adapting to the interests of the elite and being rewarded for advocating ideas from and for the elite is not change. In their view, Chicanos are supposed to adapt to the "changes" that the elite is creating and not to those that Chicanos create. This is not only Atencio's fight but our fight as Chicanos.

Many Chicanos have not been able to see that the disregard displayed by the university to individuals like Atencio and J. J. is a disregard for them also. Many of us have been satisfied with simply adapting to the sometimes toxic environment that is being created for all of us. I believe politicians refer to their colleagues who hang around but do nothing as "back benchers." It is unfortunate, but many Chicano academics have become back benchers. Such Chicano academic back benchers are even viewed as "successful" by their colleagues.

RP: Atencio belongs to one pole of Chicano idealism. Remember that this idealism of which we speak is not given in just one form to every Chicano. There is one group for whom this idealism is little more than the activism of their younger days and they now have moved around or beyond it. But there is another, more extreme, group of which you have given some examples. For them, the idealism is absolutely fundamental. Of course, there are quite a few Chicanos who are in between and who exist in varying degrees of confusion and contradiction. Sometimes it looks like they are just going to blend in. At other times they come out strong on the idealist side. Obviously, it is not beyond some of these individuals to use the idealism as a vehicle to achieve personal agendas. The idealism of which we speak is deeply rooted psychologically. It therefore has a lot of power. Such power can be both used and abused. People like Atencio make this power possible. There don't really have to be a lot of people like him to keep alive this psychological power. It is akin to religious power where only a few people are really needed to keep it going at a deep level. But as long as they are there, the rest of the people will form rings around them and keep the faith going in various forms that are not quite as pure as the form preserved by the true believers.

So taking the Chicano collectivity, what stands out is this idealism that becomes noticeable both in its pure form and in the other forms that are not quite so pure. The pure form is what drives the Chicano *movimiento*. Only a very small proportion of Chicanos actually live by this idealism but it has become the paradigm that moves everything along. It is this paradigm also that stands so starkly in contrast to the Anglo way of life in the universities.

MM: But it does not create any reaction by the universities. In the Black situation, for instance, there is a reaction among the powers that be to the Black condition in whatever form it has manifested itself. The relationship between Whites and Blacks has deep psychological roots and has been impacted by the idea of White guilt. It is a real thing. With regard to Chicano idealism and their sense of social justice, these things do not have the same kind of play with the people in power as in the case of Blacks. They have no impact.

RP: It is a totally different dynamic. The Black - White dynamic is not only one of guilt, but one that demands some kind of compensation. There is pointing of the finger: This is what you did to us. With Chicanos, it all comes out much more abstractly, it is more value driven. In a sense, one can say that what defines the Black experience is the idea of master and slave. Everything else derives from that. Racism in this Black and White case is clearly based on the master - slave relationship.

The Legacy of Las Casas
RP: In contrast, the nature of the Chicano dynamic must be sought in history, particularly in the Indo-Hispanic clash of the sixteenth century. It is there that you will find the prototype of the problem we as Chicanos are having with the universities. A discussion very similar to the one that you and I are having now occurred in the the middle of the sixteenth century between Bartolomé de las Casas and his opponent Francisco Vitoria. The argument has to do with the status of the Indians in the new world. The question was: Are Indians basically the same as other human beings, say Europeans, or are they less than human and thus Europeans have the right to enslave them with impunity? If they were ordinary humans, then the Europeans had the obligation to treat them as such, and, under church doctrine, to bring salvation to them. If they were subhuman, then there was no need to bother with these acts of generosity. This was truly the first modern debate on what we now call human rights. Down the centuries, the protagonist of this great debate, Las Casas, has been characterized by his opponents as a rank idealist because he held that the Indians were just as human as the Europeans (never mind that the British on first contact also considered the Irish as savages).

But think for a moment about the context for this debate on human rights. In the middle of the sixteenth century, Spain was at the apex of its imperial glory. It had conquered a good part of the world. Its ships were sailing the seven seas in their endless search for gold, trade, and conquest. Everyone from swine herders to aristocrats was trying to get part of the action. For the would-be conquistador, there was an opportunity to bid for power. If you had the strongest arm you would triumph. The formula actually was quite simple: Get on a ship, cross the ocean, conquer some Indians and teach them who is the boss, send some gold and plunder back home to the king, then say to him, "Look at all that I have done for you. Now give me a land grant. And by the way, why don't you throw in a few hundred Indians. I am sure that I can Christianize them. But it will take some time, and for this service you should let me use them for labor." According to the conquistador, all of this was just because he was doing right by God and king.

It is in this context of conquest and empire building that one hears the voice of Las Casas saying that it's all wrong. Values are important, he says. We must recognize the humanity of the native peoples.

Remember that idealism is based on a set of ideas: such as justice, morality, all mankind is one, and so on. Las Casas was pointing an idealistic finger at the institutions of his day. It is important to note that rhetorically he carried the day. That's what accounts for the establishment of the *Nuevas Leyes de las Indias*, perhaps the first modern expression of human rights. But in reality the exploitation of the Indians continued.

My basic point is that this great debate was a defining moment in the history of Indo-Hispanic peoples, of which Chicanos are but one expression. Too bad that Anglo historians do not recognize its true importance and thus largely ignore it, and certainly leave it out of the school curriculum. But in this historic debate one can see a tension within European culture itself. There is one part of this culture that has strong idealistic tendencies and another part that is driven by material concerns. The two parts of the culture exist in a permanent state of conflict.

The second point is that, in a curious way, the conquistador paradigm may apply to today's universities as well. Professors are like the Spanish conquistadores. They toil in an intellectual foreign land, perhaps conquer a few of the natives and claim that they have hit pay dirt. Then, of course, they ask for their just rewards from the ruling powers of the universities.

The Chicanos came to campus saying, "Wait a minute. What about social justice?" Like Las Casas, they were looked at as idealists or worse. And like Las Casas who got the *Nuevas Leyes de las Indias* approved, Chicanos get their Chicano studies programs approved. We got the Hispanic Research Center approved. So what? If you look at the real players in the university, they are playing their hand just like the conquistadores who in many ways personified what Freire would call the oppressors.

So how can one compare the epic Las Casas debate with the Black slave and White master dynamic? The idealistic moment also can be very potent, but you have to elevate yourself to a higher plateau to discern it.

Outside of Anglo History

MM: Two points: first, the influence of Las Casas is undeniable. Hugh Thomas points out that Las Casas hurt his cause because he exaggerated the role of the Spaniards in the destruction of the inhabitants of the Indies. They died not from Spanish carnage or disease (that came later) but from a loss of spirit. It is this loss of spirit that should concern us most. What happens to a people who lose their spirit? In the spirit of historical accuracy, it is also important for us to remember that in his zeal to protect the "Indians," Las Casas advocated not the abolition of slavery but that slave labor should be imported from Africa — a position he later came to regret.

Second, Hispanic historical experience in the Americas is not a recognized part of the Anglo American experience. Except for the War of 1848, which really did not involve that many Anglo Americans outside their resources and their power, they have been outside of this tradition. Their war involvement did not involve their consciousness except for a few renegades who protested the Machiavellian intent of the war. The best-known dissenting figure was Henry David Thoreau, who promptly landed in jail and wrote his famous essay on civil disobedience. If you look at the reason for the war, the taking over of one-half of the Mexican territory, you can see the myths that were created around the Alamo, the injustice attributed to Santa Ana, and the alleged stupidity of the Mexican army. There almost is a justification for the war from the point of view of the naive historian. You can understand that ours is a whole different dynamic, and it also dictates that we cannot succumb to being influenced by the para-digm of the Black - White relationship. It does not fit us.

RP: By the time the English came to the Americas, it was well over a hundred years that the Spaniards had been here. But anything before 1600 or so has no meaning in terms of conventional American history. So the big debate that Las Casas stirred up and that had such an impact in shaping the Indo-Hispanic experience is largely outside the consciousness of the aver-age Anglo. So it is not part of their cultural understanding. Likewise, this formative experience is outside the cultural experience of Anglo institu-tions, whereas they understand full well what happened with the Blacks and they are trying to deal with that.

MM: They also have fear of Black violence. Increasingly I am begin-ning to think that it is less White guilt and more a type of fear that Whites have toward Blacks. Perhaps even more fundamental is the realization by both parties that they don't want to deal with each other in an authentic manner. They are willing to divide up the pie and go their own ways. This, of course, works only in the short term. It is a decision that the elites have made so that the younger generation will have to deal with the issues later. It is the same type of decision that elites are making with regard to matters like social security and the environment.

RP: And what do elites fear about the Chicano paradigm that we are talking about? That someone might become too idealistic?

MM: There is a war raging in this country that people have not come to terms with. It is a chaotic resistance war that Blacks are fighting on many fronts. A lot of it is against themselves, but it is a war. The war is not exclusive to Blacks. Many Mexican kids involved in gang activities see their activities as a testament to their Mexican pride. It is a form of resistance against the terrible treatment that they receive from the police and the schools. I grant you that it is dysfunctional, but nevertheless if we viewed it as resistance it would give us a whole different view of what is occurring in the inner cities. It would force the society to see these issues as social problems, as injustices, and not as deviances separated from the concerns of the larger society.

There are many examples of incidents that hint at this war: Recent revelations about the burning of Afro-American churches, the Rodney King beatings, the O. J. Simpson trial, Bernhard Goetz, the so-called vigilante gunman, the inmate Willy Horton and his role in the election of Bush to the presidency, the killing of Blacks in Howard Beach and Bensonhurst in New York City, and, of course, the riots in Miami. I could go on with many other examples.

RP: And we are getting drawn into it because we are not immune to what happens in the larger dynamic of society. The real challenge facing the Chicanos is a moral challenge. At least that is the way that I am trying to phrase it. Chicano idealism must be counterposed to the hedonism and selfishness of the eighties. That's really what the Chicano should be about. In some sense, the Chicano represents an even greater threat to the hedonistic society than the Blacks. You cannot take Chicanos and jail them en masse because they are idealists. If Chicanos were to work their way into key positions in the society and truly follow the idealistic paradigm, that would be far more likely to change the dominant culture.

MM: You are more of an idealist than I am.

RP: That is the way that Chicanos have chosen to position themselves ideologically. At least this is true to the extent that there is anything to talk about in terms of a Chicano perspective or critique. Otherwise it is simply a question of assimilation. The more important question is whether this idealism, or more precisely the critique implied therein, can be spelled out clearly. I am not yet convinced that Chicanos have spelled out our idealism (i.e., our critique) with great clarity. But it can be intuited, if somewhat vaguely, from our behavior. Assuming it can be spelled out clearly, especially as a critique, it remains to be seen whether such idealism will prove to be advantageous or not. Perhaps it can only exist in isolation from the mainstream culture in certain interstices of society, like universities, that can tolerate that sort of thing. Or perhaps it is simply a utopian vision.

Yet, I don't see idealism as fundamentally alien to western thought. In fact, a lot of our idealistic vision is framed by western thought. Perhaps we as Chicanos are exhibiting a variation of the idealist Western tradition that has been shaped by our own historical experience. *Quizás es un matíz del pensamiento Europeo. Del pensamiento judeo-cristiano.* Chicano idealism has been filtered through the Indo-Hispanic experience as opposed to, say, the Protestant Reformation and the industrial revolution, more typical of our Anglo brethren. So you see, my friend, in calling you an idealist I simply was turning you into a synecdoche for Chicano idealism.

Chapter 3

University Autonomy

The Appointment of a Latino Dean

On 10 September 1975, the university president appointed a committee to select a dean for the School of Social Work. This dialogue summarizes the turmoil that occurred in the hiring of the dean, an Hispanic. At first glance, the details of the search process appear fairly routine. A search committee was appointed by the central administration, community groups put pressure on the university and thereby gained representation on the search committee, criteria were developed for judging the applicants, candidates were rated, recommendations were submitted, and a dean was appointed. However, along with these routine activities were undercurrents of political intrigue and "bad faith" that in the end compromised the university's autonomy and academic integrity.

The seed for the controversy was an excerpt from appendix B of an obscure publication, the proceedings of a 1971 WICHE Conference on Ethnic Minority Content in Social Work. The excerpt stated that "all faculty positions being vacated for whatever reasons should be replaced by Third World people or left vacant . . . [and] The present deans of schools of social work must make arrangements to replace themselves with Third World people within the next three years" (WICHE, 1971, 79–80). The excerpt was distributed to various parties interested in the dean's search as if it were the work of then candidate Ismael Dieppa. It was distributed without Dieppa's knowledge and without informing the search committee (except for the chair). Dieppa had in fact been a keynote speaker at the conference. His speech also was published in the proceedings, but it reflects a different perspective from the excerpt that came from appendix B of the publication.

Dieppa's speech was not circulated along with the excerpt from the appendix.

The central players in this incident are the three candidates for the dean's position, including Dieppa, who eventually became the dean, a faculty member who shortly thereafter became a dean elsewhere and later joined the faculty of the University of California, Berkeley, and a third individual who was affiliated with the Mormon church and who also later became a dean at another university. In addition, there was the chair of the search committee and one of his colleagues who, along with the chair of a community advisory committee whom we will refer to as a "right-wing activist," were the major opponents to the Dieppa appointment. Also, there were two state senators involved: Senator Stan Turley, who served as an advocate for the faculty who got in trouble for what was defined as unethical professional behavior by the National Association of Social Workers (NASW), and Senator Alfredo Gutierrez, who at the time was the majority leader of the Arizona state senate. Gutierrez was a central player in providing protection against the accusations made by Dieppa's opponents. Finally, there were various faculty members who are mentioned in the following dialogue.

RP: The Dieppa incident from the midseventies can set the stage for our discussion of the eighties, which are the main focus of this book. Through this incident we may get a sense of what it was like for Chicanos to be in the university during the seventies.

MM: This was one of the first Chicano confrontations with the university that had some Chicano political players involved.

RP: What was the confrontation about? In the beginning of the process to search for a new dean of the School of Social Work, did you anticipate getting a Chicano dean? Or was it simply that there happened to be a search for a dean and a Latino became a viable candidate?

Johnson's Legacy

MM: It was like any other confrontation in the selection of a dean. I don't think it was one or the other—there was an interplay between the two. In 1974, when I first arrived at the university, the dean of my school had announced that he was going to retire. I arrived from Berkeley as a visiting associate professor. When I decided not to return to Berkeley, my faculty position at the university was regularized. At the time, the department was very happy to have me. I am not sure that such would be the case now.

When the dean of the School of Social Work, Horace Lundberg, decided to retire, Dieppa was an associate dean at the University of Denver. He and I had talked about the dean's position. He was part of a small group of social workers who had been involved in the organizing efforts with the

Council of Social Work, which later led to the development of the School of Social Work at San Jose State University. The small group consisted of twenty or so Chicanos nationwide. You will recall that because of Johnson's War on Poverty, resources were abundant at that time. It is amazing that you could get to any place in the United States. The War on Poverty made it possible to hold conferences, and to consult with the federal government, and this created many possibilities for networking. Many Chicano organizations sprang from these early organizing efforts. Organizations like the National Council of La Raza were created in part because of the access people had to one another through networking. Dieppa was part of this network. I informed him about the dean's position and encouraged him to apply. He always wanted to be a dean. There were no internal candidates, and as far as I know the job was not wired for any one person.

A Routine Search

RP: Was the search committee constituted in an unbiased way, or was it loaded in one direction or another?

MM: It was routine university politics. There was nothing out of the ordinary. The chair of the selection committee was the most powerful member of the faculty. The other members of the committee included Eddie Brown (a Native American), who later became the head of the Bureau of Indian Affairs. There were two minority persons on the committee out of five members.

There was a lot of lobbying going on among interested community and professional groups, such as the National Association of Social Workers (NASW). So the committee had to make some accommodations. These groups got included in the committee. It is the regular politics of a professional school. There was nothing out of the ordinary.

The important issue is that the view of minorities by nonminorities was different at that time. In 1975 you could count the number of Chicanos at the university on one hand. There was no real animosity toward them. One of the things that I have noticed since 1975 is that at that time there was more freedom to be invited into the circles of semipower. It was an era when the school was more of a collegium. People related to one another on ethnic grounds less than now.

In summarizing the Dieppa incident, I have tried to preserve the language of the time. This is important because the School of Social Work was different from most other departments in that it included more women. Social work is a woman-dominated profession even though at the time of the Dieppa incident the hierarchy was mostly men. There has always been the presence of women in social work and our university was no exception. The language used to carry on fights and disagreements can change over time. I try to reflect the language of the time. For example, there was an instance where a faculty member accused one of the applicants and a Mormon of saying that "a woman's place is in the home." That is an early example of what we would now call sexism or the use of that type of woman power to attack an opponent. The word "sexism" was never used at the time of the incident to attack somebody's behavior.

Another important aspect of this incident is that the documentation is extensive. Everything that is said, with the exception of a reference to a rumor, is supported with letters or other reports. Not only did I personally witness many of the incidents, everything that is said is documented and that which cannot be documented is not said.

RP: So the committee and the selection process were routine. What happened then?

"When the Mess Started"

MM: All the usual routines: Selection criteria were established, announcements were sent out, people applied, a subcommittee was appointed to check out the top applicants, give-and-take occurred within the committee, and finally the applicants were whittled down to a short list of five. From this short list, the finalists were to be invited for interviews. That's when the mess started, when it became evident that Dieppa, who was on the short list, had a chance to be hired.

We had advocated Dieppa within the committee all along. But there were other good candidates. The top candidate was Michael Austin, who later got a dean's job someplace else and now is a professor at the University of California, Berkeley. He is an accomplished scholar. The third candidate was Kay Dee, who is a dean now but was not seen as a strong candidate at the time. These are the people who emerged.

RP: Clearly, the Berkeley professor was head and shoulders above the rest?

MM: I think so. He was the most accomplished scholar.

RP: Why didn't the committee simply rally around him and say, "He is the one we want"?

MM: Because in all matters like this you never forward just one name. I recall that after the two top candidates emerged the chair issued a minority report adding other people to the list.

RP: Unilaterally?

MM: That is the prerogative of the chair.

RP: No longer. This is how search committees have changed over the years. It is unusual now for a chair to go outside the decisions of a committee. First of all, you cannot unilaterally add to the short list because of affirmative action stipulations. In any event, adding names to the short list by anyone would signal to the provost that you wanted to start over the search. Or if the chair is simply out of order, the additions would probably just be ignored and the search would most likely be seen as conflicted.

MM: While all this was going on, there also was turmoil over the "Third World excerpt" (which is described in the introduction to this chapter). Two parallel processes were going on simultaneously. First, there was the regular process where people followed the rules. Then there was a sub-rosa process through which some people were trying to undermine Dieppa's candidacy. For example, when the search committee met, the chair pushed very hard to expand the short list of candidates. He had a five to four majority on this issue until one of the members of the committee reversed her vote when she saw the shenanigans of the chair. She said, "I am going with whomever is selected, and it will probably be Dieppa." It was at that point that the chair wrote a minority report.

RP: So there wasn't much irregularity in the process until after the short list was submitted? It seems that the political effort to derail Dieppa's candidacy was started after it became clear that he was one of the top three candidates.

MM: It was the chair and a faculty member on the committee who distributed an appendix from the proceedings of a conference on ethnic content in social work. These types of conferences always included a minority position statement put out by a caucus composed of students and young assistant professors or lecturers who were not familiar with academic routines. The caucuses were always making outrageous demands. The appendix in question stated that all deans of social work were to replace themselves with minorities, and that every faculty vacancy was to be filled by a Chicano. The chair and a faculty member of the committee took this excerpt, copied it, and distributed it to various people to give them the impression, either implicitly or explicitly, that it had been authored by Dieppa and that it represented his educational philosophy.

RP: And this was supposed to be a mortal blow to his candidacy?

MM: Yes, because of its militant posture. This is a conservative state. If you recall, the chair of the community advisory committee called the community people "Birchers," many of whom were Mormon. Senator Turley is Mormon. He later served on the Board of Regents for a short while. He was a very powerful man in Arizona politics. He was the leverage that the opposition used. There would be no way that a militant like Dieppa could possibly become dean.

RP: So their strategy was to short-circuit Dieppa's candidacy by going to outside community groups who would then pressure the university president and the vice president not to make an appointment regardless of the wishes of the search committee?

MM: Remember Richardson's model of cultural diversity where he says that minorities are the ones who go to outside community groups? In this situation there was a lot of outside activity by Anglo groups, much more than we could have imagined on the part of Chicanos. Yet, Chicano political powers converged that allowed Dieppa to be hired. I was a friend of the majority leader of the state senate, Alfredo Gutierrez. I was also a good friend of the state's affirmative action officer, now U.S. congressman Ed Pastor. They were both connected to a Chicano governor, Raul Castro. It was this convergence that got Dieppa hired.

A Confrontation of Wills and Politics

RP: The point that you are making is that the scenario was set for a confrontation of wills and politics between a Chicano agenda that was politically supported and the opponents of Dieppa who also were enlisting political influence from outside of the university.

MM: However, what has to be remembered is that the appointment of the dean of the School of Social Work was a very small part of the pie. It was incredibly insignificant. For me or Dieppa or for Eddie Brown it wasn't insignificant, but it was insignificant in the total scheme of things. It was nothing for the president of the university. If you analyze the budget of the School of Social Work it would represent maybe 6 percent of the total budget of the university. So in that context, most of our fights in the total scheme of things are insignificant.

RP: The actual stakes during any particular struggle may be quite modest within the context of the entire institution. So one does have to ask why it takes so much energy and conflict for such small stakes. What does this indicate? What accounts for it?

I believe that this is where racism and interest-group politics come in. It takes so much energy for Chicanos to fight for these relatively small stakes because the opposition is engaging in blocking actions. It is the finger in the dike sort of thing. Blocking someone from becoming dean is a way of blocking that person from becoming vice president, which is a way of blocking the person from becoming president. One particular block at a low level of the organization is not all that significant if it is seen in isolation. But if you understand the whole organizational scheme of academia, blocking someone from getting tenure is important, blocking someone from getting full professor or department chair is also important because these are critical points in a trajectory to power and control of the organization. So there is contention for power every step of the way. In the ordinary scheme of things, once Dieppa was appointed dean, the next battle should have been for a vice presidency.

MM: That analysis is too conspiratorial. What I think happens is that there is intense competition for each and every position, and that usually Chicanos are outgunned within particular departments for promotion and appointment as chair. Under these circumstances, it is only when those in power are willing to intervene that Chicanos are promoted or appointed to the lower-level positions. The situation is analogous to the civil rights types of changes that were made from an elitist perspective. Elites decided to make changes at the lower levels of society when those at the lower levels were unable or unwilling to make changes. This does not mean that Blacks did not have to fight; it only means that they could not have done it without help from the elites. Dye has an analysis of this phenomenon in one of his books. This model is worth examining. At any rate, there is no way that Dieppa could have become vice president or assistant vice president here.

RP: I agree about the contention for power at all levels of the organization and that Chicanos are typically outgunned in terms of power and control. However, the process that I described need not be conspiratorial, because the ethnic prejudices operating, which are often used by the opposition as leverage points, do not have to be made explicit. They are part of the shared culture of the opposition that operates almost invisibly. That's where the power of prejudice comes in. The opposition does not have to confront its prejudices; they are simply used as a set of unstated cultural assumptions. In any event, we do agree that the struggles we engage in are exaggerated in the sense that we have to use enormous amounts of political capital on campaigns involving relatively small stakes.

An Anonymous Document

MM: That is a very good insight that explains why people in power often operate in a single direction. Organizations are designed to favor them at the expense of others. Corporate taxes are a good example. But let me tell you what happened during the Dieppa incident. This was a peculiar situation in that the majority faculty rallied around Dieppa when they found out that the chair of the committee and one of his colleagues had helped circulate the so-called radical document. This document, which was part of an appendix to a 1971 WICHE conference on ethnic minority content in social work, called for the hiring of Third World people (or else leaving positions vacant) in all faculty positions being vacated for whatever reason and also that the sitting deans of schools of social work make arrangements to replace themselves with Third World people within three years. The individuals circulating this document claimed that they were "inquiring" whether Dieppa had authored it. There was no evidence that he had written the document. The document had no authorship and the only link to Dieppa was that he was one of the speakers at the conference. The faculty assumed responsibility for accusing of unprofessional behavior the professors who circulated the document during the dean's search. This is what is intriguing about the incident.

RP: The college faculty took the renegade professors to task because they were violating norms?

MM: Yes. The faculty took an ethical position. They fought the allegation.

RP: But these ethical faculty were brought back into line very quickly by the central administration and the outside political influentials. So their sense of justice was evident but very fragile. I am not quite convinced that these faculty would have gone to the mat for Dieppa, in spite of the egregious infractions of their own norms by some of their colleagues. Clearly, the majority faculty had the professional obligation to respond to the abuses. But I am curious about the degree to which they responded.

MM: They asked an external committee on inquiry to look into the matter because they felt that it could not be done internally. They first went to the American Association of University Professors (AAUP). However, the AAUP said that the matter was outside of its jurisdiction; it suggested that the matter be handled by the professional social work association. So the request to the AAUP got bounced around and finally ended up with the University Grievance Committee (UGC). The chair of the UGC assured the faculty that the process was not going to be adversarial, and that only people from within the university would participate. There was to be no participation by individuals outside the university.

In fact, however, a whole delegation of politicians, including an activist from the right, participated in the process. The UGC found that there was no misbehavior on the part of the two accused faculty members. Thus, the university succumbed to political pressure.

Or you could also say that there simply was no wrongdoing on the part of the accused faculty. However, faculty from the School of Social Work responded to the committee's decision by writing a position paper in which they reminded the committee chair of his promise not to allow any outside influences on the committee. By allowing state senators and other people from the community to participate in the review process, the committee had invalidated the review process. Therefore, the faculty resubmitted the charge of violation of ethics against the two professors to the National Association of Social Workers (NASW).

The Failure of Self-Regulation

RP: So according to the complaining faculty of the School of Social Work, the institutional mechanism for self-regulation failed?

MM: No, it did not necessarily fail. The faculty failed to get the outcome they wanted. You could argue that the accused faculty were exonerated, that there was no wrongdoing.

RP: Yes, but according to the dissatisfied faculty the system failed because it allowed outsiders to infiltrate the review process and perhaps to exert improper influence.

MM: Yes, because at that time Senator Turley wrote a letter to the university president, with copies to various people, saying that the issue had been settled with the internal review and the actual hiring decision that had been made. In fact, Dieppa was in the process of getting hired. So Turley suggested that everyone drop the matter and go forward. In effect, he was saying that we should not make things any dirtier because the accused professors had been exonerated.

RP: But here again we have influence from outside the university. So it turns out that there were at least two key points in the search process and subsequent procedures where outsiders were calling the shots. The first point of intrusion was during the actual search process and the second during the grievance hearings. So the university was not really settling its own affairs internally and autonomously.

MM: In fact, it was opening itself to increased outside intrusions.

RP: So what you have described are the dynamics of the academy itself. It was not Chicanos who were driving the process per se. The professors who challenged the activities of the two errant professors were not Chicanos. Likewise, the people who wrote the internal and external complaints were not Chicanos. In a sense, the Chicanos were to a large degree witnessing the academy wrestle with its problems. There was one Chicano and one Indian on the search committee who witnessed all of this. What was their response?

MM: We went with the flow of the faculty; we were part of the faculty. It is the most effective political posture to take.

RP: So you did not bring in the outside Chicano community as a counterbalance to the political influence from the right?

MM: We were meeting with Senator Gutierrez at the time. We told him what was going on, that Dieppa was being attacked. We were working in conjunction with the faculty of the school of social work.

RP: When the formal grievance process was under way, was there a parallel effort by Chicanos at least to keep the Chicano community apprised of what was going on?

MM: Senator Gutierrez, like Senator Turley, wrote a letter to the university president. Remember that Senator Turley wanted to drop the whole thing. Gutierrez did not want the matter dropped. If the accused faculty were not guilty, he argued, they should be exonerated. He did not want the matter dropped. It needed to be settled.

RP: Why did he take this position? Is it not idealistic? After all, the others may have been taking a much more pragmatic position even though it undermined the institution's autonomy and credibility.

MM: No, because Senator Turley saw that they had lost, and that Dieppa had been hired.

RP: You see it as a tactic on their part? They wanted to drop the matter because they had lost the battle for the dean's appointment?

NASW Was Offended

MM: They lost not only because Dieppa got hired, but because their folks were under attack for violation of the profession's code of ethics. The faculty shifted their attack against the errant professors when they filed a formal complaint with the NASW. By this time, many of the school faculty refused to join in the complaint; they wanted to stop the whole thing.

RP: So there was a group of faculty on whom the Turley admonition had an impact? In effect, they agreed to a political deal: Dieppa got the deanship and the errant professors got exonerated. It was a gentleman's agreement.

MM: Absolutely. Several faculty did drop the complaint, but other faculty members submitted a request to the NASW Arizona Committee on Inquiry to look into the matter. There is a lot of documentation on this. The Arizona affiliate of the NASW decided that it could not handle the matter locally, so it was kicked up to the national association. There was a rumor that the right-wing activist was still exerting pressure. One of the committee members from the NASW Arizona chapter worked at an agency headed by the right-wing activist either as a director or as a board member. I don't really know. At any rate, as the matter got kicked up to the national association more faculty dropped from the complaint.

RP: So at that point only a few faculty members from the school were carrying the load? What was NASW's response?

MM: NASW's response was interesting. In effect, it said, "You filed this complaint and we are going to look into it." So it was not going to drop the matter. It is strange. The thing took on a life of its own. I think that if a vote had been taken, the faculty would have stopped the complaint. But by then the entire matter was getting out of hand. The faculty was getting pressure from the administration, from the agency heads, and from the right wing. But NASW went ahead and said that there indeed had been a violation. It recommended censure of the errant professors. Further, it was offended by the faculty who had not gone through with the grievance. The next thing was the appeal. That's another story.

The Appeal

RP: The decision of NASW was appealed?

MM: Yes, by the accused professors. First, they told the dean, "This issue was dropped and we have been exonerated, and you are still pushing this thing. We are being treated unfairly." That was one way of looking at the situation, and these people may have had a point.

RP: Provided that the University Grievance Committee had been functioning in good faith, and without undue outside influence. If the committee was influenced politically, then the accused were not exonerated at all. They were exonerated only by political pressure groups, and a university faculty that did not have the guts to stand up to the pressure.

MM: In the appeal, the chair argued that the notorious appendix, which contained the radical proposals, was more in agreement than disagreement when compared with Dieppa's authored chapter. He stated that the excerpts from the appendix that were circulated could well have been Dieppa's position. So the chair reversed himself.

RP: But originally he maintained that Dieppa was the author of the appendix. He was not really reversing himself; it was a different way of maintaining his old position. Originally he argued that the appendix represented Dieppa's own educational philosophy. Then he was pressed, charged, and censured. So he did his homework. He analyzed Dieppa's speech and compared it with the appendix. He then concluded that while the two were not identical, there were clear connections between the Dieppa speech and the appendix. It all amounts to the same thing: that Dieppa was a radical.

MM: And thus there was justification for bringing out the appendix during the search process. The chair of the search committee also said that "I was asked" by the right-wing activist, who was the chair of the advisory committee, to get him the information. Now, where the hell would the right-wing activist learn about this obscure document in the first place? Then, of course, the right-wing activist supported the search committee chair and said, "Yes I asked him for it and as a matter of fact I talked to members of the Board of Regents, senators, and others, and they all said that it was legitimate to have raised this issue."

RP: So the committee chair argued that he distributed the appendix in response to an inquiry from an outsider. That sounds to me like a retroconstuction of the matter. But the argument about the content of the Dieppa speech is interesting. It is not an argument that is dismissible out of hand. He argued that after he had read the piece authored by Dieppa along with the anonymous appendix, he found concordance between the two. This supported his view that the matter had to be looked into by the search committee. Moreover, there were other people who agreed with him about the relevance of the material contained in the appendix. This position cannot be dismissed outright.

MM: From their point of view, it was an effective vehicle of attack.

RP: Of course, one would need to confirm that the content analysis justified the conclusion of concordance between the two parts of the book. He may have reached an invalid conclusion. So what was the response?

MM: The response was made by one of the social work professors who charged that the chair on several occasions admitted circulating the appendix material of his own volition.

RP: So that's how they got him. The point was not whether the appendix was in agreement with Dieppa's speech. The point was that the chair took the anonymous appendix material and selectively distributed it to various people in an effort to undermine Dieppa's candidacy. This material was not part of the official proceedings of the search committee. Therefore, the material could not be used in assessing Dieppa's suitability to become dean. That was the chair's mistake. If he had distributed this information openly to the entire committee, and then asked Dieppa to respond to it, there would not have been a case of impropriety and he probably would have been very effective in undermining Dieppa's candidacy.

MM: That is the way it would be done now. In a situation where you have total power, you can do it any way you want.

RP: That is where he made his mistake, in thinking that he had the power to act without restraint. He made a strategic mistake by going counter to the norms of the institution and his profession. That is what created all the problems for him. Of course, someone had to stand up and challenge the behavior before there could be a problem.

Rifts among the Faculty

MM: That's where the other part of the story comes in. There are letters in the files, going back to the early seventies, of rifts among the faculty in the School of Social Work. There is a letter, for instance, where the dean's administrative assistant and some faculty members complained about a professor turned administrator in the college who also was a member of the search committee and an ally of the chair. So the faculty's motivation in filing the complaints was not necessarily to protect Dieppa or to honor a code of ethics, but to get back at certain people for past behavior.

RP: So here is another example of how apparently small, personal agendas feed into larger conflicts. In this case, old scores were going to be evened or power positions were being solidified. The two censured individuals gave their opponents an opportunity to get back at them.

MM: Exactly. The documentation indicates that people who had been previously ousted later submitted letters against the chair's ally about unethical behavior.

RP: So in the Dieppa incident there were many things that converged: the agenda of the right wingers from Mesa, Arizona, the Chicano politicians who happened to be particularly influential at that moment, a particularly active professional association, and the ongoing internecine fights among the academicians. The Dieppa candidacy may just have been a catalyzing agent. It was only marginally a Chicano fight.

MM: There were some who believed in social justice.

RP: That's right. Especially within the context of the idealized university where things are supposed to occur in an orderly way and where outside influences are to be kept at bay. The political rhetoric of the university was used by the winning side. But the political pragmatism of the losing side managed to limit the damage that it sustained. And Chicanos had enough political muscle to get Dieppa the job.

MM: Several points should be noted about what happened to some of the players in this drama. The chair of the search committee was gone the following year because his relationship with the new dean had been irreparably damaged. He was a productive scholar and he could go elsewhere. The other faculty member was not and stayed. It is interesting to note that some of the people who were active in his defense later had a falling out with the new dean and eventually left the university.

RP: You are implying that Dieppa's candidacy was a central concern for them to begin with. I am suggesting that it wasn't. There was always the possibility that they would have a falling out with Dieppa because he was only a catalyst to the problems that arose during the search process. The struggle was really about internecine warfare within the School of Social Work among the regular faculty. That is what this story is about.

MM: But the fight was really only against one or two people. These were not warring parties. There were only two antagonistic persons, one of whom was influential, the other was not.

RP: And it got played out under color of ethnic concerns. Dieppa was not the top candidate. Dieppa was perhaps the second candidate.

MM: Probably they would have wanted the candidate who eventually went to U. C. Berkeley. Then they also knocked out the other candidate using the allegation that he was "sexist," although no one used the word. I actually know him, and he did not seem like a sexist to me. I don't believe that the allegation was true.

RP: There may be a story to be told there, too — how the third candidate got knocked out of the race. How do we know that there wasn't some internecine politics going on within the Mormon community itself that caused the attack on his candidacy? Once he was out of the race, and it became clear that the Chicanos were going to support the Hispanic candidate, the others had little choice but to try to reopen the search, especially if they had someone else in mind for the deanship.

MM: In the demise of this candidate, one can see the beginning of the sexual harassment strategy.

RP: Yes, that is significant especially in that it was used against a Mormon. I think that we should look for a connection there. Since then the sexism strategy, now called sexual harassment, has been used increasingly against Chicano males because everybody presumes that Chicanos are *machistas* and sexists. So they become very easy targets for political attacks using the sexual harassment strategy. To make a sexual harassment charge against a Chicano is almost to include the conviction of sexism automatically. That is a very powerful political strategy.

MM: We have two very good examples going on right now.

RP: That is the point, although it is only a side note to the present discussion. The main concern now is to try to understand the ethnic element in the Dieppa incident. From one angle, the incident appears to be a confrontation between ethnics and the university. And there are certain elements that point in that direction. But my conclusion is that the Dieppa incident was really a forerunner to the Chicano struggles within the university that were to manifest themselves during the decade of the eighties.

MM: Absolutely, because during the Dieppa incident there were actually majority faculty allies. The faculty were acting in tandem to achieve one aim.

RP: Because there was a convergence of interests. The Dieppa supporters found themselves in league with the majority faculty who were settling old scores and who wanted to control the deanship.

MM: There was a real injustice that was perceived.

RP: There *was* a real injustice.

MM: It depends. If you are exonerated by a committee, you are found not guilty.

RP: Provided that the committee's procedures are fair. Otherwise the committee's decision can be appealed on the grounds that it broke its own rules. The university temporized during the Dieppa incident. It processed the complaint through the University Grievance Committee, and looked the other way when it turned out that this committee broke its own rules by letting outsiders participate. Then there was no further appeal internally.

Who Governs the University?

MM: In this case it indicates the university's inability to govern itself. At that time, it seemed like people were still struggling to play by the rules, and deviations from the rules were more apparent. I think that today people don't have as much difficulty breaking the rules because the rules are not as clear. You identify what you want and you go after it. The rules seem secondary. It is difficult even to find out what the rules are. The university is now open to outside interference. This was an instance where people grossly broke the rule of self-governance. The university should not open itself to outside interference, and still expect to keep its autonomy and integrity.

This obviously was not the first time that outside influences have interfered in university processes. It would be interesting to document how often legislators, regents, community leaders, and local politicians have influenced student admissions and financial aid, faculty hiring, and the hiring and firing of administrators. This type of interference is and was common, although few would be willing to acknowledge it. It is hard to escape the fact that this is a public institution and therefore subject to public scrutiny and political manipulation. I heard later in the process that Governor Raul Castro, the first Chicano governor of Arizona, did in fact end up calling the president of the university. I would love to have heard what happened in that conversation.

I can't help thinking, however, that the behavior of some members of the faculty was the beginning of the demise of the school of social work. This truly was a defining moment, and an excellent example of how actions and decisions have a cumulative impact on later events.

RP: It raises the question of who actually governs the university. That is the more fundamental question. The university basically was reacting to outside pressures, and the decisions that were made were not made internally. They were greatly influenced from the outside—by the Chicano governor, the professional association, and the Mormon senator who in the end was trying to limit his losses.

MM: The senator came out real clean in the end. He wrote a beautiful letter. It was a letter about brotherhood.

Chapter 4

The Rationalist Turn

The Trip to Flagstaff

On 9 September 1982, Ismael Dieppa, Luis Aranda, and Raymond V. Padilla traveled to Flagstaff, Arizona, for a meeting that included Chicano affirmative action officers from the three Arizona state universities and then-member of the Arizona Board of Regents Tio Tachías. During the three-hour trip between Tempe and Flagstaff, the trio discussed the Chicano situation in higher education and the steps that might be taken to improve it. The trio agreed to three new initiatives: (1) to organize a statewide conference on Chicanos and higher education to identify specific issues and solutions that would subsequently be communicated to the proper authorities; (2) to propose the creation of a statewide Chicano advisory council to the Arizona Board of Regents that would work with the regents and university administrators to improve the educational services available to Chicanos; and (3) to ask then-governor Bruce Babbitt to support the establishment of a statutory commission on Hispanic affairs.

The Roots of Our Problems

RP: I first came to the university on December fifth of 1981 after having spent more than ten years as an academic activist involved with Chicano issues. During those years of activism I gained a lot of experience and understanding about institutional processes and about ourselves as Chicanos.

MM: That is reflected in your dissertation. Do you recall what you said about Chicano academics and the community? You said that both Chicano academics and students were interested in getting involved at the grassroots level but they did not understand the nature of universities.

RP: Yes, the problem that Chicano studies participants experienced in those years is that ideologically they wanted to involve the community as such in the universities in a way that was resisted by the universities. They really did not have a clear idea about what role the Chicano community ought to play; they simply had no experience. They developed their ideas as they went along. So when they met serious difficulties in trying to bring the Chicano community into the university environment, all kinds of strange things happened.

Yes, that is part of the experience that I brought with me. Remember that the four years that I spent as a graduate student at Berkeley were spent largely as a participant observer, particularly of the Chicano studies program and its participants. In addition, some of the graduate students tried very hard to get the School of Education to recognize the needs of the Chicano community, but without much success. That story in itself could fill a volume.

On top of all that, when I graduated from U. C. Berkeley I went back to Michigan to become the Latino education coordinator for the Michigan Department of Education. It was there that I had the first opportunity to work on Chicano issues on a statewide basis. That experience was important because people who don't have experience at the state level are often too local in their perspectives.

The roots of our problems are often at the state level. I have made this argument for a long time, but it has fallen largely on deaf ears. Remember that during the late sixties the Chicano strategy was to leapfrog local and state institutions and go straight to Washington, D. C. Chicanos expected that the solutions to our problems would come out of Washington, and that those solutions would be forced down the gullets of the intervening layers of state and local governments.

I was critical of the Washington approach as a strategy and changed my practice accordingly. So I got valuable experience by working on educational issues at the state level. I also tried to organize the Chicano community on a statewide basis. All that was part of the experience that I brought to the university.

Caught in a Time Warp

RP: When I first got to the university I did not know what to expect. I had driven through Arizona only once in my life. As a kid I lived in Texas but as a teenager I grew up in Michigan. Michigan is a big industrial state. But I lived in rural Michigan. During my graduate studies, I spent almost five years in the San Francisco and East Bay area. In spite of living in different places, I had no idea what Arizona was about.

As soon as I got here, I noticed something about the Chicanos in Arizona. There was a staff member at the Center for Bilingual and Bicultural Education named Ernesto López. He did not have regular faculty status; he was not on a tenure track line. Thus he was temporary help, although I am not sure that he saw things that way. He also was a committed community activist. But he was not well anchored in the university. One has to wonder to what extent his maneuvering was really an attempt to anchor himself more firmly within the university.

What struck me is that his status in the university was very similar to the status of Chicanos that I had known ten years before. In other words, he was very weakly anchored to the institution. Like many of his earlier colleagues, he did not have a faculty tenure track position or even a very substantial staff position where he could more or less count on a long tenure. López seemed to me to be stuck in a time warp.

MM: It was toward the end of an era when Chicanos were calling for a presence in the university. This presence usually was out of bilingual programs or out of Chicano studies efforts. I recall the initial efforts at U.C. Berkeley when Chicano graduate students and part-time employees were teaching and administering the beginning efforts of ethnic programs. There were few Chicanos teaching as tenured professors during those times. Here at our university, as well as other universities, there were some professors teaching in Spanish departments. Martinez was here and Rosaldo at the University of Arizona. There have always been professors in the Spanish departments.

RP: But those professors in Spanish departments represent a different generation. Many of them were not Chicanos. They were Hispanics, Spaniards, and Latin Americans mostly. You still have the remnants of that generation here at ASU.

Anyway, López was facing the kind of weakly anchored situation that I just described. This was very different from my situation because I came as a tenured professor or that of Eugene García, the director of the center, who also was a tenured professor. So things finally were changing a little bit on campus; a different set of players was beginning to assemble, those with tenured or tenure track appointments. But people like López were still driving the activist agenda on campus.

MM: When I started working at the university as a research assistant on soft money in 1967, there were very few Chicanos on the faculty. After leaving in 1969 and returning in 1974, there were some changes, but not many. The school of social work had hired one or two, there were a couple of Chicanos in history, two or three in education. But most of them, I guess, were in the Spanish department. You arrived at a time when things had already started to break. We were the first influx of Chicanos after the few who made it as a result of the G.I. Bill after World War II.

Shouting Matches

RP: One of the things that I heard about is that López and a group of community people made a proposal to the university to set up a center in the community dealing with Chicano students. We have a copy of that proposal that dates back to 1981. The document is anonymous. What I noticed is that the arguments made in the proposal were very much like the ones that were made ten years before when Chicanos first approached the universities with proposals for action. In fact, the proposal was still dealing with many of the issues that were hot during the late sixties. Of course, not much progress had been made in resolving those problems.

But the basic strategy behind the proposal also did not seem to have changed much: nonacademics from the community and a few weakly anchored Chicanos in the university would approach the highest levels of the administration demanding that something be done.

As it turns out, the actual proposal was technically quite good. It was very well thought out. Apparently, ten years of experience with universities had taught Chicanos like López how to produce a proposal that frankly should have been received by the university with open arms if it were judging the proposal strictly on its merits. It wasn't. The proposal was totally ignored.

MM: How do you know it was ignored? There are two stories to everything. One can be told through documentation, and the other through what really happened. Toni Morrison makes an important distinction between "what took place," that is, how a newspaper would describe a particular incident, and "what really happened" or what is to be understood after careful reflection. We all know that reviewing the "sanitized" documentation of certain incidents does not really tell you what happened. This is one of the reasons why we are having these conversations. As a matter of fact, your story about this trip and subsequent events that occurred in the Board of Regents is illustrative of this distinction. But please go on.

RP: I am saying that nothing happened because there is no trace of anything left from that proposal. There is nothing in the institution that you can look at and say that it was started way back with the López proposal.

But the proposal did have a different kind of impact. López organized a group of Chicano influentials, including state politicians, who met with Executive Vice President Paige Mulholland. The meeting was very public, with TV cameras whirring, and very confrontational. It fact, apparently it turned into a shouting match between the Chicanos and the vice president. Later I found out that the vice president wasn't all that put off by the shouting matches. So it seems that everybody enjoyed themselves and possibly saw their picture in the evening news.

As someone on the sidelines, I wondered why we were doing that sort of thing. I mean, it seemed so ineffectual. Besides, I knew that universities would try to pretend that they would not respond to community pressure from minority groups. That incident reinforced my notion that we needed a new strategy. The strategy being used by López and others was antiquated and largely ineffectual because universities had developed strong defenses against it during the ten or so years that it had been used.

It's about Jobs

MM: You will recall that most of the confrontations with the administration rarely revolved around programmatic issues. I don't remember this particular incident. But most of the confrontations involving community groups and meetings with administrators were focused around protecting someone's job. I would not be at all surprised if the shouting was around someone getting fired. The same conditions exist even today. People tend to get riled when someone's job is being threatened or someone is vying for a job. That is the easiest problem that the administration can have. If someone has been fired, it is usually too late to intervene, but sometimes you can prevent someone getting fired by creating commotion in the community. For the university, it is a very simple concession either to keep someone or to hire someone, particularly if it is a minority-oriented job that makes little difference in the larger scheme of things. Many of these folks later serve as effective gatekeepers. We also see some Chicanos just hanging around looking busy but not really being effective players. For chicanada, it is a lot of effort for almost zero benefit.

RP: You may be right because at the same time there was a huge row surrounding the Chicano director of admissions or someone like that. I think that he got fired and there was an uproar in the community. When I found out about the incident, I asked if the individual was in trouble why did he not come forward to solicit support from the chicanada before he was fired? That way we could have negotiated internally with the president to reach some kind of agreement.

MM: Although I don't recall the details of this specific fight, it is not difficult to identify patterns in many of these incidents. I have already talked about the Chicano gatekeepers and their role in the university. I recall that in this particular incident, a relative of one of the Chicano gatekeepers got axed by one of the vice presidents for some type of infraction that had to do with mismanagement of money. He may have been a financial aid officer — I don't really remember. It is not important for the point I want to make. As is the case with most gatekeepers, he had some political clout, having served in a minor post with a Republican governor. His position at the university was part of the progression of how many of these folks get their jobs. Anyhow, when the administration made its move to fire his relative, he tried to mobilize the community to place the calls to the president and vice presidents to reverse the decision. There was, however, very little support from the community. He could not get much community support because the administration had done its homework and through its own contacts found out that many in the community were pleased with their decision. Many Chicanos don't realize that administrators have their own contacts with the various ethnic communities. They are aware, more than people realize, of the great divisions within the minority communities.

I think that some Chicano university officials need to reconsider the manner in which they relate to students. They use, I think wrongly, the little power they have to reward students in the form of financial aid or scholarships as if these resources were their personal property. This sends a very distorted message to students. Obviously, many non-Chicano administrators do the same thing. There is a basic dishonesty in the way that our bureaucrats operate in relationship to the community. Students have little idea of the financial aid infrastructure, and are intimidated by obviously opportunistic university employees. I have seen students beginning to incorporate the mannerisms of some of these individuals thinking that this is proper behavior — visibility rather than courageous action in the community is the criterion for achievement. This is corrupt and unethical behavior. We should not tolerate our public servants confusing students by making them believe that they are handing out favors when in fact they are merely doing their jobs. This type of "networking" is destructive to young people. Some of these minority programs often are cliques that exclude those who don't share the adoration of the director.

RP: I don't remember for sure what the shouting was about. The point is that a shouting match occurred in an attempt to get things done at the university. My reaction to this was that the methods being used by some of the Chicanos on campus were totally antiquated. Moreover, I felt that it was useless to try to get someone reinstated in their job. I have seldom seen people get reinstated after they get fired by a university. There is very little recourse. I thought that trying to get someone reinstated after they were fired was basically an impotent gesture.

I suggested that Chicanos had to be much more astute. If someone was in trouble, or they were being treated unjustly, then the group should come together in an informal kind of way, apply pressure, and give the university an opportunity to solve the problem without losing face. I was specifically concerned about those Chicanos who were being treated unjustly. I am not discounting the possibility that some of the individuals in trouble may have deserved to be ousted.

MM: This raises another issue. Which fights do we take on? Some are not good fights, either because they can't be won or because they are simply wrong. Some fights simply are not justified because the individuals may be incompetent or corrupt. Perhaps we should adopt a code of ethics where we could explicitly outline the values that should guide our actions. Anyhow, the point is that it is wrong to protect someone simply because he or she is Chicano.

RP: If you want to call it protection. The efficacy of these actions is questionable. I suggested that the Chicano group get together informally, dialogue about the situation, then determine whether or not we would defend the person under fire. My point is that this dialogue is important if rational objectives are going to be agreed upon and effective actions taken.

MM: I'll tell you an interesting side note to this. It has to do with the firing of one of the gatekeepers several years back. I got a call from the administration asking me if I would serve on its team to evaluate his performance. They had already decided to fire him and they wanted justification to do so. If they had my name on the evaluation team, it would have made things easier for them. Even though I did not like or respect him, I chose not to participate.

Un Pinto as Mentor

RP: What you are saying is that none of the parties was completely honest. The gatekeeper may have had his faults, but the administration also was not totally aboveboard. This notion that everyone is following their own agenda brings something to mind. For many years I have been using a "test hole" approach to activism. I am using the term metaphorically after the way that petroleum engineers drill test holes before they invest a lot of money drilling oil wells where there may be no oil.

MM: You are consciously doing this?

RP: Yes. But you have to understand that I did not invent this. Whenever you find yourself in a new situation, as I did coming to Arizona from Michigan, you have to find out systematically what is going on, who are the key players, and what are the important agendas. Most important, you have to qualify the people with whom you come in contact. I was taught this qualification idea by a friend of mine who had been a *pinto*.

MM: There is a fundamental difference between Michigan or California and Arizona. The difference is that in Arizona everybody knows everybody else. Even though Phoenix seems like a very large place, you are dealing with a very small group of people. In Michigan or California that is not the case. In those large states there are many small pockets of power that make it possible to initiate activities with little interference from other quarters. For instance, at the University of California it is possible to operate independently from one campus to the next. In Arizona everyone knows everybody. That is a fundamental political difference.

RP: There certainly is a difference in scale.

MM: It is not just scale. It is necessary to tap into particular networks if you hope to be effective. If you fail to do so, you will get stopped and you won't know what happened.

RP: Almost everything I know about *la política* I learned from the Chicano ex *pinto* that I mentioned. He was a very smart *pinto*; you and I should be as smart. I began my political training as a post doc, if you will, when I became the statewide coordinator for Latino education in the Michigan Department of Education just after I received my Ph.D. The department had more than two thousand employees and the only game in town was turf. I had never been involved in this type of situation before. I had no idea what was going on. My *pinto* friend helped me with advice, but even more valuable was watching him interact with the organization.

When I got the job he stayed on with the department for about a month to help in the transition. His tutelage consisted of a simple strategy: that I identify all the key players, not just in the organization but in the community, the legislature, everywhere. He was a walking Who's Who, Where's Where, and What's What. He particularly advised me to pay attention to who each person was, what each one could do, and what each one wanted.

The second major point made by my ex *pinto* mentor was that each relevant individual had to be "qualified" — a peculiar term that was new to me. He was a natural-born salesman with a business master's degree to boot. So I suppose that he borrowed the term from the sales field where a potential customer is always qualified by the salesman if a deal is to be made.

But he was using the term "qualify" more generally to mean that you don't simply take people on the basis of whatever appearance they give to you consciously or unconsciously. If the person is a player in your arena, you have to determine exactly what that person has to offer vis à vis your own agendas, that is, you must qualify the person. But you don't qualify people just by looking at them. You have to test them. You have to test them constantly to see how they are positioning themselves and to know what you can expect from them. You should interact with them in a way that is advantageous to your agenda, but you can't do so unless you know something about them. Every person has to be qualified — the key players for sure. It is a very extensive and ongoing process.

My friend's tutelage had the force of a hurricane. He would share his own assessment of each person to whom he introduced me. His knowledge was encyclopedic. He pointed out particularly the Chicano cleavages along party lines: Republicans and Democrats. Then he explained how various individuals or groups would jockey for control within the various factions. He noted leverage points, identified who had what agenda, and warned me not to crisscross these agendas in strange ways that would make it impossible to get things done.

This was sophisticated stuff. He was very good at it. He knew exactly what to do because he knew what everybody could do. He knew which buttons to push and how long to hold them. So I learned a little bit about how to work within a political situation, how to make changes, and how to prosecute an agenda.

MM: Explain how what you are saying is different from the gatekeepers we were talking about who go around manipulating people for their own ends. What is the difference?

RP: It is the same difference that exists between wantonly killing an animal or slaughtering one for food or as a sacrifice to a god; it is also the same difference as murdering a person in cold blood or executing a criminal for some heinous crime. There is a difference between actions that are taken to promote some selfish interest and those that promote the common good, even though on the surface there may appear to be similarities between the two.

A Simple Agenda

RP: So when I got to Arizona, I proceeded to behave in the way that I was taught. I wanted to find out who were the various players in the university and the surrounding community. This meant everybody from the academic senate, to the university president and the Board of Regents. Once I identified and qualified the various players, then I could begin work on my basic agenda: to get more Chicanos to become college educated in the hope that this would lead to advancement in the Chicano community. That was my agenda.

MM: Why this agenda?

RP: My conclusion was that the chicanada could profit by becoming university educated in ever-increasing numbers; higher education in and of itself was healthy for the community. I thought that part of our problem was that we just had too low a level of educational attainment. So I wanted to open up universities to greater Chicano participation. Our university simply became part of that strategy. It is as simple as that. Of course, I knew that the university would never open up to chicanada of its own accord. Universities are not proactive in that way.

Agreement to Some Extent

MM: I agree with you to some extent. However, to a large degree the population demographics dictate the social agenda of the times. For instance, if you look at the demographic shifts just from 1970 to 1990, you see dramatic increases in the minority populations. There are about 22 million Hispanics in the United States. This includes Mexicans, Puerto Ricans, and Cubans — an increase of over 50 percent. About 60 percent (13.5 million) are Mexican Americans, and about half of these are recent immigrants arriving over the last two decades.

RP: How does having more minority people make the problem better?

MM: What one needs to realize is that the demographics themselves and the circumstances of the time forced administrators and the Board of Regents to begin to look at minority issues and that we as Chicanos are participants in those endeavors. Minority issues emerge out of a set of circumstances that includes Chicanos but not exclusively. As our numbers grow, it makes sense that we will have a greater presence everywhere, for example in prisons, business, and higher education. The way you are framing the situation seems to imply that if it weren't for our intervention nothing would have happened. Such is not the case.

RP: Your thesis is tantamount to saying that things will take care of themselves. I am not saying that the university administrators don't know that there are problems related to Chicanos and minorities. Of course they do. I am arguing that if they are going to do anything about these problems there has to be pressure put on them. But even if you apply pressure there is no guarantee that they will do the right thing from an ethnic point of view.

I am also saying that you can continue to be the underdog whether your population is big or small. Numbers are not central when it comes to making you either powerful or not powerful. Look around the world. If numbers alone were at the heart of the matter, then South Africa wouldn't have had to go through so much turmoil. After all, Blacks have been in the majority there since time immemorial.

MM: You misunderstand what I said. I said that the numbers and the demographic shifts automatically forced people to attend to these issues. It does not necessarily mean that they will do it in the right way. The changing demographics become part of the "problem" that higher education has to deal with because ultimately people have to make certain types of policy decisions. In the case of the Black community, a decision has to be made about whether Black youths are going to be placed in jail or sent to school. A decision has to be made about what to do with unwed mothers who now account for two-thirds of all births in the Black community. These are demographic imperatives. The choices are clear; they were not clear in the beginning, but they are clear now.

RP: Yes, but your meaning is that to attend to the problems is "to do something." That is not what I am interested in. I am interested in Chicanos proposing our own solutions.

MM: The issue then is not that the nonminorities don't care. They do. It is just that they don't care about the same things or in the same manner that you want them to.

RP: They care about themselves.

Two Examples

MM: It is not that they just totally ignore the existence of Chicanos. They have a different vision of what the problems are and what to do about them. Let me give you a couple of examples.

Darrel Brown argues that it is the White person's conception of race and racism, and not that of Blacks, that is used for understanding and acting against racism. Brown wants people to know that he knows people are aware of racism but that it is not his conception that they understand.

When I served as chair of the Commission on Ethnic Minorities for the Council of Social Work Education, which included Blacks, Chicanos, Puerto Ricans, Asians, and Native Americans, one of the issues that we pushed during the 1970s was to include "ethnic content" in the curriculum of the schools of social work. Through the politics of the council, we instituted the requirement that ethnic content had to be included in the social work curriculum. Social work was a leader in the development of cultural diversity strategies.

RP: That was your solution. The council didn't come up with it.

MM: Wait, that's my point. At about that time women started getting into the picture. So women's content got included in the curriculum also. Then the gays got into the picture and gays are now included as required content in the curriculum.

RP: That is what you all wanted.

MM: Remember the point that we are talking about: How different people view problems differently . . .

RP: But you still gave them the "correct views."

MM: . . . I am now reviewing two books on cultural diversity and ethnic content. I read the Black and the Chicano sections, which include fairly congratulatory thinking. It is politically correct thinking to the point that nothing Blacks have done is wrong, nothing Chicanos have done is wrong. Then I read the gay and lesbian section and again the same refrain. There is no wrong behavior; it is simply another perspective on the world. There is no difference among people; we are all the same: Blacks, Chicanos,

Anglo women, and homosexuals.

RP: Where does diversity come in if we are all the same?

MM: That is one question. The question I am alluding to is whether all behavior is acceptable merely because this or that group says it is. Let's get back to the issue of Anglo elites examining and judging curriculum materials on minorities. Is it not possible that they are examining our curriculum material in the same fashion, or with the same perplexity, that one might express about gays or immigrants?

RP: Absolutely, yes.

MM: In the case of minorities, you have students scoring one standard deviation below the norm. There is little question that African Americans, Hispanics, and Native Americans do worse on standardized tests, attendance, and graduation rates than other groups, including Asians and Whites. If I want to increase the pool of minorities, as an Anglo administrator I am forced to set up admissions that are below the norms of the regular student body. There is irrefutable evidence that this happened at Berkeley. If you are a White, Asian, or Jewish parent, your views on this matter will be quite different from those of Blacks or Hispanics. Do you see my point about how Anglos could be viewing the situation differently? They have a totally different analysis. It is not that they don't want to do anything about it. Their solutions may be different from the ones that we propose as Chicanos.

RP: Very different. They might tend to keep you where you are, too.

MM: But the point is whether there is justification in their position as opposed to my position.

The Imposition of Will

RP: Let's look at the issue in smaller pieces. There is no question that university administrators have their own perspective, or that it is a well-defined perspective. That is not the issue. It is also not an issue that their perspective may be different . . .

MM: It may not be the issue, but I want you to address it.

RP: . . . That it is likely to be different from those who are outside the system, in the sense that they are not receiving largesse from it.

The issue that you are raising is that when a demand is made of an institution, regardless of whether the demand is made on the basis of race, religion, ethnicity, gender, sexual orientation, etc., is the demand justified and who decides whether it is justified or not? Clearly it cannot just be the people in power who make these decisions from their own perspectives. There is no good a priori reason to make them the arbiters of these kinds of demands. Nor is it necessarily the case that those making the demands are totally justified in making them.

This is the quintessential situation from which our adversarial system of justice has developed. One person makes a claim on another and then there is an adversarial procedure to determine not just who is right and who is wrong but to what extent one party is right and the other wrong.

What we have here is an adjudication paradigm. However, this paradigm becomes very problematic when the demands that are made are highly political. Under politicized conditions, there is no proper venue like the courts to handle the competing claims. Nor is there a set of codified laws that can be applied consistently to the issues at hand. In fact, the laws themselves may be at issue. The only recourse that we have is to engage the political process. In a political situation you are dealing fundamentally with the imposition of will. The political system is designed to see whose will shall be imposed on the society.

MM: You are using "political" in a broad sense. Is it political behavior across all institutions?

RP: I am talking about civility, about civilization, which in a sense is maintained by politics. The fact that somebody asserts a right does not automatically make it a justified demand. The problem is how to adjudicate such a demand, and the only thing we have been able to come up with that makes much sense is the political process. There are other possibilities. You could have warring clans that would simply fight it out. Or you could have a dictator or a king or a pope who would make the determination and then lay down the law. Should you find yourself outside the law, you would most likely be punished. If you live in a society such as ours, the only way to adjudicate such demands is through the political process, which includes the appointment of justices to the supreme court.

Getting back to the main point: when people make a demand, should it be granted automatically? I say no. When people have the power to deny a demand, should they do so automatically? Again, I say no. It becomes a matter of political will to determine what the outcome is going to be. In order for Chicanos to make demands of the university effectively, there has to be a collective political will to do so. Then we have to possess political skills sufficient to accomplish the task. Otherwise, Chicanos will not drive the solutions to our problems.

That was my view of things when I began to think about putting demands on the university with the expectation that they would be satisfied. I knew full well that there could be a university reaction to the demands that would either deny them or fashion solutions that at bottom would not satisfy our needs.

What Happened to Dialogue?
MM: Let me raise one other point here. What happened to the idea of

resolving issues through a dialogue rather than the political process that you described? In a real dialogue people with divergent positions talk through a problem. It requires a setting where there are horizontal and not vertical relationships. It is a setting where justice reigns, where people do not talk past each other and there is fair play. I have rarely witnessed such dialogue in the university. As a matter of fact, we rarely talked about academic issues during my tenure in the vice president's office; we rarely dialogued about fundamental issues. The discussions usually revolved around how to protect the university politically, not about what was right. Are we now at the point where we can only settle issues through a political process or through a confrontation of wills as you put it? Is there any room for doing the right thing? For really trying to understand another's point of view? Does the university capitulate only on those issues that benefit those in power or are not threatening to the institution or the people who run it?

RP: I don't think there ever was a public space in which a dialogue of the type that you describe could occur. You remind me of Habermas's idea of the ideal speech community, which precisely describes the kind of setting that you are alluding to: a situation in which issues are argued out rationally and where there is no coercion other than the force of the arguments made. The truth will come out because there is no coercive element intruding into the process; there are only the rational faculties of the discussants. I think that with good reason he calls it the ideal speech community.

MM: Is this not the purpose of our dialogues? Is it not possible to achieve that?

RP: I have not seen it achieved at the institutional level. It's quite an idealistic proposition. Could it be achieved? I think it could be approximated. We are doing it in part. We are trying to do it. But we are here in my home, not in the middle of the student union, or in a lecture hall, or in the president's office.

MM: We are here because the university allows us a certain kind of lifestyle. It is Friday morning.

Cosmologists, Toilets, and Fools

RP: Miguel, the university is a multifaceted institution. Now we are equivocating about what we mean by the university. It has a lot of lofty ideals and it serves a wonderful purpose when it allows these kinds of spaces. But that does not say much about the university as a political institution. Perhaps it is in academic debates that the university comes closest to the kind of ideal speech situation that you were alluding to. Even academic debates can get very dirty. Have you looked at *A Brief History of*

Time by Stephen Hawking? At the end of the book he presents some vignettes about the great minds of Western civilization so that we can get a glimpse of their personalities as well. We see that, like you and me, they also were embroiled in petty little life situations, and that they dealt with them in petty little ways.

MM: I am trying to get out of that, Padilla. Don't use the phrase "you and me," just say you.

RP: Montiel, I am just trying to tell you that even Hawking, the great cosmologist, could not resist showing us a little bit of social reality. All of us, even the great minds of western civilization who debate the leading issues in cosmology, have our feet firmly planted in the mud.

MM: In one of the most important books that I have ever read, Norman O. Brown reminds Protestants that Martin Luther got his inspiration for the Protestant Reformation from the tower—it was the medieval toilet. The point that he is making is that all of us are always close to the mud. We are creatures who will die and decay. It is the source of what Kierkegaard referred to as "angst." We tend not to ever face our mortality. We should never forget this. This is what makes human beings such nasty creatures; it is also what makes us humble and godly. We do not have to act like fools all our lives.

RP: But regardless of our genius, at some point or another we are going to act foolishly.

A Simple Strategy

RP: Going back to my original point, I am trying to say that I had a very simple strategy when I came to Arizona. I was going to poke around in various institutions and organizations to see who were the relevant players. Then I would try to initiate some activities that would begin to move us away from the antiquated tactics that I mentioned earlier regarding access to higher education.

One of the players that I met was Luis Aranda, then assistant to the president for affirmative action. He was a lawyer and professor in the College of Business. I went to his office just to meet him and talk. I did not have any particular plan, only the general strategy that I mentioned.

MM: Are you assuming that the people here in Arizona did not know what they were doing? You are approaching this from an elitist perspective: an outsider coming to show these people from Arizona the right path!

RP: They knew perfectly well what they were doing. The issue was whether we should be doing what they were doing or something else. I did not tell anybody about what I was doing. I approached the situation like a stranger, like a foreigner coming to a strange land and trying to understand what was going on. But I had my own set of organizing tools and skills. I decided that if I was going to be a player, I was going to develop strategy from my experience, since things were not going very well for the chicanada from what I could see. That is why I did not talk about my approach to anyone. I didn't join anything. I didn't become president of this or that group. I simply began systematically to find out who the players were and what agendas were in play.

I had a pleasant conversation with Aranda and told him that I was interested in some of the problems facing Chicanos in the university and left. Later, I got a short note from Aranda inviting me to a meeting of Chicano affirmative action officers that was to be held in Flagstaff. They arranged for a lunch with Tachías, at the time a member of the Board of Regents. How many professors do you know who would take time off to go to this type of meeting? Not many. So why was I doing it?

When I heard that there was a Chicano regent, I wanted to see who this person was because he was likely to be a player in my activities. This was an opportunity to meet him, and begin to qualify him to see what were the possibilities with him. I had never worked in a university that had a Chicano regent. I saw this as quite an opportunity. Together, Aranda, Dieppa, and I drove up to Flagstaff to meet with Francisco Alcocer, who was hosting the meeting. I think that there might also have been a representative from the University of Arizona.

Qualifying Two Potential Players

RP: During the drive I tried to qualify the Chicanos who were with me and who had important posts in the university. What kind of individuals were they? Would they push the institution? Were they mostly interested in looking after their careers? Did they have much personal power? How committed were they to bringing about changes that might help the chicanada? What were their agendas?

Along the way I commented that things were not going well for Chicanos at the university and that there were tremendous needs that were not being met. The first step in qualifying them was to propose some things to see how they would react. I told them that we Chicanos often cannot state clearly what it is that we want. We do not know what to ask for as a group. If we wanted to make demands of an institution, we would need to have a foundation so that we could make demands that represented a collective view. Administrators would always ask us, "What do you want?" and it wasn't clear that we could respond in a coherent and convincing way.

MM: Remember when we used to meet with Burton Barr—the majority leader of the Arizona House of Representatives? If you said to Barr, "We want social justice; we want equal education," we would be talking in large terms about an idealistic vision of society. Barr could not connect to something like that. Nor can most administrators. He would say, "Yes, but what do you want?" There is a disjunction between different people's worldviews. There is something else operating with administrators, however. Administrators will ask if you want an office of minority affairs. If that is what you want, they will set it up but they will also make sure that it doesn't work. When they see that it makes minorities happy, and that it makes little difference to their agendas, they will set up the same type of office in student affairs and in community relations. If that is what you want, that is what you are going to get. These additions are not designed to produce any concrete results or to implement a grand vision. They simply create gatekeepers who serve to negate our ability to make significant change. This is the dilemma.

RP: What you are saying is that you'd better be careful about what you ask for. I was very conscious of that problem. That is exactly the point that I was trying to make to my two colleagues in the car on our way to Flagstaff. The problem is that if you get ten Chicanos in a room and ask "What do you want?", you get twelve opinions. And most of them want a job, or something like that. Getting a job is not trivial, but it's not very lofty either.

I said to my friends that it made sense to develop a Chicano agenda on a statewide basis. Then we could all go to our respective institutions and say, "Here is what we want!" Naturally I did not expect that anything would be granted immediately. You would expect the university to ask us to prioritize our suggestions. Once we did that, months later they might send us a note asking if we still wanted what we had asked for. Finally, if they did decide to do something, they would most likely establish a task force that would just issue a report.

MM: But I was clear on what I asked for. As the interim director of the HRC, one of the issues uppermost on my agenda was space. Elmer Gooding, who at that time was the interim vice president for academic affairs, was the first person I approached. After I explained our long-term need for space, he instructed me to go see the space manager for the university. After I gave the space manager my spiel about growth and the Hispanic Research Center, he sent me to the dean of the College of Liberal Arts and Sciences, who then sent me to the budget man in his college. I went to the budget man and he asked me why of all people I was coming to him. He showed me some useless classroom. However, he was honest enough to ask me why I was talking to him. These visits took about six months to complete. Finally, I again was referred to Gooding. By that time I was an assistant vice president and he had lost out on his bid for the vice president's job. So we had similar titles. I said, "Elmer, six months ago I came to you about finding space for the Hispanic Research Center. After six months of visiting people, I am back to you because you are the person who makes the decision."

RP: That's a great story! Another suggestion that I made to my companions during the trip to Flagstaff was that we set up an advisory council to the Board of Regents that would advise them on ways and means to improve the higher education services available to Hispanics. Incidentally, years later the Board of Regents created a commission on women. They never established an advisory council or Commission on Hispanics, even though we asked for it much earlier.

The last suggestion, in addition to developing a collective agenda and establishing an advisory council to the Board of Regents, was that we establish a statutory Hispanic affairs commission that would advise the legislature and the governor on how pending legislation would affect our community, and that would serve as an advocate on statewide issues affecting Chicanos. These were all reasonable and basically bureaucratic responses to our situation. But it wasn't so much the proposals that mattered. I wanted to get a reaction from my colleagues, to qualify them. Outwardly they agreed enthusiastically. Then I pressed them.

MM: They held gatekeeper positions. So anything that put pressure on their bosses would be unacceptable.

RP: I sometimes have fun pointing out to people that in voluntary collective work all you have is an opportunity to volunteer your own time and effort. Many people think incorrectly that in collective volunteer work you can give orders, as if you were an army general, and everyone just follows them. In reality, all you create in voluntary collectivities of this type is an opportunity to shape a public agenda for the group and then to work your butt off to accomplish it. The key to this enterprise is to turn your private efforts into public efforts so that you won't be out in the desert shouting all by yourself.

I wanted to see how the Chicano players at the university would get involved. So I pressed them for an implementation strategy. Of course, I had already made up my mind that I would be willing to put some effort into all of this. I was prepared to make a commitment. That is how I was going to start my agenda. Aranda asked me to write out my ideas. I agreed and volunteered to prepare a concept paper for a statewide conference dealing with Chicano issues in higher education. Aranda agreed to draft a proposal for the advisory council to the Board of Regents. And I think that Dieppa agreed to draft a proposal for the statewide Hispanic affairs commission. I believe that he didn't want to become overly committed. He did it in a nice way. I also understood that my companions probably believed that nothing would come out of that conversation.

MM: That is the case with people's intentions. Even if they intend to do something they rarely follow through. It is the way people are. They don't have that kind of will.

RP: What you just said is that they don't have a great understanding of politics because politics involves the imposition of your will.

MM: Maybe that was not an important issue for them. It could be many things. People's rhetoric rarely gets actualized.

The Importance of Following Up

RP: That is probably what they assumed. The day we got back I wrote the concept paper for the conference, and sent it out to both of my collaborators. Implicitly I also was asking them for their drafts. I could see that they were not going to do anything. So I offered to help Aranda sketch something out for the Advisory Council to the regents. By doing so I was tightening the screw one more turn. I am sure that they were not eager to get involved in this type of activism.

I also asked Aranda to convene the conference since he was in a better position than I to do that type of fronting. I also asked him to present the advisory council proposal to the Board of Regents. I waited a long time for Dieppa, but eventually I gave up on him. I wrote the letter to the governor suggesting a commission on Hispanic affairs. A few months passed before all these moves came to a conclusion. By then I had a sense about how far my two colleagues would go. Aranda was willing to work on organizing the conference, and he did present the advisory council proposal, which I wrote to the Board of Regents. Dieppa basically did not do anything.

MM: Are you saying that all the efforts to bring him in as a dean during the seventies were for naught?

RP: I was simply trying to qualify him to see how far he would go with an activist agenda as I was defining it. He did not go in the direction that I was leading. Maybe he was not in a position to do so. Maybe he felt that it could compromise his effectiveness as dean. I have no idea what he was thinking. I do know that he agreed with the ideas while in the car on the trip to Flagstaff. He even took responsibility for doing one of the proposals. But I wrote him off as a result of his subsequent nonperformance. You didn't know that, did you? Aranda was trying to help and he did push some things. Shortly thereafter, he quit the affirmative action job and became a nonplayer.

In short, in the early eighties I came on the scene as a new player. I had an activist methodology and an agenda to prosecute. I assessed the scene. I engaged in an inductive learning experience. As part of all this, I came up with three ideas that seemed sensible but about which I had no real conviction that they were going anywhere. As those initiatives moved forward, they began to produce institutional reactions over the next ten years. They also spilled over into the community and the larger political scene.

Montiel's Lament

MM: One of the results may have been the development of the Arizona Tri-university Commission on Minority Recruitment and Retention whose job was to set up a statewide strategy for minority recruitment and retention. When the regents developed the Tri-university Commission, which I cochaired, there was no recognition on the part of the commission of the work that came before. The commission came as an idea from the regents that had no connection to anything else. There is no documentation about what happened.

When we developed the recommendations from the Minority Advisory Council to the president, the university came out with a twenty-one-point Action Now program that made a very powerful statement. The ideas came from the Minority Advisory Council. Yet there was no recognition of their work. They were not invited to participate in the process.

A couple of years ago I spent one full year working on a pilot project to set up the campus communities program at the university. I was asked to do this by the president of the university. I postponed my sabbatical and I was happy to do it. I don't think I have ever refused a request from a university official. Anyhow, I had a most interesting year. I had to work closely with the Honors College, and even dabbled with the possibility of trying to raise money for the program. I recruited the students, housed them, set up a course, and set up volunteer opportunities. I wrote an extensive report to the president, and he acknowledged my efforts with a very nice letter. Do you know, however, that after my report not once has anyone asked me about the campus communities? I learned a great deal about the idea and about what can and does go wrong. It is as if there is no transition from one idea to the next. It is a very interesting phenomenon.

RP: Let me show you something. This is the Volume five, number ten, December 1982 issue of the *Newsletter of the Arizona Board of Regents*. It tells of the establishment of the ad hoc regents' committee that was later to create the Tri-university Commission on Student Recruitment and Retention. What you don't see is that at the same meeting the regents turned down the proposal to establish a Chicano advisory council to the regents. Clearly we hit a nerve by making the proposal. Although the proposal was not approved, sympathetic members of the Board of Regents seized the moment and used it to create the ad hoc committee that would lead to many other things.

Montiel's Conjecture about Change

MM: It is possible that what you are trying to do is explain not how one can change the world, but how one fits into the scheme of things. Things almost naturally go in one direction or another. The key to a successful player is to go with the direction of change. Chaos theory states that from the initial conditions you cannot predict the outcome. I think we have found this to be true time and time again, for example when we were discussing the Dieppa appointment and in the trip that you were just discussing. You do not cross the currents; you find out what currents are possible. This is not determining change per se, but going with the direction of things. There are so many players in these situations that what really happens is that we find the stream and ride it. In those situations where we are successful we call this success. Take the campus communities project. When we started the project, the idea was to set up campus communities around substantive interests. For example, students interested in public service would study and work together; students interested in languages would live and speak the languages together. However, when the cycle was completed we ended up with ethnic and women's programs. I did not expect nor did I want that outcome.

I think that this is why resolving the educational dilemmas is critical. It is not simply a matter of getting kids through school, but instilling in them the spirit of being warriors or priests so that collectively the currents that we ride point toward larger things than merely jobs. When enacted properly, ideas such as campus communities could provide a good opportunity to our students to acquire the virtues of priests and warriors.

Chapter 5

Change From the Top Down

The Arizona Board of Regents' Policy
on Minority Affairs

The Arizona Board of Regents appointed the Ad Hoc Committee on Minority Affairs in December of 1982. This committee in turn appointed the Arizona Universities' Study Group on Minority Student Recruitment and Retention; this was the so-called Tri-university Study Group, which was composed of individuals from each of the three state universities: Arizona State University, Northern Arizona University, and the University of Arizona. The study group's report of April 1984 recommended that each president of the three universities emphasize the importance of recruitment and retention of minority students. The study group was composed primarily of minority professors and administrators. It also included representatives from student affairs as well as regular faculty members. Miguel Montiel served as one of the cochairs.

The Arizona Board of Regents adopted a policy on minority affairs on 12 October 1984, which was derived from the Tri-University Study Group report. The regental policy recommended specific actions that universities needed to take to improve the recruitment and retention of minority students.

The Locus of Change

RP: I want to critique the goals and actions of the Arizona Board of Regents as it tried to bring about changes in the universities that were similar to the changes that had already been proposed by the Arizona

Association of Chicanos for Higher Education (AACHE). In doing so, I am conscious of the fact that there are at least two basic philosophies on creating institutional change. The predominant philosophy is that change can be made from the top down. In this approach, the people in authority can use their power to reshape the institution over which they have control. The other approach is change from the bottom up, about which we will speak later.

I certainly appreciate the top-down approach, but by 1981 I had concluded that Chicanos generally were outside the circles of power that control public institutions. My years in California made this problem painfully clear. There, Chicanos had very little influence on the legislature, the Board of Regents, the president's office, the chancellors, deans, full professors, or even tenure track professors. As a result, we did not have the wherewithal to engage in change from the top down.

Nevertheless, I was interested in meeting with Tachías because as a board member he was indeed positioned at the control level of the university, and I wanted to determine whether he represented any real possibility for developing a strategy for change from the top down. Even as I explored this possibility, however, my own inclination was to use a bottom-up approach to change. Through the bottom-up approach, institutional changes can be brought about through a process of self-empowerment by those who are outside the system. This model of institutional change is not covered very well in the formal literature on university administration. But you can see it in other places, such as labor unions and community organizing at the grassroots level.

Earlier we discussed the proposal that Aranda made to the Board of Regents for an Hispanic advisory council. In 1982 the regents rejected the idea, but to my surprise they created the regents' Ad Hoc Committee on Minority Affairs that was chaired by Esther Capin. Our proposal apparently piqued the interest of some sympathetic members of the regents who supported the creation of the ad hoc committee and subsequently the Tri-university Study Group on Minority Student Recruitment and Retention.

I notice that the study group was composed mostly of minorities.

Minorities Speak

MM: The group included Rebecca Robbins (a Native American), Don McTaggart (a European), Morrison Warren (an African American), and me.

RP: So three of the four people were minority representatives. This was also the case with representatives from the other universities. The study group was loaded with minorities. Was this intentional? The way I see it, the difficulty was not that minorities did not understand the problems of recruitment and retention. We generally knew what needed to be done.

MM: Don't assume that people knew what had to be done. This was a study group for the Board of Regents. They wanted knowledgeable people to give them advice on the issues. They got very knowledgeable people. I have never served on a committee where there was such focused intent on doing a good job and where there was so much cooperation among the three universities. The regents selected people who were willing to work.

RP: Was this an attempt to create a rainbow coalition of minorities?

MM: That is overstating the case. It was a balanced group. I don't think that the minority composition of the study group became an issue in the deliberations of the commission. What is your point?

RP: I am wondering whether it would have been a better political strategy to include in the study group the responsible nonminority administrators from the various universities — have them come up with the plans and ideas for improvement. When the regents asked for recommendations on minority recruitment and retention, the presidents appointed mostly minorities to the task force.

MM: They chose people with credibility: for example, John Woods, a highly respected anthropology professor, and Anthony Roth, an African American administrator, who I understand later became the dean of students at Northern Arizona University. There were people from student and academic affairs. They chose people who could deliver.

RP: That is not my point. They did appoint quality people, but they were mostly minorities and a few White liberals. So the task force produced mostly a minority report. Of course, they took the charge seriously. They had an opportunity to express a minority view under the mantle of authority of the Board of Regents. If you look at it this way, with the regents' ad hoc committee, whether they intended to or not, they created a mechanism through which the minority voice could be expressed.

The Solutions Proposed

MM: Let's get specific. Let me outline the organizing themes of the study group's recommendations. First, to organize efforts cooperatively. The problems of recruitment and retention were not seen as minority problems, but as problems that implicated everybody. This shifted the Board of Regents' view of these problems away from minorities alone and toward everyone else. Is this a minority view?

RP: It is a minority perspective that got a chance to be heard.

MM: Would not Richardson, who argues for a cooperative approach to minority student issues, agree with this perspective? Richardson and one of his colleagues developed a model for altering institutional environments aimed at providing equal educational opportunities for underrepresented groups. The model focuses on resolving tensions within the academic community between diversity and quality, which are often seen as mutually exclusive. Administrators must forge a working consensus among those whose cooperation is essential for creating an environment that will support achievement by diverse learners without sacrificing quality.

RP: Richardson had already published in this area. But the minority point of view had never been articulated from such a high perch. This was the first group to clearly articulate a well thought-out minority position.

MM: The second organizing theme was to link together the state's educational system. Not only do people have to work cooperatively, but also they have to develop formal links throughout the various levels of the educational system.

RP: You were reaching down. You told the universities that the roots of the recruitment and retention problems went beyond freshmen students. You wanted to include the community colleges, the high schools, the junior high schools, and the elementary schools.

MM: The third principle was to improve basic proficiencies. This is an admission that a great deal of the problem lies in the preparation of minority students. When minority students arrive at the university, many of them lack the preparation in mathematics and English to successfully compete in the world of the university.

The fourth theme was directing students' university experience. This meant that the university had to take more interest in minority students. We wanted the universities to be more intrusive in the lives of students. It was the idea of in loco parentis of the early sixties.

The final theme was to involve faculty and to allocate more resources. Included here was the old problem where minorities claim that they are always expected to do things over and beyond the expectations of other faculty, and then their efforts don't get rewarded. I don't know if this is true, but that is the argument. These were the themes of the study group as I understood them.

The Minority Critique
RP: They also did something that was interesting and very important. The study group inquired into the existing recruitment and retention activities of the universities. They took each activity — the summer bridge programs, tuition waivers, providing tickets to football games, and so on — and critiqued it.

MM: We reviewed the literature, talked with experts (you will recall that you were one of our experts), and inquired into the strategies used by various universities to recruit and improve the performance of minority students.

RP: You did a summary evaluation of each major activity area. If you look closely, these evaluations were basically negative. The study group concluded that on the whole what the universities were doing was fragmented, and that not enough resources were being committed to the various efforts. The study group also concluded that much more could and should be done. This is an important point. I agree with you that the report of the study group was thorough, direct, and supportive of a minority agenda.

MM: Remember that we were constrained as to what we could recommend because our charge was limited to issues dealing with minority student recruitment and retention.

RP: That is one of the points that I want to highlight. When the regents decided to look into minority issues, their focus was almost exclusively on student recruitment and retention, specifically on increasing the numbers enrolled and the graduation rates. This is a consistent theme over the last ten to fifteen years. The regents seem to have turned the demands of the Chicano community for greater participation in universities into the goal of increasing the number of students admitted to the universities.

One possible explanation for this regental perspective is that it is easier to count noses than, say, determine if hiring practices are equitable. After all, one should be able to count the students attending universities, there is a fairly well-defined bureaucratic structure that deals with admissions, the numbers are large, and if something positive occurs it is highly visible in the minority community.

From this perspective, it makes sense to focus on student recruitment and retention. But how does recruiting more Chicano students change the university? Or, to put it bluntly, is increasing the number of Chicano students in the university the best strategy to change the institution in fundamental ways?

MM: Yes, and don't we celebrate this with such events as the Hispanic convocation as the crowning moment? This tends to give the impression to parents and the community that this is it—that this is all there is.

I think that it is erroneous to believe that the regents were attempting to change the universities. It is a wrong assumption. At best they were trying to get the universities to adapt to minority students. I am jumping ahead a bit here, but if you look at the presidents' responses to the recommendations, you will find that the student affairs units of the various campuses always claimed that what they were doing was correct, but perhaps not enough. In other words, the general response from the units was that everyone was doing their bit, and there was no need to change, unless they got more money. And even then they would only do more of the same activities they were already doing. There was no acknowledgment on the part of student affairs units that they needed to change the way in which they were operating.

This is a fundamental insight about the presidents' collective response: It reflected the view of their vice presidents for student affairs to keep everything the way it was. Universities are committed to their organizational routines. The continuation of these routines was most obvious within student affairs because the recommendations of the study group impacted on student affairs more than any other unit of the university.

RP: That is my point. The regents should have had the intent to change the universities, but they also lacked the power to achieve change. We are saying the same thing. Even the limited goal of increasing minority student recruitment and retention was futile, at least in this early round. I cannot believe that Regent Capin did not have it in her mind that the universities had to change in order to accommodate the demands of minority populations. What you are saying, and I agree, is that the universities basically refused to change their routines even after the regents pressed them to do so.

MM: The regents do not act in a vacuum. When the minority policy was adopted by the regents, the universities had already signed off on it. The universities decided before the policy was formally enacted whether or not it was acceptable to them. The regents do not dictate to the universities. There had been previous negotiations on the nature of the proposed policy. The policy was partly the universities' creation.

RP: I understand that. But the formulation of that policy was more complicated. The actual enactment of the policy was late in the chronology of events. You also have to look at the report of the study group. The presidents did not tell you what to put in the report. You and the other members of the group had a free hand.

MM: No, not exactly. Let's use Manuel Escamilla, the director of minority affairs at the University of Arizona, as an example. He had a vested interest in the issues. His job was built into the university routines, into the old ways of doing things. He recommended the things that he was already doing. There was no willingness to jump beyond those things that were constraining the system.

RP: Perhaps he didn't feel constrained. Maybe he simply wanted to increase his resource base. He could have proposed new initiatives, but why not get more money for what he was already doing? I wouldn't necessarily say that he was being insincere. He could have genuinely believed that his APEX program was the right thing to do, and he certainly could have used more resources. Remember that the programs evaluated by the study group at some point were created as reactions to outside pressures for change.

The Presidents' Response to the Regents

RP: Going back to the regents' Ad Hoc Committee on Minority Affairs, their objective was to stimulate the universities to do a better job in meeting the needs of minority students. We need to ask how successful the regents were in pursuing this minority agenda. The answer to that question is evident if we look at the responses of the three university presidents to the study group's report. Their responses represent the first opportunity that university administrators had to speak to the essentially minority perspective that informed the study group's report.

MM: As a matter of fact, at our university the president established a task force that was charged with responding to the recommendations contained in the study group report. In its response, the task force included short-term goals, current programs for recruiting and retaining students, a priority ranking, a timeline, and an estimate of required resources for each of the recommendations in the study group report. The response of the task force was submitted by the president to the regents along with similar reports from the University of Arizona and Northern Arizona University.

RP: So there were three separate institutional responses to the study group report. By looking at those responses, we can see how the universities reacted to the regents' minority initiative. First, the institutions repeated the litany of programs and activities that were already in place. Notice that the study group had already done this and determined that these efforts were fragmented and lacked sufficient resources; the study group felt that much more needed to be done. So in spite of the fact that the study group found that existing efforts were inadequate, the universities simply listed what they were already doing as a response to the study group's recommendations!

MM: The general response was that every unit was doing its bit and that there was really no need to change, unless they got more money. And even then, it was not so much that they would change but that they would do more of whatever they were already doing.

There was also a reluctance to be accountable. This has always been the case. The university always bucks requests aimed at monitoring its activities. Remember when you and de los Santos tried to implement an accountability system for the minority programs as part of the work of the Minority Advisory Council to the university president? To this day it has not happened. This same attitude is reflected in the president's response to the study group's recommendations. Such an attitude reflects a commitment to organizational routines. To tell the truth, the response was kind of insulting.

Two Key Recommendations

RP: Let's go back to one other point of the study group's report. It contained two very important recommendations that implied new activities on the part of the universities. These recommendations were very specific. The first stated that each institution should establish an office of minority affairs within the academic vice president's office. This represented an effort to make student retention a responsibility of the academic affairs division, as opposed to student affairs. The Office of Minority Affairs was supposed to address the weaknesses in the ongoing activities: lack of coordination, piecemeal efforts, lack of resources, lack of planning, and lack of program coherence. In short, the office was to develop rational plans for the recruitment and retention of minority students, and this was viewed as an improvement over the way that things were being done.

Second, the study group recommended the establishment of a developmental year during which students could earn credit for courses taken, but the courses would not apply toward a degree. This recommendation implicitly acknowledged that minority students might not possess the requisite skills to succeed in the university. The study group faced this issue head-on not only by recommending a developmental year but also by suggesting that the universities had the responsibility to help the high schools and the community colleges to do a better job of preparing students to handle university-level work.

MM: There was very little support at the university for the developmental year. It was totally rejected. But the recommendation was not altogether that unreasonable. We knew that it would be difficult to implement the recommendation at the university level, and that the university was not necessarily the most appropriate place for the developmental year, but by raising the issue we thought that it might be taken over by the community colleges. I don't know to what extent the community colleges have been open to this idea.

I know, however, that the community colleges have always rejected the idea of informing people about the number of minority students from the colleges who continue on to the university level. It is very difficult to obtain these data even with de los Santos there as vice chancellor. I recall that there was an increase of only eleven minority students who went to the university from one year to the next. You and I have talked about the famous article written by Burton Clark, "Cooling the Mark," where there is a frank discussion of the true role of the community colleges. They often serve to quarantine students so that they won't show up where they are not wanted. Certainly this is why the community colleges developed in Cali-fornia where there is an obvious caste system that segregates students into three separate and distinct systems of higher education. It is minority students that end up in community colleges and the vast majority never make it to the University of California. It is not difficult to understand why that information is not readily available. Anyhow, it was very difficult to sell the idea of a developmental year. It is a difficult issue to take on.

RP: My point is that suggesting something like the developmental year demanded fundamental change from the universities. The committee was suggesting something to the universities that demanded a real change in the way that they see themselves, and how they use their resources.

MM: That is the key. The recommendations of the study group that had anything to do with interrupting organizational routines or with reallocating resources were rejected out of hand. These were the key criteria that determined whether or not the universities would do any-thing. What is important is not so much whether a recommended program works or not, but whether it interrupts the status quo. That is your point, is it not?

The Social Responsibilities of the University

RP: Yes, and more. I am also interested in institutional rationales. I agree that the university did not want to establish a developmental year, but what argument did it use to oppose the idea? It is precisely the argument that you already presented, namely that it is the role of the community colleges to do such development and not the universities. I believe that such a response is basically a cop-out.

MM: Those discussions also took place in the study group. It is a legitimate argument.

RP: Not necessarily. This is where history is useful. What the study group was saying implicitly is that our system of education is not capable of producing large numbers of minority students who can benefit directly from university instruction.

MM: And the university responded that it cannot be a high school and still be a university.

RP: Indeed! But let's turn back the clock a hundred years or so when the public universities were first established as ongoing concerns. The universities were created well before there was a well-established public school system. In fact, it was not until about the 1930s that the majority of the U.S. population earned a high school diploma, the gateway to higher learning.

Remember that in the last half of the nineteenth century, the federal government stimulated the creation of the land grant universities throughout the country. This had the effect of greatly expanding the capacity of universities to admit new students. In fact, the new universities had far more capacity to admit students than there were students prepared to handle university-level work.

So what did the universities do? They established high schools within the universities, which were essentially prep schools. Thus they were able to admit students from, say, the rural areas, educate them through the prep schools, and then admit them to the university. In this way, the universities could maintain relatively high standards and still meet their social responsibilities to the communities that were supporting them.

MM: It is not exactly a parallel situation. Today there are many high schools whereas in those days there were very few.

RP: It is not exactly a parallel, but it is a similar problem. Today we have large numbers of minority students who are not qualified to do university-level work because the schools are not functioning properly, and the universities must take a proactive role. They have to meet their social responsibility just as they did over one hundred years ago.

MM: If you are a rational taxpayer, are you going to stand for the university doing a developmental year?

RP: I don't think that the university's decision on this issue was driven by concern for the taxpayers. This decision reflects the university's view of itself.

MM: What I am saying is that choosing a developmental year would not be a wise decision. We know the reasons why the university rejected the developmental year, and they are not honorable. The point, however, is that it makes sense for the university not to take on that added task.

RP: It makes sense under a rationality that holds that there are other levels in the educational system that are going to take care of the problem. My point is that the other levels are not taking care of the problem so we have a situation where thousands of minority students are not equipped to handle university-level work. So it does not matter that we have a multi-level educational system. If it is not working for a large segment of the population, the universities must accept part of the responsibility for solving the problem.

MM: One of the basic operating assumptions of the study group was that the problems of minority students implicate everyone and that the various institutional levels have to be linked together to address them.

RP: The study group not only made a strong pitch for a developmental year but it also urged the universities to reach out and help the lower levels of the educational system so that they would be more effective in preparing students who could handle university-level work.

Here an industrial analogy may be useful. If an auto manufacturer learns that a supplier is producing faulty parts that lead to poor cars, the manufacturer either eliminates the supplier or demands that standards of quality be met. This kind of vertical influence on suppliers goes on all the time. So why can't universities, which are perched on top of the educational system, demand that their "suppliers" produce a quality "product"?

MM: Again I have to jump a little bit ahead. Actually, the universities engaged in various substitute activities that did not get as far as the developmental year. For example, one of the responses from the university was to set up the Hispanic Mother/Daughter Program. This program has some good points; for example, it links both mothers and daughters in the educational process as early as junior high school. It is, however, a program that has netted few graduates and thus is quite expensive.

Valle del Sol, a community-based organization, started a science and mathematics program that eventually grew into a major program of the university for minority students. The program, once it got funded, unfortunately severed its links to the community. When I was in the vice president's office, we succeeded in transferring directly to one of the departments in the College of Liberal Arts and Sciences around $200,000 from money that was to have gone to the office of student affairs. Another example is Project PRIME (a program to improve minority education), which was brought to the university by Gary Keller. It was a collaborative effort among a group of Hispanic administrators, the Educational Testing Service, and the university. Keller and I served as codirectors of the project in its early stages. This program, unlike the science and math program that brought students to campus and had little to do directly with the high schools and teachers, focused its efforts on setting up partnerships with the middle and high schools. PRIME tried to prepare students by assisting parents to secure funds for the college education of their children, providing linkages between the middle schools and the high schools in the teaching of algebra, and training students so they could do better on college entrance exams. There are other efforts. We have found, however, that it is difficult to set up linkages with the schools. Here I am talking only of the linkages and not the teaching paradigm at the university.

The Fragmentation of the University

RP: Such programs have the characteristics described by the study group. They are uncoordinated, fragmented, lack resources, and have no long-term planning. There is no one really in charge to make sure that things are done correctly, and there is no effective program evaluation. These are the things you and the other members of the study group said about such programs.

MM: That is a good point. You are right. But in fact, those are the kinds of programs that were developed. Let me tell you a bit about a program in the College of Liberal Arts and Sciences that focused on science and mathematics for high school students. It was a war because the vice president for academic affairs took on the vice president for student affairs on my behalf to transfer a quarter of a million dollars from student affairs to the Math Department.

Politically, I had to get assurances from the Math Department that this money would be used to get kids involved in math as well as in English. There is a letter where the Math Department agreed to use some of this money for other related activities. I remember the letter very well. It specifically requested that the vast resources of this project (in the vicinity of a quarter of a million dollars) be used to expand its programs by linking with other interrelated projects in the university, thus utilizing funds more efficiently and providing more rounded services to students. Furthermore, it called for the formation of a steering committee to ensure accountability not only within the university but in the community as well. This also would enhance communication between the community and the university.

It is important to remember that this project was conceived and originally funded by a community group. Arrangements were under way to create an electronic community between the high schools and the university. The intent was to encourage faculty to become involved in the education of minority high school students. I am saddened to say that none of these things was ever done: no steering committee, no electronic community, no interest in working with the high schools on an equal footing, and, what is most devastating, no well-rounded minority students. I don't know if this happened because of "bad faith," a reluctance to merge too many ideas together, laziness, or some other reasons that I have not yet contemplated. Often it is simply the need for personal aggrandizement. The important point is that we lose many opportunities to address issues holisticly because there are too many forces operating against ideas that address our problems holisticly. And most of the shortcomings have little to do with racism. Many of the problems are of our own creation.

It does not matter whether minorities are involved or not. Everybody behaves the same within the university. People try to accumulate resources and refuse to see beyond their noses. If people perceive that their interests are threatened, they are not interested in working with others, even though the administration sometimes tries to push for more expansive activities. Your point is well taken: Every response further fragments the university.

The Office of Minority Affairs

RP: Fragmentation is what the study group observed and wanted to prevent. So it recommended the creation of an office of minority affairs.

Why did you resist that idea?

MM: Yes, I have always resisted the idea. It is instructive to look at what happens to these offices. At the university we already had an office of minority recruitment that was not even linked to the admissions office. It was separate and apart from the admissions office. The admissions office had all the power to recruit and admit students. The people in the minority office did not have the power to admit students. These minority programs are always marginal.

RP: Not necessarily. The situation that you described was a local artifact.

MM: I am telling you about our university. They are always marginal. Not only was the minority recruitment office marginalized from academic affairs, it was marginalized from student affairs as well. This office was the creation of the vice president for student affairs. It was their way of keeping minorities separate and apart from the routines of the university. That is why I fought against the minority affairs office as proposed by the study group.

RP: But the example need not be elevated to a general principle. I am not saying that the minority affairs office, had it been created, would have been a great success, given the institutional climate at the university that you have described. But the situation at the university was aberrant. When I became the Chicano admissions officer at the University of Michigan in 1970, we had the very same options that we are now discussing. At Michigan the director of admissions made it clear that he did not want the minority recruiters to be anything other than regular admissions officers of the university. He did not create a minority recruitment office. He simply hired admissions officers who happened to be minorities, fully empowered them, required that they learn the mechanics of the job, and expected them to make special efforts to recruit minority students.

MM: The vice president for student affairs seemed philosophically opposed to that. When I got into the office of the vice president for academic affairs, I took that fight on and even to this day we have not succeeded in moving minority recruitment into the regular admissions operation; it is still separate. Administrators have a vested interest in keeping things that way. The other side is that minorities themselves seem to want it that way because they seem to think that having positions within these enclaves gives them power.

RP: But, as you said, there was no power in such an arrangement.

MM: It does not matter. The point is that you are director of something, and you don't have to deal with the outside politics of the university. A lot of the fragmentation is maintained by minorities themselves. It is our own creation. The lower you are in the organization, the less you seem to appreciate the manner in which decisions are made.

RP: I remember very clearly that some people involved with the minority recruitment program came to me and objected strenuously to the fact that they were not part of the regular admissions office. I am talking about Beatríz and others. They were very conscious of the fact that they had no real power and that the program was ineffective. They also knew the solution: to move the program into the regular admissions office and empower the recruiters to be regular admissions officers.

So I don't think that it was minorities who were causing the problem. They simply did not have the power to change the situation. You said it was the vice president for student affairs who was making these decisions. Perhaps it was even the president.

MM: It was the whole infrastructure of the university that wanted these programs marginalized. It is important to remember, however, that in the last few years many minorities have become complacent and comfortable with their jobs in established programs. One of two things has happened: First, they have become isolated and now have little to do with the larger efforts of the university. One cannot work in isolation from the main action. In cases where people have found a "comfort zone," there is great danger that these same people will fight against any changes that need to be made. The evidence is overwhelming. The same obviously applies to the faculty. I am beginning to see a great deal of reaction against Chicanos within departments. This is something that we should be concerned about. Anyhow, let's not forget how many of these minority programs were started. They started as a reaction to pressure. Minority recruitment was set up in a separate office because this way it did not disturb the existing routines.

RP: It depends. If such programs become powerful they can affect routines.

MM: But they are not. How can they be powerful units if you put them in student affairs and then within student affairs they are marginalized. They are away from the action. Look at where many of these minority programs are situated. They are more to appease the community than to get things done. Minorities in these positions are happy with the arrangements.

RP: If you structure minority programs in the fashion that you have described, they are not powerful by definition. But minority programs can be designed that can be very powerful. What you are describing does not mean to me that Chicanos are responsible for maintaining fragmentation. Nor does it mean that the university is incapable of seeing the contradictions and that it does not know any better. What you are describing is an institution where Chicanos have very little power to reshape the institution and where the people who were running the show have the power to resist change.

The Board of Regents, through the work of the study group, tried to change these arrangements by recommending the creation of an office of minority affairs. Clearly, the problems were larger and embedded in an institutional history and culture that prevented the institution from opening itself to minority participation. Thus, minority participation was very weak. Minorities came to the universities in a fragmented state, outside established lines of authority, and outside of any rationality that could be brought to bear on the situation. It was either that or nothing.

What I am saying is that the regents put a lot of stock in the proposed office of minority affairs. Especially since some of the other recommendations of the study group were made the responsibility of such an office.

Moreover, the University of Arizona already had an office of minority affairs, so for them this was a superfluous recommendation. Their office, however, was in student affairs and not in academic affairs as suggested by the study group. Arizona State University had no such office. And it was relatively willing to establish one. Northern Arizona University made a nonresponse. They stated that the recruitment and retention problems should not be approached by creating new units but by having the entire university address them — from the president to the deans and chairs. That is exactly the opposite strategy of setting up an Office of Minority Affairs.

The Strategy of Infusion

RP: Let's critique the infusion strategy adopted by Northern Arizona University. I agree with you about the dangers of setting up minority offices when they are set up as a useless exercise. But the NAU position can lead to lack of focus and can be most naive about institutional dynamics.

MM: If you take into account the Chicano assistant to the president at NAU, it was not naive at all.

RP: What you are really saying is that de facto NAU had an office of minority affairs. But that is not how they proposed it. The Chicano assistant to the president does not appear in the response. They were very clear about their position: They did not want an office of minority affairs. They wanted the whole institution to move forward.

The problem with this approach is that no one is made responsible for anything because it is not possible to make each unit respond the way you want it to. You can press them hard and they will respond in some manner. But they will not deliver the goods. Further, there is no effective advocacy because there are not, in each of the relevant units, enough people with power who are sympathetic to the goals and who will try to realize them.

Instead, what you get back from the units are piles of paper saying the things that you have already mentioned: We are already doing things; we are willing to do more but need more money; attached is our decision package to get new money to address these issues, and so on. That is the danger of not having some specific unit assigned to be responsible to advocate within the institution. Advocacy is the advantage of a truly effective minority affairs unit.

MM: An institution that has "goodwill," that includes representation of minorities as chairs, deans, as assistant vice presidents, and even one or two vice presidents, will not need an office of minority affairs. By definition such an institution takes minorities into account in the routine deliberations of the administration.

RP: Maybe, but a lot of people who hold such administrative positions are very opportunistic; they will go along with a minority agenda only as far as their horizon of interest. I accept one of your premises that many of the minorities who hold administrative positions are not going to act much differently from other players in the university. They work out of self interest even though they are under pressure from community groups and others to do more. But many of them are very successfull at merely shuffling paper.

MM: It will be interesting to see what has happened at the University of Arizona with a Chicano president. I have not followed the situation. It would be interesting to see if my hypothesis is correct or not. Whether decisions that affect Chicanos adversely are avoided merely because the president is Chicano.

RP: In any event, the university did create an office, which you directed, and it was called Assistant Vice President for Academic Affairs and Director of the Office of Minority Affairs.

Advice vs. Advocacy

MM: Do you recall the major task of the Office of Minority Affairs? It was to develop a long-range plan for the integration of minorities into the regular routines of the university. That was my job.

RP: That is what the study group said should be done. You were following the recommendation of the study group. I suppose that was the answer to the fragmentation, to the lack of coordinated effort, and so on. Did the office function the way you anticipated?

MM: Let's look at what my task was. It was to develop a plan. The first thing we did was to set up the Minority Advisory Council whose purpose was to set up a plan. In fact, that is exactly what it did.

RP: First of all, why did you need a minority council? Again you were going to outsiders and to minority groups. About half of the council was composed of community people. The charge given to the office of minority affairs was to work explicitly within the organization. That is where the problems were, and the recommendations for change had already been expressed by the study group. You did not need much more advice than what had already been provided by the study group. What was needed was to push the bureaucracy into action, not to come up with another report and another set of recommendations. That is the way I saw it. Why did you choose to establish another committee? Another minority perspective?

MM: I remember sending a list of the advisory council recommendations to Richardson. He wrote a very powerful letter stating what you have already said. Why were nonminorities not included in this? It makes little sense. It erodes the potential power of the recommendations. In fact he was correct. Why did we have a committee with minorities only?

RP: I don't see why the Minority Advisory Council was necessary for the functioning of an office whose agenda had already been established by the study group. There was no need to beat the bushes again to come up with another report. What was needed was for that office to do what the advisory council later told it to do. Namely, to shake up the organization, include academic affairs in retention efforts, bring coherence to the various ongoing programs, and determine which ones were doing a good job and which ones were not. What impediments did you encounter to that strategy?

MM: The role of the advisory council was not really to devise a new set of recommendations, but to serve as a leverage point on the university. It is not that we did not know what needed to be done. The issue within the university was implementation. That is a political process. How do you get the university officials to buy into the proposed changes? Exactly what changes needed to take place? How do you get the academic departments to begin to hire minority faculty, to become sensitive to the needs of minority students? It is not merely reading a report. The trick is to get the power of the vice president's office to begin implementing these ideas. That is one issue.

The other issue has to do with the Division of Student Affairs. My running battle with student affairs was that they had marginalized minority issues, and that much of what they were doing rightly belonged within academic affairs because as long as academic affairs did not assume responsibility for some of the programs, student affairs was home free.

Think about this. Tutoring programs were within student affairs. It does not make sense. If students have problems in algebra they should be taken care of by the math department. The task of the Minority Advisory Council was to begin to get the various parts of the university to buy into these ideas. That is why we worked with student affairs, with academic affairs, with the procurement office. The intent was to get the university to respond in concert with the minority business community. It was a strategy with a wide perspective. It was an advocacy strategy.

RP: But the Advisory Council never interfaced very well with the different players in the university.

MM: After we submitted our first report, one of the tasks that the president assigned to us was to start interacting with the various units of the university. We met with the vice presidents for business affairs, academic affairs, and community relations on several occasions. There was that kind of intent. The question is, was that the best strategy?

RP: I guess that is what I am asking. I think what happened is that we spent too much time in the Minority Advisory Council working in isolation rather than creating the kind of coordinating mechanisms that would bring together all those people in the university. This is what the study group's report called for. But that was a very tough order.

MM: Why did the university officials not have the will to do these things? Why did we have to go through a charade? Why did the president not take action to begin with? Remember that eventually the president did act through the twenty-one-point Action Now plan, which we will talk about later. Don't you see the process of incrementalism? In a large organization that is probably the only way you can bring about change. The university is not going to change from one day to the next.

When we finished the study group report, we sat around and had a beer and wondered what it was that needed to be done. I recall Morrison Warren saying that what was needed was a "home run." He is an old jock from the Jackie Robinson days. He was one of the first Blacks to play for the university, and he tells a story of the time he played fullback and the "White" guys would not block for him. I think he tells it metaphorically, but he makes the point in a very funny way. His idea of the "home run" was to put the squeeze on the university president.

We sat down and drafted a letter. I recall that we misspelled the word colleague and none of us picked it up. In the letter we told the president that the honorable thing to do was for the university to address these issues in a coherent and comprehensive manner. The letter implied that if the university did not move on these issues we were prepared to discuss the matter with Regent Capin. We could no longer operate the way we are operating. We needed to do something dramatic.

The vice president for community relations called me and wanted to know what we were trying to do with that letter. I reminded the vice president that no copies were sent to anyone. The president was the only one who got the letter. We did not show the letter to anyone. We were asking the president for a response. I think that the letter and that communication convinced the administration to set up an Office of Minority Affairs within the vice president's office. I think that this was the case, but you never really know. Remember that the original university response did not buy into this idea. But the vice president for academic affairs did buy into it. What you are raising is the possibility that we wasted our efforts—in fact, the possibility that that part of my life was a waste!

RP: It is incremental. We were learning.

MM: Incremental means that I am rationalizing my life. It is a valid point.

RP: I don't think it was wasted, but I don't think we got much out of it. This takes me to the next point.

The Lack of Political Leverage

RP: My conclusion about the regents' Ad Hoc Committee on Minority Affairs of 1982 is that the universities basically sloughed off its initiatives. By and large, through this effort the regents were not successful in bringing about top-down change in the universities.

I think that Regent Esther Capin must have realized that they had been successfully resisted by the universities. But to her credit, she did not give up. What all this tells me is that even with powerful people leading the charge, a minority agenda could not be successfully implemented. The lack of success reflected the absence of one very important component, which I think some of the members of the Board of Regents came to realize: namely, the absence of participation by the governor and the legislature. Capin approached the universities from a rationalist paradigm. The professors in the study group argued for more planning, coordination, and resources—the kinds of things that rationalist people always bring out. But what was really needed was political pressure on the universities.

MM: The central operating political component from my point of view was getting people to buy in. If you want things to change within the university you need to get the deans to buy in.

RP: That is my whole point: What are you going to use as leverage to get them to buy in?

MM: Persuasion.

RP: There wasn't even much of that. The regental effort at top-down change failed because it lacked a political component. There was no political muscle behind it. As a result, the universities were successful in deflecting it. The initiative was washed out at the point where the university presidents responded to the study group report. They basically dismissed the effort in their responses.

What happened as a result of that? The regents learned their lesson. If they wanted the universities to change, they needed to show political muscle. So three things happened: one, they started working with the legislature. They worked out a deal where the legislature appropriated to the universities a token amount of money ($2.8 million) for minority programming. Second, they co-opted the governor's initiative to do an external review of the universities by establishing their own Commission on Effectiveness, Efficiency, and Competence. Finally, the regents created a new group called the Ad Hoc Committee on University Access and Retention.

I took all these initiatives to be round two of the regental effort to bring about top-down change in the universities.

MM: That is the subject for our next conversation. However, let me make some concluding comments about the first initiative.

The Tri-university Study Group was a serious effort whose recommendations were adopted by the Board of Regents whole cloth. It was truly a tri-university, multicultural effort. Our efforts at the university, however, never achieved the "home run" that Morrison Warren hoped for. Morrison Warren, who to this day is a dear friend, applied for the assistant vice president job, which I eventually took. I had never been interested in administration, but my need to change jobs without leaving Arizona, and the opportunity to try to implement these ideas, drove me to apply for the job.

Several points have been made that perhaps need to be highlighted. First, university officials have insisted all along that they have always been on the right track with respect to their efforts on behalf of minorities. To some extent this posture has continued. Second, there has been a reluctance to accept accountability as evidenced by the absence of any impact studies on minority programs. Third, the university responded to the recommendations of the study group by creating the position of assistant vice president and director of minority affairs, but there has yet to be a dramatic reallocation of resources over a long period of time. Fourth, there has been a reluctance to change the rules of evaluation with respect to minority faculty. Up to this date there are only two Chicano regents professors. Fifth, I have to conclude that community pressure is a questionable strategy at best. The reason for this is that the university is a low priority for community people, there are serious divisions within the minority communities that hinder action, and there are split agendas even within the Hispanic community itself. Many are merely interested in football tickets, and, as a matter of fact, this is one of the most potent levers to keep our leaders quiet. Sixth, the affirmative action office has been of no help to Chicanos. This we can discuss at a later time.

The Complexities of University Administration

RP: We have noted that the basic response of the universities to the study group's report was that the universities already were doing what was being recommended and that more money was needed if any new initiatives were to be undertaken. Further, the universities simply refused to comply with those recommendations that threatened established routines, as in the case of the developmental year where the universities argued that this kind of activity rightly belonged to the community colleges.

MM: As I mentioned before, the universities did provide fragments of the developmental year. Programs like the Hispanic Mother/Daughter Program, the Math/Science Project, Project PRIME and many others are fragments of the developmental year concept. So the idea was not rejected out of hand as much as it might appear at first. When it gets down to it, the university simply continued what was already under way.

RP: More broadly, the university's response exemplifies the way in which universities change as discussed by Derek Bok, the former president of Harvard University, in his book *Higher Learning.* He explains how apparently nothing appears to happen when a new initiative is introduced in a university. Yet, after a while, say two or three years, the idea emerges from within the organization, but it emerges without recognizable authorship and it only resembles what was originally proposed. So the change process becomes subterranean and anonymous. Ideas are reconstructed along the way. Change does not occur when or how you expect it to happen. When change does occur, there is no apparent agent involved. Ideas take a life of their own.

MM: That is a fascinating insight because it has to do with some of the things we have talked about. Namely, that very few things that are planned in the university get implemented by the people who planned them. It is possible that things happen accidentally. Will is not as strong as we imagine it to be.

Tolstoy's idea is that history is not a function of the great man. All people influence the course of events, and it is difficult to control the direction of change. In *War and Peace,* Tolstoy compares Napoleon, an aggressive planner, with a Russian general who, unlike Napoleon, waits for the right moment to act. He lets the Russian winter and the spirit of the Russian people be his allies. And we know what happened to Napoleon.

The Diffusion of Authority

RP: Complexity, and perhaps confusion, has many aspects. For example, there is complexity in the pattern of power and authority within universities. Bok did not have the power to impose a set of activities on the faculty.

MM: In fact, Bok had a lot less power than the university presidents in Arizona. Harvard is more department and faculty driven, and accordingly the power of administrators is far less than it would be at our university. My impression is that many professors are more committed to their own narrow interests than to any discipline and profession. Many are alienated individuals who simply do nothing for their institutions or communities, and at the first sign of trouble simply leave and do the same at the next institution. It is no different from people moving out to the next neighborhood when things start falling apart. It is a very American trait to have no sense of place or loyalty.

RP: Nevertheless, it seems to be the case that power and authority are diffused in most universities. There are small, medium, and large centers of power distributed throughout the university in complex patterns. You cannot say categorically that the faculty does or does not have power. Some faculty, some departments, some colleges have more or less power. It is the same with administrators—some may have powerful positions yet exercise very little power. It is difficult to decipher.

The Turnover of Administrators

MM: One of the interesting things about the university is the rapid turnover of administrators. In the last ten years there have been eleven academic vice presidents, which accounts for much of the lack of coherence in policy and decision making. This also accounts for many of the gaps in the implementation of policy.

Turnover also applies to deans. Several years ago, for example, deans in the college of liberal arts and sciences and in the college of education spent much of their time looking for jobs at other universities. It would be interesting to examine the calendars of some of these deans. This explains much of their behavior. It explains much of the equivocation in implementing the recommendations of the Board of Regents.

RP: I agree with you, but with a slightly different twist. The turnover of deans at the university actually is fairly stable. They stay for four or five years. The presidency also has been fairly stable. With the exception of interim presidents, there have been only two presidents during the last twelve years. That is a reasonably stable tenure for a president. But the position of provost has been incredibly unstable, and quite a few people on campus know it. Given that the provost is the chief academic officer of the university, the high instability of the position has debilitating consequences for the university.

MM: Why is the provost's position so unstable?

RP: The presidents of large universities typically do not get involved very much with the academic affairs of a university. They generally deal more with outside constituencies. This makes the provostship the most important and powerful academic position within the university. But the provost is only one small step away from the presidency. This creates some very interesting dynamics.

In our case, these dynamics include the peculiar characteristics of the university. Ours is a very large university. Although it is not yet in the very top tier of universities, it is not an insignificant university. In fact, it is a very good stepping stone into the presidency of some other university of equal status or one step below (which still would make it a very good institution). So from the moment that a provost arrives, he or she begins looking for a presidency elsewhere. As a consequence, the provost manages his or her office in a way that will not jeopardize his or her chances of achieving a presidency. Remember that the tradition in higher education is for search committees to check an applicant's performance at their previous place of employment.

When it comes to high-profile issues dealing with conflicting minority and gender agendas, for example, the provost cannot afford to make a controversial decision that will follow the provost into the next interview for a presidency. I have seen plenty of examples where provosts and vice presidents made decisions that hurt Chicanos, and the university as a whole, because they were trying to protect their interest in getting the next job higher up the administrative ladder.

The same argument can be made about the deans. They are on their way to a vice presidency. If they run a large college they can literally walk into a presidency, as did the dean of the college of liberal arts and sciences. In spite of the fact that the deans at the university have a lot of power, they also are very much aware of their career advancement. So they are reluctant to make decisions that will jeopardize their chances of being hired into the next administrative level.

There is irony in all of this. First you have a provost's office that will not act for fear of jeopardizing the incumbent's future career moves. So power shifts downward to the deans. Power cannot shift upward because the president is not in a position to make use of it (that is why he hired a provost to begin with). So, in theory, the university has some very powerful deans, which results in large measure from the provost's reluctance to act. But the deans also are playing the "let's get promoted" game so they too avoid making controversial decisions. Thus, the organization can be paralyzed for lack of the proper exercise of power.

I remember when we approached the vice president for student affairs about increasing the enrollment of Chicano students. She wanted to be a president, and the last thing she was going to do was get involved in a controversy dealing with Chicanos that would jeopardize her chances for a presidency. She would rather turn down Chicanos than incur the wrath of other groups. I have noticed that most administrators, if forced to,

always choose to burn Chicanos.
    MM: Why is this?

Career Choices vs. Policy Choices
    RP: Administrators are in a national job market. They realize, for example, that women's issues are likely to be just as strong in Nebraska and Wisconsin as in Arizona. Chicano concerns, while they may be strong here, will probably not follow them to Wisconsin. They are better off zapping the Chicanos than women or Blacks, for example. This kind of logic has led to our being zapped constantly in very ugly ways.
    Too many administrators have concluded that they will not have to pay for zapping Chicano interests. Sadly, I have to agree that too often Chicanos have not brought political pressure to bear on administrators who have sold our interests down the river. Chicanos must take to task such administrators if positive changes are ever going to be realized.
    MM: Is it a matter of politics?
    RP: It is not just politics. Administrative behavior is conditioned by career trajectories. Administrators may feel sorry for having zapped someone, especially if one assumes that it is not in human nature to behave routinely in this fashion. But it is in the nature of administrative work that often someone will have to be zapped when competing demands cannot be reconciled.
    Right now we are having to fight the provost. The fight is not direct, but it is a fight nonetheless. It has to do with his decisions, based on his own career interests, that impacted negatively on the hiring of Chicano professors. I think he will never acknowledge the damage that his decisions have done to Chicanos and to the institution in general. Such things never get discussed publicly so he is never taken to task for having made them. There is no way that the president will take him to task, and surely not in a public way. And Chicanos don't take him to task because we are too damn disorganized to understand collectively what is happening.
    MM: It is not an easy matter to take him to task. Administrators very effectively play one group against another. They play Blacks against Chicanos, women against Chicanos, and so it becomes very difficult to attack the damaging behavior because the provost will encourage competition among groups. If you are correct that administrators decide issues not on their merits but on the consequences for their next job, it is difficult to envision that Blacks and women won't exploit this vulnerability.
    It is important to assess the impact of administrator instability on the university. We know that it causes the deans to accumulate power. But it also fragments the university, making it difficult for all parts of the institution to follow a common path. An example of such fragmentation is

the fights that went on between the college of business, the college of liberal arts and sciences, and the college of education. The resources went to the college of business, which was hiring assistant professors at two and three times the going rate for professors in other colleges. As a result, the liberal arts and sciences college was terribly understaffed. At the same time, the university shifted the focus of the college of education from teaching to research. This proved to be disastrous to the state of Arizona.

Several years back, I recall visiting the high school districts in Maricopa County and getting assaulted for the university's negligence in providing service to the local community. I wrote the report on our visits, and in spite of the strong message for the university to pay greater attention to the schools in the county, there was absolutely no improvement in developing better relationships between the university and the school districts. As a result of this, most school administrators chose to work on their advanced degrees with Northern Arizona University.

RP: Why is it that in higher education so many administrators don't seem to work for the university?

MM: Part of the answer lies in the infrastructure of higher education where policies like those related to retirement (TIAA/CREF) create a license for people to go from job to job without accountability to their place of work. For example, judging from the actions that you described earlier, it could be argued that many administrators at the university, including deans, might as well be working for a university in Michigan, Ohio, or Connecticut for all the good they do the people of Arizona. Up until recently, when it began to look at local issues like the concerns of minorities (Blacks, Indians, and Chicanos), our university had little to do with significant sectors of the people of Arizona. Many of the people who work for the university have no local connections.

Another example is the West Campus. It is a branch campus with little minority presence at the administrative level, even though they promote equity rhetoric in their publications. But they have zero Chicano administrators, zero Chicano deans, and few Chicano faculty with any power. I think that things will change somewhat now that the people in power are getting ready to apply for the permanent position of provost that is now open. There will be some token appointments. I had occasion to apply for a job there a while back and what struck me is not only the disdain exhibited toward minorities ("I like him as a colleague but not as a dean" is what I heard one faculty member said about my application) but the distance that they have created toward the main campus. There is actually an antipathy for the goings-on at the main campus. This speaks to the lack of power of the administration to create the idea of one campus with branches. I suspect the same thing may be happening in the newly created East Campus. My feeling is that this behavior will have an adverse impact on the state of Arizona. There is, however, another side to the story, namely, Chicanos had a chance to impact the direction of the West Campus but failed. There was a Chicano provost who for various reasons failed to mobilize the community, to hire Chicanos, and overall simply failed as an administrator. Perhaps his failure reflects on us.

RP: Take the English department. They have many experts on British literature but very few on Chicano literature, which is being produced right here in Arizona and elsewhere in the Southwest.

MM: Let's talk about the Spanish department and its apparent disdain for so-called local Spanish. It is no great mystery why many Chicano kids speak "poor" Spanish. They have not had any formal training in the language. There is, however, a base of language competencies that teachers could use to strengthen the students' language skills. Many Spanish instructors fail to see this and in their ignorance "put down" and intimidate these kids so that they fail to realize their potential. This is not only a pedagogical mistake, but also an absence of humanity largely due to the lack of connectedness with the Chicano community. The devaluing of the Spanish language is a powerful tool in the oppression of Mexican people in the Southwest. All this is reflected in the instructors' inability to help Chicano students develop their language skills. In some ways, it is a university that is not connected.

RP: I think I understand why administrators behave the way they do. If you accept my hypothesis of the importance of career trajectories, then their optimal behavior is to stay in a position for the shortest time possible because it minimizes the opportunity of creating, or bumping into, controversy.

MM: Look at the impact on the budget of administrators who spend a great deal of time looking for other jobs at the expense of the taxpayers of Arizona. I may have mentioned this to you before, but I know of one case where an administrator took a job at the university and during the first week applied for yet another administrative position at another university. We all know of deans who are never around to take care of the affairs of their colleges because they are out interviewing for new jobs. In my judgment, these issues raise profound ethical dilemmas in higher education. These anecdotes support your theory that often what administrators do has little to do with the problems of the university and more with their career interests.

RP: While they are doing that, their strategy is to stay on the job as short a time as possible and to be uncontroversial. You cannot leave your past completely behind. Administrative inertia can be explained as resulting from a set of behaviors that aims to appease as many interest groups as possible. Likewise, administrators try to snuff out or discourage independent initiatives because it is not in their interest to create activities that may get out of control.

Institutional Amnesia

MM: An extension of the theory might be the idea of the "new start." Administrators think that work at the university started with their arrival. There is little or no continuity. You see this also in minority programs where each program thinks it owns the answer to the problems of minorities. The problems that ethnic minorities have in trying to be heard and understood lie in these kinds of arrangements. There is a tendency in these cases for administrators simply to be ignorant of a particular setting. For example, I recall one vice president coming in and immediately arranging the minority issue strictly as a Black/White issue with absolutely no idea of the existence of other groups. He would make decisions, such as the appointment of search committees, the allocation of resources, and the selection of administrators, on the Black/White human relations model. This is partly a function of ignorance and partly out of advantages that may accrue in keeping people fighting among themselves; it is a type of opportunism that is not seen as unethical because it is supported by the infrastructure and ideology of universities. Also, these difficulties are partly the result of the absence of leadership.

RP: That fits in with the administrator logic that I am talking about. One way of getting rid of controversy is to leave an institution. When things get hot, administrators bail out before an adverse situation gets out of hand or turns into a scandal. A new administrator then comes in, reframes the issues, and forgets what went on before. Everyone else will go along with the organizational amnesia, waiting to see how things are going to move.

The Disruptiveness of Transitions

MM: There is also another pattern. Every time a new vice president is hired you have to redefine your position, and by the time you redefine your position the administrator is gone and so forth in an endless cycle.

RP: The same thing happens with presidents. That is why some years ago we supported President Nelson while everyone else wanted to get rid of him.

MM: Is this when coaches were running around naked?

RP: No, this is when the university made an illegal contract with one of the coaches. The main reason that we decided to support J. Russell Nelson is that we felt that it would take one year to search for a new president, another year to get to see him, and yet another year to present an agenda to him. It would have taken three years to get anything going.

So we asked ourselves, What has this guy done to us that we would want to join the crowd and ask for his head? We could not come up with a good answer to that question so we agreed to support him. You could say that we supported him because it was too costly for us to bring in a new president.

Faculty Are Not Rooted in the Local Community

RP: I want to continue examining the lack of connection between university people and the taxpayers. In this regard, faculty are no different from administrators. There is a corresponding set of behaviors among the faculty that leads to a situation analogous to what is going on with administrators. Faculty are not rooted to any given university or college or even to their home departments. Faculty are rooted to a discipline, which by definition is geographically distributed nationally and in many cases internationally. The discipline is what determines their professional identity. They promote that identity by meeting with their colleagues on a periodic basis at professional meetings. Such meetings are held anywhere in the country or in the world.

So faculty have no great loyalty to any particular university. Their loyalty is to a discipline or a profession. If a faculty member is not being treated well in a given department, he or she simply puts himself or herself on the job market. If the person has a good reputation, he or she simply picks up and leaves. It turns out that cross-institutional mobility is one of the few ways that faculty have to gain advancement and salary increases. Universities are fairly good about attracting faculty, but not as good at keeping them.

MM: We are really talking about the context of why things don't work. What we are saying is that the interests of local people are not paramount for administrators and faculty. Ask yourself, who needs the most help in a university?

RP: The students.

MM: And in particular minority students. Now, if the most powerful players in the university — administrators and faculty — are not inclined to serve local needs, how can we expect to implement mandated policies of the regents or even to articulate clearly what needs to be done? I think that this is the key contextual factor for understanding what is occurring in the universities.

RP: What you are saying is that part of the reason that the agendas of Chicanos have not been implemented is that there is something fundamentally wrong with the paradigm of the university as it is currently constructed. Universities no longer fit the pattern of mostly denominational institutions of the eighteenth century that trained the clergy and the higher-level functionaries of local society. Harvard was set up to develop clerics and to educate the Boston elites. In this sense, it was locally rooted. But this is not the pattern of the modern multiversity. Today's large universities are best compared with an industrial plant that produces knowledge, and where managers and technical workers are fundamentally driven by career or disciplinary considerations. They maximize their interests by moving from one institution to another in a vast archipelago of institutons of higher education, government bureaus, philanthropic foundations, private research organizations, and so on.

MM: Harris, an anthropologist, wrote a book entitled *Why Nothing Works*. The book tries to explain why the help does not help, why televisions break down after a designated period of time, why there is violence in the streets. He argues that the oligarchies, with their centralized power, do not have accountability at the local level. Things are allowed to break apart because people are not linked to one another on a personal level. Decisions that negatively impact people are far removed and thus administrators and leaders are not accountable for their actions. In some ways, this is one reason why the schools need to be scaled down.

RP: There is no longer a moral calling to be responsible. People are simply following their economic and career interests or worse.

Developing People with Souls

MM: What is going on in the universities is about merely producing knowledge, and not about developing people with souls. One has soul to the extent that one has control over one's own destiny. I guess it is another way of saying that we need to create institutions where people can create meaning in their lives; where we can be conscious of our history and where this history will be respected. That is one of the things that these task force reports never take into account.

What kind of human beings are we creating? What is our notion of the ideal man or woman and of the ideal society? These ancient questions must be answered by each generation. One has to ask these questions of oneself and of our institutions, and then one has to act on the answers. This is my beef with many of our minority programs: It seems that they are initially set up out of good intentions, but they quickly erode to serve the needs of those who are heading them. The programs become monuments to those who run them and weapons to manipulate our youngsters. Sad to say, youngsters begin to see power and not justice as the ruling ideology. It is very tough to transcend these interests, but I have noticed people in student affairs working hard to get more unity among their programs. In this vein, a committee at Arizona State University recommended that major generators of data on quality and diversity should routinely exchange data and meet once a year for a two-day retreat to develop a short report to the president and the campus communities on the insights they have gained from the evaluation and discussion of the data.

What is the role of faculty and administrators in all this? Many university people are not oriented to the needs of the people they are supposed to be serving.

RP: Should we succeed in increasing the number of minority students, you can expect that most minority graduates will behave pretty much the same way that we have described for the system as a whole. So we must challenge the underlying paradigm of the contemporary university: the knowledge factory where people pursue their own individual economic and career interests, where the local community is no longer important, where knowledge is construed as universal, and where there is no responsibility for how that knowledge is used, including whom it might benefit or whom it might injure. These issues are seldom raised in the current university system. What is considered legitimate and important is to prosecute your individual agenda and to promote your career. Only these things are considered the legitimate preoccupation of the academic mind.

MM: A key problem is how university people connect with one another as human beings, and as long as universities operate in the fashion that we have outlined there is no way that any of these regental task forces is going to come up with ways of creating better human beings.

The Need to Change Values

RP: The most that we can achieve with these types of initiatives is to produce brown professors and brown administrators who essentially will have the same characteristics as the people who are already there. This is one of the great ironies of our situation. Our discussion is drifting back to the notion that there is a basic clash between the values prevalent in American universities and Chicano idealism. What you are saying is that what needs to be changed are the values of the university, and this has very little to do with the regental reports.

MM: Yes, but those values are man-made. There is an intent behind them. The Board of Regents can change the way that it operates. It is possible that the board may not be reflecting on these kinds of issues. My thesis is that most of us get carried by events, and if I have learned one thing from my role as assistant vice president, it is that I got carried by events. What I mean by this is that one has a tendency to operate by going through the motions rather than by acting critically on our world. This is very easy to do if you get caught in the whirlwind of administration. Administration is a continual whirl of activities — meetings, handling complaints, appeasing this group or the other. It is a very difficult job and it is easy to get lost.

Regents can get carried away by events just as easily. It is possible that members of the Board of Regents may not be aware of what they are doing, and may be inadvertently promoting the narrow interests of individuals at the expense of the community. It is not in the best interest of regents to perpetuate institutions that are not serving the local community. After all, regents are usually people who are connected to the local economy. Why should they be interested in perpetuating the interests of academics and administrators at the expense of the people in Arizona?

RP: They should promote the interests of academicians to the extent that academicians benefit their communities. After all, the regents are supposed to represent the interests of the people who pay the bills.

MM: Exactly, and they are not. The Board of Regents should be amenable to a critique of how they have lost hold of higher education. Their current vision is no different from that of administrators as exemplified by the various reports of the past ten years. The regents have lost hold of the institutional reins because the proper analysis of their predicament has been absent.

Failing the Community

RP: Don't you think that Regent Art Chapa, who is a Chicano, is on the right track when he argues that a certain minimum proportion of Arizonans should be admitted to the law schools? Look at the negative reaction that he got!

MM: Absolutely. He is correct in wanting more Arizona residents to benefit from Arizona schools. This would obviously benefit minorities since they are so underrepresented but pay the same taxes as other citizens. The problem with arguing that point is that it is too trite. People do not make the connection that needs to be made. As I said earlier, calling someone a sexist, an ageist, or a racist does nothing to explain the underlying problem. Regent Chapa is kind of in between someone who calls the institution racist and someone else who explains what the trouble is with the universities from the point of view that includes interest in the local community. His approach has a bit more class, but it does not explain sufficiently. We need to explore ways of creating a balance between the individualized interests of the faculty and the administration and the collective interests of the community. In the case of the engineering and business colleges, I do think that they have helped the local community and particularly the monied interests. It is questionable whether the education college has done even that much.

The College of Social Work provides an interesting example. It was originally set up to promote the interests of the less advantaged among us. This is a historical mandate going back to Hull House in Chicago and people like Jane Adams whose mission was to help immigrants with their problems in the big cities. At the university there was a similar intent in establishing the College of Social Work. The mission statement of the college calls for working with disenfranchised communities. Thus it seems to me that the college would want to hire people with interests that are consistent with this idea. In fact, this is not the case. The interests of the people who are hired are more in tune with the training of therapists; they are people who view minority groups as their enemies rather than their allies. Perhaps it would be more correct to state that they operate from a medical model where they view individual pathology rather than social or community pathology. In many ways, the responsibility for this situation has to be placed on the administration that supported not only the change of mission but, also as important, the nonsense that has occurred in the college over the years: the firing of Hispanic faculty, the lack of enforcement even of the college's own feeble rules because a minority was hired as dean, and the absence of commitment to the Hispanic community. Certainly social work has lost its soul.

Clearly the university has failed minorities and particularly Chicanos and Native Americans. In doing so they have failed the total community. Consider the costs involved in paying for minority kids in correctional schools and in prisons, on the welfare rolls, and consider also the tremendous number of people in Sun City on social security. They also live off the public dole even though they refuse to acknowledge this fact. They use their voting power in antisocial ways. For example, they voted themselves out of educational jurisdictions arguing that they did not have school-age children. Who supported their children when they were in school? Everything is connected. Someone has to pay.

RP: The study group recommended that special incentives be provided to faculty who were advisers to minority students. The study group knew that minority professors who spend time with minority students receive no reward for their efforts, and, in fact, feel punished for their activities. This idea, and the reaction from the universities, connects to our earlier conversation about the interests of the faculty and administrators. In this case, the minority faculty wanted the reward policies of the university to reflect the local interests. This is what the study group was echoing. Minority faculty were saying that they were paying attention to local interests and they were getting absolutely no rewards for it. Through the report of the Study Group, the minority faculty had the audacity to say that the local interests were important and those who serve them should be rewarded. They wanted research moneys to be set aside for faculty who participated in these activities both as a reward for community service and in recognition of the fact that successful academics have to produce and publish the results of research.

MM: How did the university respond?

Deconstructing the University's Rhetoric

RP: The university's response was very harsh. It was almost like talking back to the Board of Regents. It is one of the few recommendations that the university actually threw back into the face of regents. Here is how the university responded to the regents who are supposed to control the university:

> [The university] believes that this recommendation is not viable for two reasons. First, reward in the university derives from performance in research, instruction and public service, and advising students is considered part of institutional service. Once one system of special incentives is established then other groups can call for additional special incentives for their special projects.

Clearly, the university did not believe that to increase the number of minority students is to engage in public service; they placed student advising under a brand-new category called institutional service. I always thought that student advising was part of the instructional process. Here you can see the social construction of reality by the university.

The university's response continues:

> Secondly, eligibility to compete for research funds is wholly unrelated to advising. It is the quality of the research proposal which is singly germane not an individual's devotion to advising that should determine research funding. [The university] recommends that a system for advisement of minority students be established without any special incentives except for released time for overloaded faculty advisors. Minority faculty are often overloaded. Department chairs must see that this does not occur by granting them release time or by providing additional advisors for minority students.

Let's deconstruct this response. First, it is based on a discourse that favors the kind of university that we have just described but that stands on a pedestal of high rhetoric. They would have us believe that the university engages in only research, teaching, and public service and that it is immune from political pressures. However, the high-tech industry of Arizona mobilized the business community and the legislature to put up millions of dollars to retool the college of engineering. But the university wants to pretend that in conducting its routine business it is insulated from this type of outside pressure. It wants people to believe that it has a pure vision of itself, and that it is immune from outside pressure.

Second, the response promotes the fanciful idea that the quality of the research proposal is "singly germane." This claim is connected to the myth of the meritocracy, the notion of intellectual purity, the claim to high standards of quality, and the belief that the university is an apolitical institution. You have to be a total outsider not to realize that in matters such as judging the quality of a research proposal, making tenure decisions, or granting salary raises, personal connections and personal interests can be just as important as the quality of the proposal or the impressiveness of the individual's scholarly productivity. This self-centered and political modus operandi drives the universities as much as anything else. But instead of projecting that image, the universities project a totally fictitious image of themselves and use it as a shield to fend off needed change. This is the way that the situation has been for a very long time, and why the regents have not been able to promote change. How could change take place in this type of environment?

MM: I think that this is why I try to be committed to the idea of service, and I try to take on challenges that seem unconventional but are at the core of what I think you are talking about: Changing the paradigm of the university. One thing that is critical is to involve ourselves directly with other institutions and teach out of those experiences. This is why last year I worked for the City of Phoenix analyzing its youth-at-risk programs. I taught a course at the same time and tried to integrate my students into the reality of the city. This year I am trying to do the same thing with the Phoenix Union High School District. It wants me to examine the alternative education programs that have been accumulating over the past twenty years or so. This is a follow-up to the work you and I did ten years ago when we conducted a dropout study and just recently an assessment of their alternative dropout programs. I think that these are worthwhile projects. Unfortunately, faculty sometimes get penalized for taking them on. Nevertheless, we need to keep trying.

Critique and Political Muscle

RP: My conclusion is that the study group's report, and the subsequent actions of the Board of Regents, were highly ineffectual, not because the report did not say the right things, but because it embodied the perspective of the minority community in Arizona with no effective vehicle that could carry forward the actions advocated in the report. The report failed because it did not have enough political muscle. The legislature was not involved, and the Hispanic advisory council that we had proposed, and that could have been used as a pressure group, was not implemented. No mechanisms were in place to exert ongoing pressure on the universities. Instead, the universities were left alone to offer a countercritique of their own. Where was the continuing pressure going to come from? It could have come from the Hispanic advisory council, which was never formed.

MM: There are problems with community advisory groups. Many community people do not have the time to devote to this type of activity. Second, they don't have the commitment to the university that would be needed. The university is not a high priority in their lives. Fundamentally, however, there is no transactional relationship between minorities and the university. Also minority faculty are distanced from the community because most of us live outside of those communities.

So I don't agree with your conclusion. I don't think that one more interest group is the solution. I think that it is important to remember that no matter how many more Hispanic groups we develop there will always be counteracting forces that are much more powerful than ours to dictate a different direction. One of the problems with existing theories that claim that minorities go outside of the institution to get concessions from universities fails to recognize that other groups are also operating in a similar manner. Moreover, and perhaps most important, it is the power within the bureaucracy itself that yields the most benefits. Outside influence is interpreted as merely "political noise." What is needed is a retooling of values. Unfortunately, it will take a crisis of major proportions to get things moving in a different direction.

RP: Perhaps, but I think that there are ways out of that problem. These referent groups, if not organized properly, can be a disaster. They should always work with a carefully chosen staff person who can provide them support and serve as a liaison to the Board of Regents or whomever they report to. Nominees to such referent groups should have an abiding interest in the issues of the university and at least some of them should have technical expertise. The groups must be well balanced.

MM: We have concluded that the ethos of the university precludes attention to local concerns. This is not only a minority problem. Why would you not want an advisory committee that would include more general issues, issues that would impact on the role of the university in terms of its local responsibilities?

RP: There is nothing to prevent an Hispanic Advisory Council from taking on these issues.

MM: Why not be more inclusive so that people would pay attention to it.

RP: No, I don't think so. This is not a rainbow coalition.

MM: I am not talking about a rainbow coalition, but about a group whose concerns would be transcendental. The problem is not merely the recruitment of minority students. The problem is the inability of the university to take care of the interests of local students.

RP: They take care of middle-class students. If the university did not take care of middle-class students, it would not get funded. The critique of the system must come from outside the system, because outsiders are in a better position to present alternatives than the people inside the system. That is the power of what we might call "the ethnic moment." It is because of this power that I have worked within an ethnic context during my professional life. I have tried to harness the critical power of the ethnic moment. From a theoretical and practical point of view, the ethnic moment is precisely the probe that you want to use to see what is going on in our institutions and to envision viable alternatives.

MM: It cannot come about if the university is producing people who are unable to do the critique.

RP: Society has the capacity to produce people who can do the critique. I am saying that in addition to the universities, or in conjunction with the universities, minorities have the power to produce insightful critique. That is the contribution that diversity can make.

The Board of Regents did not have, on an ongoing basis, the power of critique that could be brought to bear on the entrenched position of the universities. Moreover, the Board of Regents was politically isolated on the minority agenda. The political moment came subsequently when the Board of Regents began to work with the legislature.

MM: The political moment, however, can be wrong. That is, politics can push in the wrong direction or create greater fragmentation. Political pressure may be a necessary ingredient but it is not sufficient to change the direction of the university if, in fact, we are correct in arguing that the current university paradigm is incapable of serving minority interests.

RP: I am talking about external politics — the legislature, the governor, the business community. In one way or another, the university has to respond to these pressure groups. The regental minority initiative failed because it was detached from these significant outside voices. An Hispanic Advisory Council might have at least kept the critique going.

A Lesson Learned

RP: But the board learned its lesson. Remember when Governor Mecham wanted to reform the universities because he thought them wasteful and inefficient? He was an unpopular governor, but his points on this issue were exactly on target. He wanted to set up a commission to look into the universities and recommend ways to make them more effective, efficient, and competitive.

The Board of Regents responded by setting up its own commission to circumvent the governor's initiative. Interestingly, the regental commission supported a minority agenda. One of the most important recommendations made by the commission was the simple idea that the universities should increase their minority enrollment by 10 percent compounded annually for the succeeding five years.

At about the same time, the legislature provided a token sum of money (about $2.8 million) to fund minority programs at the universities. The bill required that the universities develop comprehensive plans and report their plans and progress to the Board of Regents.

Soon thereafter, the Board of Regents established the Ad Hoc Committee on University Access and Retention. This committee can be seen as the second minority initiative of the Board of Regents. The Access and Retention Committee (as it was called) included significant involvement by members of the legislature and other influentials. The committee's report, titled *Our Common Commitment* (August 1989), incorporated many of the ideas from the study group's report. Most important, it incorporated the recommendation of the Commission on Effectiveness, Efficiency, and Competitiveness that minority enrollments increase by 10 percent compounded annually for five years. After some fidgeting, the universities accepted this "formidable" challenge.

What is noteworthy about the regents' second initiative, besides its much stronger political foundation, is that the regents simply gave the universities a goal without telling them how to do it. That is a much more effective strategy than trying to tell the staff how to go about recruiting more minority students. That is not the real problem. It is not simply a question of how to do better recruiting. The issue, as we have analyzed it, is that the universities simply did not want to alter their established routines because they represent the existing configuration of vested interests. In setting the 10 percent annual increase in minority students, the regents simply told the universities the results that had to be achieved. In this case, the regents exercised their authority and the presidents simply complied. It is rare to see this type of organizational clarity. However, it still does not address the paradigm issues that we talked about earlier. It plants some seeds only.

MM: Another difference is that the three universities responded as one. As a matter of fact, the minority data that are reported to the regents are aggregated across the university system.

Also, one has to wonder whether the 10 percent goal required that much effort from the universities. It may not have taken much effort.

RP: When the presidents accepted the 10 percent per annum goal, they said that it was a "formidable challenge." Five years later, we see that the formidable challenge was met readily. But there was never an explanation as to how the formidable feat was accomplished, who was involved, how much money it took, and so on. Everyone is too busy developing

arguments about why 10 percent per annum increases in minority enrollment for the next five years are unreasonable. We'll just have to wait and
see what the regents' next move will be in their efforts to change the
universities from the top down.

Chapter 6

Change From the Bottom Up

The AACHE Plan for Chicano Higher Education in Arizona

The first Arizona conference on Chicanos and Higher Education was organized as a result of the Aranda, Dieppa, and Padilla conversation that took place during the trip to Flagstaff discussed in chapter 4. The purpose of the conference was to answer the question, "What do you want?" that was asked implicitly or explicitly of Chicanos whenever we met with university officials. In order to provide an answer that carried political weight, Chicanos needed to dialogue at the state level to identify the key needs in higher education and to recommend solutions. In addition, the conference was intended to give people an opportunity to get involved.

Two assistant professors were recruited to cochair the conference. They were supported by an executive committee that included professors from Arizona State University and the Maricopa County Community Colleges. As a first step, the conference cochairs conducted a statewide survey of Chicano educators to determine what they thought were the key issues facing Chicanos. The results of the survey were used to organize the conference program and became the foundation for the recommendations that eventually appeared in the Action Plan of the Arizona Association of Chicanos for Higher Education (AACHE), which was compiled and edited by Padilla and Montiel.

During the conference, Raul Cárdenas, then president of South Mountain Community College, suggested that recommendations be made to each individual higher education institution rather than to all institutions collectively. He reasoned that Chicanos at each institution would know best what needed to be done at their respective institutions, both in terms of limits and opportunities. Implicit in this approach was the idea that if we were going to take risks to make institutional changes, only those who had to face the consequences of those risks had the right to say what needed to be done.

This idea was elevated to a cardinal principle of the newly founded AACHE organization and it also became a key ingredient in the formulation of the AACHE plan. However, the single institution approach threatened to weaken the political muscle that AACHE was expected to exert on a statewide basis. The solution was to develop individual institutional plans, then overlay a statewide initiative that would reflect common concerns. These would be expressed in terms of recommendatons for action to the state legislature, the Arizona Board of Regents, and the state board of education. In addition, AACHE would provide state support to local chapters as they attempted to implement the individual institutional plans. This was the basic model that came out of the AACHE conference and that was reflected in the organization of the AACHE plan.

Perspectives on Higher Education

RP: With very few exceptions, the Chicanos that I have worked with over the years generally have not spent a great deal of time studying universities. In contrast, I spent almost five years at the University of California, Berkeley, studying higher education. So there is a great deal of theory and conceptual work that informs my own personal experience in these institutions. Most Chicanos have only experiential knowledge of universities because their special training is in other subjects. When I approach the university, I do so as a scholar/practitioner whose focus of study and field of action is the university itself; so I have a different frame of reference from my colleagues who only work out of universities.

MM: In the last few years, I spent a great deal of time doing administrative or related work. This past year, however, I have done some intensive reading in this area. I am kind of in between someone who is grounded theoretically as well as experientially. In reviewing my activities over the last few years, I find a great deal of naïveté in my manner of operating in the university.

RP: Many university people are naive about universities or, in any event, not very critical.

MM: The question becomes: Would I have been more effective had I possessed greater knowledge of the university?

RP: Or might you have behaved differently? You have to realize that at Berkeley we spent countless hours discussing how universities have changed or not changed throughout their history.

MM: While I was in the vice president's office I spent a summer at Harvard University studying higher education. My colleagues were all administrators and I got a different idea about higher education. It was at that point that I decided not to go into university administration.

I came out of the Harvard experience impressed with the intelligence of the people, but many seemed consumed by getting ahead. I realized that higher education administration is more about personally getting ahead than with doing anything else. You do things mostly because of how you are going to look—the presentation of self—but not really to advance a substantive agenda. Such perpetual fronting is a very consuming kind of life. I realized that I do not want to live that way. That insight helped me decide to return to faculty life, so the Harvard experience was good from that perspective.

Freire's Legacy

RP: I want to turn now to the subject of this conversation, change from the bottom up. Many years ago, I realized that we Chicanos simply did not have sufficient strength at the controlling levels of universities to effectively use top-down change as a strategy to improve our situation. I saw us mostly as strangers in academia. The university experience was alien to us because many of us came from the working class. The idea of sending their kids to college was not typical of this population. This lack of college-going experience impacted us in many ways, including not having effective leadership. We also did not know how to create and maintain viable communities within academia.

But once we became participants in university life, we quickly realized that we were at a historic turning point. We as Chicanos would either regenerate ourselves as a people, as a community, or face extinction through some form of assimilation or through being permanently designated as lowly players in the society in which we lived. We might become a surplus, marginal, useless population that could only pave streets or clear the crap off of them. So we needed to create a new generation of able leaders who would be able to lead us out of our historic stagnation and transform us into a viable society again.

Early on I was influenced by the Brazilian educator Paulo Freire who made good use of the idea of a "project." Freire's way of educating the people was not to do it abstractly or through moralizing but through projects. I had also noticed that people with very high skills and demanding tasks also worked on the basis of projects; take as an example Kennedy's project to land a man on the moon within a decade. The project idea is powerful because it channels human behavior constructively at both the individual and social levels. Freire engaged people in projects as a way to empower them.

When people are in a state of oppression or stagnation, they appear to have lost the will and the power to engage in projects, that is, to engage the world for themselves. So they must be given the opportunity to engage in specific projects as a way to encourage them to reengage the world. This is Freire's idea of a project, which is quite unlike the typical American idea of a project as getting organized to efficiently carry out something that needs to be done. Freire looks at the project idea from the other end, as it were. While it is important to accomplish something external through a project, the most important result is to change the way in which the project participants see themselves and the world around them. Change is focused inwardly and is given as much importance as outward or material change.

MM: I think you point to a very important distinction. Remember one of Freire's basic tenets: "The ontological vocation of man is to be subject," which means that the essence of life is relationships. When he talks about the subject he is talking about subjective relationships as opposed to objective relationships. In the instrumental world, people are used as a means to get some material project done. In the world that you are talking about, in a world where people try to achieve critical consciousness, relationships are horizontal and people are treated as subjects.

RP: And in such a world people as subjects design projects to reshape the world around them.

MM: Which is no different from the people who design projects instrumentally. The difference is that these people do not treat other people who are involved with their projects as subjects. If you take the university as an example, administrators often operate in a horizontal manner with one another. But that is not how they relate with the students, with many of our faculty, and certainly not with our communities. I don't want to overstate the point by claiming that every administrator operates to further his or her career over the interests of the institution. It is our view that this is the case in many instances. But we are always hopeful that a Chicano, or other administrator for that matter, will advance our circumstances by advancing the interests of our students and influence faculty hires. On the other hand, some could and do argue that Chicano administrators might be seen as "plugs" in that the community cannot "hit" or take action against Chicanos, but would be able to do so if the administrators were non-Chicano or minority. It is an interesting dilemma when this arises.

RP: Freire uses projects pedagogically, actually androgogically, to change people's consciousness, attitudes, and behavior. He saw that people who are in a state of oppression or stagnation lack subjectivity. Instead of engaging projects in the world as subjects, their consciousness folds inwardly. With that enfolded consciousness their posture in the world is one of complaining or they will take refuge in hopelessness believing that action is useless. They learn to be helpless and silent.

MM: Many people believe that Freire's ideas apply only to the peasantry. They do not realize that people in universities, and in industrial societies generally, also lack subjectivity in their lives. One can have material comforts and still operate in a somnambulant way, without acting critically in one's world. I think that Freire was talking about all of us, not just the peasants in some distant Third World country.

RP: Freire's analysis includes the idea that people can get reduced to a state of quiescence. The most famous expression of this idea is his notion of the "culture of silence." The culture of silence can envelop not just peasants but also anyone else, including university professors and administrators. For example, the people who came under the spell of Hitler, Mussolini, or Stalin were reduced to a politically quiescent state. It is amazing how quickly people can become quiescent under certain kinds of pressure. But people can also become quiescent over longer periods of time when they come under epochal pressures of economic exploitation or political disenfranchisement. Their ability to function critically and as subjects is gradually eroded until they have practically lost their ability to think and act independently. Freire's idea was to use projects to get such people to exercise their agency, to regain critical consciousness, and to reengage the world productively.

MM: My feeling is that this state of what you refer to as quiescence can be manifested under conditions where people feel comfortable or complacent with their situation. One does not have to be visibly oppressed to lack consciousness. Obviously, it is not an either-or situation. There are degrees of consciousness, and it is something that one has to continually work on.

Changing Ourselves

RP: These kinds of ideas informed my thinking as I pondered the situation in which we found ourselves as Chicanos in U.S. universities as well as in the society at large: without leadership and in many ways socially stagnant. We needed to engage in change from the bottom up. We needed to change ourselves as much as we needed to change the institutions around us. So I borrowed Freire's idea of using projects to change people as well as the world. Thus my activist project in academia was aimed at changing ourselves as much as anything else. It resulted in a series of group projects that focused on changing universities because that is where we were and it seemed as good a place as any to start. If in changing ourselves we could change the world around us in meaningful ways, so much the better.

MM: A critical question is whether in fact we have succeeded with our projects. On one level we have to ask whether we changed the institutions. On another level we have to ask whether we changed ourselves in the ways that we had in mind.

RP: Those are good questions. Every project that I was involved in was designed to get Chicanos to work in ways that would increase our level of consciousness about us and the world around us. The projects were relevant to important concerns that we had about academia. The things that mattered to us were often political in character because we were challenging established views and values. We must ponder your questions as we go along.

In addition to borrowing ideas from Freire, I had also concluded that we as Chicanos were being perceived very negatively by the universities: As people who did not have a technical capacity to express our agendas within the rationalist modality that is prevalent in universities and the rest of our society. In retrospect, the power and weakness of our approach to institutional change during the sixties derived from the same source. We were somewhat successful in shaking up the institutions because we used unconventional and unabashedly political approaches. We could not get much accomplished for the same reason. Our nonrationalist approach was too alien for the universities as bureaucratic institutions. So I created an exercise—a project—to see if we had the wherewithal to engage the universities from a rationalist model knowing full well that the outward appearance of rationality at the universities is undergirded by a political system that is probably the most important element when it comes to control of the institutions. But the project was simply to demonstrate to ourselves and to others that we could approach the universities within the rationalist paradigm. In doing so, we as Chicanos would have the opportunity to engage in a rationalist exercise and possibly critique rationalism itself. The resulting project took the specific form of a statewide conference on Chicanos and higher education in which we would problematize what it was that we wanted universities to do for Chicanos and then construct a plan for action.

Critiquing the Results

RP: From this perspective, it is curious to me that awhile ago you commented that the universities have done everything that we have asked them to do.

MM: Yes, and I have the documentation to show you as reflected in the AACHE recommendations.

RP: My point is that ten years ago the AACHE project aimed to determine whether we could express to the universities what it was that we wanted them to do because before that time there was no clear, rational articulation of what it was that we wanted them to do for Chicanos.

MM: Yes, because we had not been present in universities before. The reality of the situation is that we are newcomers to the world of the university. Remember that many of us come from displaced peasant families tied to the revolution in Mexico. We are talking about a vast population that immigrated into this country during the teens, twenties, thirties, and forties as peasants; then we are also talking about the second generation that finally entered the universities. It was a dramatic event. It is not the case that American society was never responsive. That is not true. The society has been responsive. We just came into it late. I think that it is a bad rap on American institutions to say that they have been unresponsive. If you look at our situation—yours and mine—what has been accomplished is dramatic. I know that it is not wise to confuse individual mobility with group mobility but in my family, for example, five out of five graduated from college. It is a success story. We are not an exceptional family. We are the first generation and already we have imposed ourselves on the world. It is not that we are sitting back and people are not paying attention to us. Our daughters are going to have an impact on the world far more profound than we have had in our chosen fields. It is not like we sat back and did nothing. We did a lot.

RP: I agree, but there is more to it. I was stretching the point when I described our situation as stagnant. It was stagnant in the sense that our peasant parents were confronted with an industrial society on the verge of becoming a postindustrial society. So we had to challenge our thinking about where we were going, not just as isolated individuals or small groups, but on a mass level. And the strategy was to use well-educated individuals like you and me as the cadre that could engage us all in a process to transform the group. It was all too clear to most of us who first penetrated into academia that Chicanos were going to be transformed anyway. The issue was whether we would become just another anesthetized consumer group or whether we could develop a more critical orientation. Also, we were confronted by the possibility of becoming an underdeveloped Third World people within the confines of the United States. We were facing the same kinds of problems that Freire was facing in the Third World, so some of us Chicanos decided to use approaches similar to the ones that he used.

Specifically our project was to create leadership, to engage institutions in ways that could produce positive results for us, and going beyond that to cultivate a mindset among ourselves that we should not strive for mere incorporation into the mainstream society, but seek to become full participants. A fully participating individual has the power to engage and potentially to change the society.

Our project involved higher education because that is where we
found ourselves. The first step was to change ourselves, to see if we could
engage universities within the reigning rationalist paradigm. Through this
exercise we might be able to gain some concessions from the universities,
but, more important, we would have the opportunity to use and to critique
the rationalist paradigm, to see if it was something that we should buy into.

Romano's Legacy

MM: In the case of our careers, the activist project really started with
the Romano circle at the University of California at Berkeley. The historians
and the social workers had a seminar once a week with Octavio Romano in
the basement of the Penney's store on Shattuck Avenue. If you will recall,
our approach was to tell the mainstream scholars who were writing about
Chicanos that they were wrong in interpreting our existence. You'll note
the immaturity of the work. This really was our first attack on the rationalist model. You did the same thing in your work on Leonard Pitt and on
Chicano bibliographies. My project was to attack the prevalent interpretations of the Chicano family, but in my case it was quite immature. Much of
what those mainstream scholars said about our situation was in fact true.
At that point we were unable to distinguish the attack on us as people from
the substance of what was said. We threw out everything. I have been
looking at the more recent literature on the Chicano family and although
it is still very romanticized, there is a more profound reflection on our
situation. In discussions with women's groups, when women talk about
their fathers as machos, they often turn around and start to defend them.
My conclusion about the literature in this area is that it tends to rationalize
the behavior of Mexican/Chicano men. This rationalization, it seems to
me, is a mechanism to defend our families. Most people, and particularly
Mexican people, will not very easily divulge the dysfunctionalities in their
families—problems, unresolved conflicts, pathologies, etc. The saying *No
le platiques a nadie* [Don't talk about it to anyone] seems to reflect this
sentiment.

Surplus Labor

RP: We are discussing the bottom-up strategy for changing institutions and also for changing ourselves. If you look at the historical record
(the creation of AACHE, the AACHE plan itself, the various institutional
plans, the creation of research centers, and so on), it would be easy for
someone to conclude that our primary goal was to incorporate ourselves
into the universities in a manner similar to the mainstream population.
Such a conclusion would seem reasonable because the fact of the matter is
that the Chicano population during that period was almost completely

outside the universities and many were eager to get in. With few Chicanos participating in universities, we did not understand in a profound way the nature of these institutions. We found ourselves in a situation where we had to deal with complex bureaucratic organizations, but we ourselves were not well organized as a population. Our historic form of social organization was small groups that included extended families and local communities. So we were trying to survive in a complex bureaucratic world using forms of social organization that were meant for a different world order. What we really needed to do was to change ourselves as well as the mainstream social institutions around us. Both changes had to occur simultaneously. In this context, a more accurate expression of our goal as social activists within universities would be to say that we wanted more than mere incorporation. We wanted to become full participants in, and shapers of, the universities and other social institutions.

MM: Another way of describing our situation is to see Chicanos as surplus labor; that we served as an appendage to the corporate structure, mostly agribusiness. We were an appendage and at the same time we were interchangeable. We simply replaced the Chinese workers in the fields. We did not have control over our destiny. We were part of the machinery of agribusiness. I think we pointed this out in the "Framework for Action" section of the AACHE plan.

The Democratization of Knowledge

MM: You are saying that physical incorporation into universities and other institutions is not enough. Atencio has been talking about the democratization of knowledge; that we have to incorporate our own knowledge into the universities. We have much knowledge to contribute even though our knowledge is not yet systematic. You are also claiming that our indigenous knowledge and frameworks are not rational. I don't know if it is fair to say that we need to transform the nonrational to the rational, which is what I think the AACHE plan was trying to do. What we have to recognize is that we have a different framework and we have to articulate it much more clearly. It has to be legitimated. This can be done through dialogue or the *resolana,* which is a metaphor for enlightenment. Out of this dialogue will come the spiral of thought and action. Taken together, these ideas give new meaning to the notion of participation.

RP: The project approach that we used followed that kind of thinking. However, instead of the *resolana,* we used projects to create an ethnic context in which to develop community within the university. The *resolana* may or may not link to a university.

MM: This could explain Atencio's isolation. The *resolana* concept may not connect in a university, perhaps because there is no consensual validation. We cannot get people to agree and thus work together.

Legitimizing Our Knowledge

RP: The project to create the AACHE plan was in fact a project to legitimize our knowledge vis-à-vis the universities. Without legitimizing our knowledge, we would not be able to make claims on the universities and make the academy deal with them. To gain legitimacy we had to shift from an individualistic view of our situation to group consensus. We had to reach consensus about what it was that we knew about our needs. We did not need a multimillion-dollar research project to determine our needs. What we needed were social and political tools that would allow us to see ourselves as a community that could achieve collective action.

MM: The AACHE plan is rational and it even has good ideas, but it was not sponsored by a foundation or by the government. What is legitimate in the universities are documents that are sponsored by foundations or the government. Chicano documents are ignored because they are not published by the National Science Foundation or the Department of Education. They are not legitimate. The strength of these documents from our point of view — ethnic centered, participative, and democratizing — becomes the weakness from the mainstream point of view.

RP: I agree with you that such productions are not legitimate in a certain sense, but in another sense they are profoundly legitimate. Take the AACHE plan, which is indeed constructed in a rationalist mode. As such, it has to be legitimate within the rationalist framework of the bureaucratic university. Moreover, it has face validity because it was produced by the very people who were concerned with the problems addressed by the plan and it represented a collective call for action. However, I agree that the plan did not have legitimacy in the sense that it required political power to implement it, yet there was no large reservoir of political power behind it. So not all legitimate acts are equally significant. Our rationalist documents were not accompanied by the political power necesssary to impress them on the universities and thus their legitimacy became problematic. What I am saying is that for me legitimacy within the university required both rationalism and political muscle.

MM: Absent such political power, university administrators might simply ask, what advantage is there to me if I go along with this? Am I going to get a lot of flack from the faculty?

RP: Or they might ask, what disadvantages are there to me?

Ideas and Politics

MM: What you are arguing is that ideas by themselves, no matter how good they are, will not get heard if they don't have political power linked to them.

RP: I would agree with that view in general. In our case, that is exactly the situation that we found ourselves in. We had two problems. First, we could not articulate as a group and within a rationalist framework what we wanted. Second, we did not know how to make demands of universities that would be seen as legitimate, that is, that could be both rationalistic and framed within a proper political context.

MM: I am going to digress just for a second. In 1969 I attended a Chicano Conference on Mental Health in Tucson. This was the first time that Chicanos got together on mental health issues. This group has remained together as a network since then. We have all stayed in social work, and we have all had the same type of agenda. We met with officials from the National Institute of Mental Health (NIMH). As I recall, someone in the group shook a painting in the faces of the NIMH officials. The painting depicted a man with his hands and mouth tied up in silence. José Clemente Orozco painted people without faces. It is the idea of people not having a voice. So our group used the Mau-Mauist approach with the NIMH officials, holding up the painting and yelling at them. This was not a rational approach. We seem to have come a long way since then. Since 1969 our way of being articulate has changed. I don't know if things have improved in terms of people listening to us.

RP: You have expressed exactly our situation. The point is not that the expressions of pain from the sixties were off the mark. They were powerful expressions, almost in an iconic sort of way. They were an historic outburst: *El Grito*, the denouncement. Clearly, we went through a period of denouncing during the sixties. But there also has to be an annunciatory moment, as Illich indicates, in order to make really useful change. To denounce is to try to eliminate or destroy what is hurting you. But the solution is not simply to destroy what is hurting you. You must also construct something that is going to help you. We came to understand this point. There were many people who fell out of the *movimiento* because they were good at denouncing but not very good at announcing. These people did not have plans to improve things after "the revolution." By the 1980s we had concluded that we needed to be able to communicate with the universities. That meant having a rational set of goals and so on. We also knew that simple rationality would not carry the day. One also has to be able to impose one's views through the existing political system.

Participation and Consensus

RP: For me, the AACHE plan has various facets. One of those facets is participation and consensus. When your group was yelling at the NIMH officials in 1969, I am sure that they were wondering what it was that you wanted. Apparently, no rational proposal was forthcoming from your group. I found out through my activism that it is very difficult for us to articulate in plain language what it is that we really want. We have had a lot of conflicts built into our own experiences. Do we want to assimilate? Do we want simply to improve our material condition by getting better jobs or housing? Is it a matter of cultural nationalism? Is it a matter of maintaining our customs and values? If so, what does that mean? Among us there were many demands and conflicts but little or no clarity and less consensus. From the point of view of the Anglo population, they wondered why we just didn't become Americans and get on with it.

Lurking under all of this is the idea that we need special treatment. This idea of special treatment has been very problematic historically because that is the foundation for affirmative action, differential criteria, and so on.

Critique of Affirmative Action

MM: The idea of special treatment certainly has been a two-edged sword for minorities. Over the years, ideas like affirmative action have been transformed. When affirmative action started it was aimed at giving everyone an even break. There was a need to eliminate the negative impact of race and later gender. Now affirmation action is the exact opposite. For instance, job selection is based on groups. You now are not excluded because you are a woman or Black but included because you are a woman or Black. Moreover, the impact of affirmative action is felt differentially among the echelons of the society. Affirmative action does not impact the ruling class at all. They are immune from it. It does impact the professional class, the White professional class in particular. Also the middle-management level. Affirmative action has become negative in the sense that it has created the opposite spirit to what it was supposed to create. Our problem as Chicanos is that we don't fit the underlying premises of affirmative action. In many ways we are more like Eastern European immigrants. Institutions seem to hire White women rather than Chicana women. They tend to hire Blacks over Chicanos. And what has occurred is a zero-sum game. We blame one another for the hires that are made by those in power. We try to get the institutions to give us the benefits that Blacks get, but we are not perceived by Anglos in that fashion because we are not part of the American guilt consciousness. In many ways, they were at the forefront of the civil rights movement and the laws were designed to redress the wrongs perpetrated against Blacks. It creates a terrible dilemma for us.

Elusive Success

RP: As I look back over the last ten years, I see that the various projects that we undertook to galvanize Chicanos into a new social force were not very successful. I have not been able to determine why we have not been as successful as I thought and hoped we might be. It is not because we did not have the intellectual power to discern what was going on. Many of the players were tenured or tenure track professors; others were in entry-level or middle-management positions. There were probably at least one hundred members of AACHE with responsible positions. If there was any hope that we could get Chicanos to advocate our collective needs in academia, it should have been this group. After all we were working with people who were already in higher education.

But when it came down to it, the group could or would not put together rational plans that would do two things: (1) identify in clear and precise language what it was that we wanted the universities to do; and (2) provide a rationale for what we were asking. So we held a conference to move the process along. Then we created an association to develop the plan. We further decided to organize the plan on an institutional basis with an overlay of recommendations at the state level. All those things did come out in the plan, but if you look closely at the various institutional plans, only our institutional plan closely parallels the need areas that were developed at the AACHE conference. Why did the other institutions fail to stay on course?

MM: It goes back to Atencio's metaphor of the *resolana*, where people get together aided by the warmth of the sun to dialogue. In these dialogues they examine the contemporary problems of the world and themselves. What comes out of that process is consensual validation: agreement about the mutual problems of the people and what needs to be done. This sets the stage for action. The reason that those institutional plans don't fit the conference framework is that there was no consensual validation of the framework.

There is an absence of dialogue in our world: among Chicanos, Chicanos and Chicanas, Blacks and Chicanos, and on and on. Why is it that AACHE fell apart? It did not fall apart; it merely continues flat from its initial trajectory. There seems to be less dialogue now than when it began. In order to come out with political plans there has to be intensive dialogue, which is absent.

One of the problems you see in Chicano politicians, for example, is an emphasis on getting elected. What is missing is a dialogue with the community and accountability. The leaders are not accountable to the people because the people are not accountable to their leaders. There is an absence of dialogue, of critical consciousness. It is interesting to examine the trajectory of certain politicians in our community. Some of them were catapulted into power not by their community but by other powerful politicians who use the Chicano politicians to do their bidding. Such politicians also do the bidding of large business interests, often at the expense of their own communities.

RP: That is what I am trying to tell you about the AACHE plan. It was constructed by a few people. We were not successful in getting the group to collectively express its ideas in a rational way. The plan includes a section on demographics. Why did it take an Anglo to do a study on demographics that we should have done ourselves?

MM: In all fairness, if you look at the Tri-university Study Group we did our own demographic analysis.

RP: Your group was sponsored by the universities. When it came to the Chicano plan the empirical data were compiled by an Anglo. This is very revealing because it shows that our group really did not understand the rationalist model and that it was weak in fashioning empirically grounded arguments.

MM: They were not funded by resources from the federal government. It takes resources to pull empirical data together. You have to get computer tapes. Your point is why don't we have our own experts.

RP: What it tells me is that we did not know how to approach large bureaucratic organizations. The typical Chicano modus operandi was to justify our demands by telling stories about our own lives. When Chicanos approached an institution and were asked what it was that they wanted, they responded with stories from their personal experience.

MM: And, of course, these stories don't make sense to the institution. There is a tendency in these stories to dwell on our personal struggles whether in getting an education or a job. There also is a tendency to talk about our families. I've seen people do this in job interviews, and it has a detrimental effect because by and large American society separates the world of work from family life. We don't understand this. It is not necessarily a bad thing; it is just that we are a profoundly different type of people. You are right about Chicanos telling stories.

RP: All those people who sat around the tables at AACHE meetings understood the problems in personal terms, but they could not tell you how the problems affected the Chicanos in the state using empirical data. Many of them had the skills to do the empirical work, but they would not do it. Why?

My point is that when I insisted on having empirical data in the plan, I was trying to convey to those participating in the project the notion that we had to connect our needs to institutions in a rational way and that to do so empirical data are essential. The point was that outside of rationality we would not be viewed as legitimate. And I was trying to make sure that we understood this point collectively.

MM: There are two issues here. One is being able to develop the demographic analysis and the second is to appreciate it. Are you saying that Chicanos didn't even appreciate it?

RP: At that point, no, because nobody came forward to do the analysis, even though some had the skills to do so. It was only a few people within the AACHE group who understood the rationalist perspective of American institutions. Actually, by the 1980s there were many of us who understood *individually* the rationalist paradigm of universities and other institutions. We used that knowledge to write proposals to get federal and state funds, and so on. But I don't think that we accepted rationalism as a group nor could we use it to engage in collective action.

The AACHE plan also contains a set of propositions that appear prior to the actual recommendations for institutional action. These propositions form a framework that presents the social and historical context for institutional action. The framework expresses in political terms what it was that we wanted. The framework went beyond the empirical data, which clearly indicated that we were not adequately represented in the universities. It expressed our basic situation as a community that did not participate fully and richly in the social institutions of our country. So we demanded full participation and defined it as the power to change institutions, not merely to be assimilated. We wanted to participate in a radical democratic sort of way. This was quite a departure from traditional affirmative action. We were demanding political power so that we could change institutions and so that we could be responsible to them. We no longer saw institutions in opposition to us but as part of our civic life. Political power is not garnered by merely having 10 percent more Chicanos at the university or whatever. You must be able to participate fully in institutions. The statement also said that we take responsibility for our actions. Chicanos were willing to create a new covenant to promote democratic institutions.

MM: We just said that we did not carry out our responsibility.

RP: Precisely. But who is speaking in this section of the AACHE plan? It is you and I! The purpose of the AACHE plan was not just for you and me to talk to each other. The plan was intended to generate dialogue among the AACHE group and others to see if Chicanos accepted or rejected the new ideas. Yet there has never been any serious discussion or critique of the propositions contained in the AACHE plan by AACHE members themselves, let alone the larger academic community.

Getting Organized

MM: Here is where we have to get political. It has to do with the idea of organizing. If you look at the preeminent Chicano organizer, Ernie Cortéz, he says that you organize individual by individual. So if we had been serious about the AACHE plan we would have set up small meetings at all the colleges and asked people to discuss the ideas with us. Throwing out these ideas was not enough. You have to take the next step. You have to organize individual by individual so that the ideas become part of them. This is the idea of developing a critical consciousness. This is exactly Freire's idea of *círculos de cultura* or of Atencio's *resolana*, however one wants to depict it.

RP: I would agree with you as a general principle, particularly when one is working with poor and uneducated people.

MM: No, this was the essence of our conversation last time. You can have material wealth and you can still be disenfranchised. You can be a professor and be disenfranchised. You can be disenfranchised and still have a nice car and a nice house.

RP: I agree. But what I am saying about us collectively addresses a different point. I do not believe that the people who failed to engage the AACHE plan did not have the intellectual capacity to do so. I know that as professors and academics they are accustomed to engaging published ideas. They do so routinely in their academic specialties. So the question that I have is, why did they refuse to engage intellectually the ideas that were offered in the AACHE plan? In academia, when you publish a paper you don't have to go around holding small group sessions, because it is part of the profession to keep current with ideas in your field. But apparently, this convention doesn't apply when the ideas relate to Chicano concerns.

MM: It goes beyond that because we are not only talking about ideas but about a political process. The focus of Chicano politicians, for example, is to get elected and not to do anything in particular. At best they get a piece of the pie for their constituency. It has nothing to do with collective action. This is the essence of the corruption of the democratic process. We are part of it.

RP: I understand that part about the politicians, but now explain why the intellectuals, who are supposed to engage ideas anyway, refused to do so regarding the AACHE plan.

MM: Part of it is that we did not push it.

RP: We published it. That is how we push things in the academic world. We discussed it at various meetings and it was reviewed by the AACHE Executive Committee. But the academics chose not to engage it. Just as the politicians don't engage the community seriously, the academics did not engage seriously Chicano intellectual work. Why was there no intellectual follow-up? Why was it still born?

MM: As is much of our work.

RP: And not just among the Anglos. I didn't expect them to pay attention to us. But why was it stillborn among *us*?

MM: I don't really know. What do you mean?

AACHE's Failure

RP: For me, this was a great failure of AACHE: that we could not get Chicano academics to behave like academics in the context of Chicano-focused ideas. This was a disappointment for me because the AACHE project was intended precisely to instill in Chicano academics a professional interest in issues that were important to us. Historically, we have not shown much interest of this sort. You can see that on many levels. For example, you don't see many Chicano-focused academic journals. There may be two or three in existence today and that is about it. Yet, we are talking about millions and millions of Chicanos in this country. Thousands of them are university educated and many are engaged in intellectual work relevant to the larger society. But there are very few forums where these Chicanos seriously engage intellectual ideas about ourselves. Why are we not capable of doing that? What does it say about what we consider to be truly important in our lives as academicians?

What I am trying to say is that I don't think that Chicano academics wanted to buy into the idea of a Chicano intellectual life. It scared them. As such, they were cowardly; we were cowardly. We could not bring ourselves to engage an intellectual life that was ethnically focused. We could engage intellectual life in the mainstream cultural world, and we did so, but we could not do the same for an ethnically focused intellectual life. But you see, the AACHE project was intended precisely to create a larger Chicano intellectual world. And it fizzled. What AACHE turned into, and what I think Chicano intellectuals want from the Chicano agenda, is a forum, a venue, for emotional support, not a forum for critical intellectual activity. Chicanos want to congregate to assuage each other's emotional wounds. Then they go back into the "real world" and engage their intellects. The Chicano intellectual enclave has not been seriously intellectual because it has been too preoccupied with its affective needs. That is my hypothesis that accounts for the failure of the AACHE project and similar Chicano initiatives.

MM: There are many Chicano academics who do not want to engage Chicano intellectual life at all. Consider this: I won't repeat the difficulties that Atencio has had in developing a Chicano body of knowledge. However, let's look at your situation. You had a difficult time getting promoted to full professor even though by any standards you have a superior record. Many of the things they say about Atencio they also have said about you. Your promotion to professor was blocked unfairly for several years. These are not unique situations. I have witnessed them with many other professors. These situations explain why many Chicanos avoid confronting what is nearest to their hearts. There are other reasons. It is also partly a matter of experience because for the most part dialogue is not part of our public education.

Aversive Ethnicity

RP: Engaging the ethnic experience from the perch of an academic institution is very painful. You might even call it an aversive activity. Take for example Joaquín Bustos, a faculty colleague. One day, two or three of us Chicano faculty were eating in the cafeteria when he came through with his food tray. He looked at us, and in his inimitable way groaned, "Why is it that every time I see you guys I get pissed off!"

That expression communicated volumes to me. He actually said it in a matter-of-fact way. He was telling us, "Whenever I see you I am in pain. I get pissed off when I am in pain." His statement to us was rich and expressive and it captured that pain. The irony is that, like the fabled tar baby, you can't really divest yourself from that pain. Either you self impose ethnicity through your self-identity or others are just as likely to impose ethnicity on you. Others are likely to consider Bustos a Chicano no matter what he thinks. Maybe this unrelenting pain explains why people don't want to commit their intellectual resources to ethnic concerns. There are probably more mundane explanations as well that don't quite reach this deeply psychological hypothesis. Perhaps people think that it is simply a waste of time to engage in ethnic concerns because no one is going to give you a nickel of academic credit for doing so. Ethnic concerns have little or no currency value in academia.

MM: It is true because nobody ever reads that stuff.

RP: So intellectual ethnic productions become a self-extinguishing activity. There you have a more sociological explanation as to why Chicanos would not engage in intellectual productions that are ethnically focused.

MM: But we would also have to consider whether or not ethnically focused intellectual productions have any real meaning. If you look at a lot of the material in the journals it is vacuous; it says nothing.

RP: It has little meaning because once you refuse to engage in ethnic intellectual issues you are limited to becoming just one more run-of-the-mill academic. Most ethnic academics cannot break away from the scripted ethnic roles that are assigned to them, and for the same reason they have no legitimacy to speak credibly for the majority culture.

MM: There are also personal concerns. Most of us are products of very difficult circumstances. Many of our grandparents were refugees from a chaotic and cruel Civil War where more than 1 million people were killed. This created great dislocations in family life and transplantation to many places in the United States. My grandmother and her four daughters lived in four or five different places in Mexico before arriving in the United States. My mother had a difficult life. At the age of nine or ten she started working as a maid for a Jewish family. My father's story is similarly tragic. My grandfather fled the Revolution and went into the mining towns of Arizona. He died in Phoenix, Arizona, when my father was six years old and we don't even know where he is buried. My grandmother returned to Mexico and lived in extreme poverty. Others like you immigrated directly from Mexico and spent a good part of your life toiling in the agricultural fields. I can't image how difficult it was for your parents to have to raise fourteen children under those circumstances. There is a great deal of pain in many of our lives. We tend to romanticize it and downplay its impact, but it explains the avoidance of engaging in close self-examination. Some of this denial is breaking down, and we are beginning to see a more and more honest depiction of Mexican life as it was lived. Social science by and large ignores the issues; it romanticizes or quantifies our situation. I think these stories provide the secret key to many of the professional difficulties between Chicano men and women — certainly the key to the manner in which we conduct our family life, how we discipline our children. I can't help but think that our early years, particularly if not confronted, dictate our behavior to a great extent in other arenas. This is one area where we need to begin some serious discussions, particularly with Chicanas but also with Blacks and other groups.

Who Is Speaking for Whom?

RP: From a certain vantage point, we can frame the issue in terms of who is speaking for whom. Clearly in the AACHE plan we were presumably speaking for Chicanos. Who if not us should be able to speak for Chicanos? As it turns out, Anglo academics, speaking as anthropologists or sociologists, often speak for us. And they have better access to the proper academic and policy publications. So it turns out that we can become outsiders to intellectual discussions, even those related to Chicano ethnic concerns. Through self-exclusion and exclusion by others we become nonintellectual people. And if you are a nonintellectual person, what business do you have in a university? In the context of American society, our failure to engage an ethnic intellectual life destroys the possibility that we can become powerful academics.

MM: You will become an academic but be a nonplayer; you will become a backbencher. There are many examples of Chicanos holding jobs and not doing anything substantive. These are people who merely take up space.

RP: That's a terrible status. The AACHE plan was a project to challenge ourselves to leapfrog all of that. I don't see that we were able to do so in spite of the enormous energy that went into the project. That is what I am talking about.

I see Chicanos as having one of two options. Either we create an intellectual space in which the ethnic intellectual life blossoms or, through whatever means we have available, join the larger intellectual arena, such as it is. Not everyone will be allowed into the latter. And to the extent that we gain access to the mainstream intellectual world, we will wind up approaching our ethnic concerns as anthropologists, sociologists, whatever. This will not generate a genuine intellectual dialogue among ourselves.

The University's Responses

MM: At a certain level, the university did in fact respond to the AACHE plan. There was an increase in the number of minorities, resources were provided for a Hispanic Research Center, 50 percent of the HB 2108 moneys were allocated to Project Prime, and so on. On all these points the university did comply with the recommendations of the AACHE plan. Yet you are saying that it was not enough. If you look at President Nelson's response to the plan, you find that the university in fact complied with all that we asked for. What is missing?

RP: The university did many things. However, what exactly did it do and how did it do it? I reviewed one year of correspondence and it is clear that fundamentally the university did not respond to the plan in the sense that the university was opening up to Chicanos. The university was simply reacting and adjusting to new pressures. For the university, the Chicano demands were simply one more set of pressures. These demands had to be addressed at some point, but it did not have to be done immediately. Responses were made within the existing routines of the university. The Chicano concerns were seen mostly as political fires to be put out.

MM: So what? Is that not the way that the university responds to everything?

RP: Perhaps. But let me give you a counterexample. When Jack Kinsinger was vice president for academic affairs, he decided that computer technology was important. He spent millions of dollars on a microcomputer infusion project that soon led to a major transition in university computing from mainframe computers to microcomputers. It was a brilliant administrative move. I think that the microcomputer infusion project was one of the most effective things that Kinsinger did as an administrator. He took ownership of the project and put a lot of money into it. It was part of his agenda. I have never seen a Chicano project supported by the institution in that fashion.

MM: You are saying that the university response was piecemeal—that the university had no coherent strategy for implementing the AACHE plan recommendations. It simply made some concessions to appease

Chicanos. For example, it hired assistant vice presidents, which has done much to appease the community, yet those individuals do little to promote the university in the Chicano community and vice versa. It seems that a great deal of their time is spent in self-promotion or worse in promoting their bosses. I am shocked at the amount of space taken up on the Internet in congratulating one another and in awarding plaques to administrators who have done little to further our agendas. Don't you see that as our fault? Why are you blaming the university?

RP: Our failure to engage in an ethnic intellectual dialogue focused on our collective needs gets translated into lack of power to influence the university. We become incapable of acting collectively; the focus is placed on the individual. Perhaps it is only individual careers that can fit well into the structure of the university because individuals can be bought off. Everyone is susceptible to being bought off at the university.

There are large and small agendas at the university. The institution has to be seen as multilayered where agendas are moving simultaneously through all of the layers. Characteristically, an agenda is pushed by one interest group or another. What is confusing is that interest groups operate from the lowest to the highest levels of the organization but they all work within the same paradigm: they are organized into collectivities so that they can garner the political power to impose their agendas. It is easy to get confused in the maelstrom of small and large agendas that are always in play. Sometimes it is not easy to see the connections. It is complicated. We as Chicanos don't deploy ourselves at all levels of the institution to engage our agendas at various levels simultaneously. Instead, we focus on some specific items. And that is where you are claiming that we have been successful in getting the university to respond. But it has been very difficult to gain those types of concessions. Usually we have had to expend an enormous amount of political capital that is totally out of proportion to what we gain. Moreover, we tend to go to the very top of the organization in order to accomplish things that are at or near the bottom of the organization. We concentrate our efforts at the highest administrative levels assuming that the top has direct linkages to all the levels of the organization. That could be fallacious. It might be more effective to deploy our efforts at many levels of the organization and in a collective way.

MM: I have been thinking about that. Many of us have confused the process of meeting with the president with the idea of getting something done. For many Chicanos, meeting with the president itself is getting something done. There is little understanding about the kind of follow-through that is necessary. One of the things you learn in administration is that if you issue a directive about something it does not get implemented automatically. The place is manned by people and you have to follow through. For example, if you send a memo to the deans nothing will happen unless you follow through. The president is two layers removed in most situations. When you meet with the president and he or she commits to something, if there is no follow-through, little or nothing will happen. If we don't have access to the operational level to move our agenda forward, the bureaucracy will not get the job done.

RP: We have been trying to bring more Chicanos into the university so that we can deploy them up and down the organization. But influence is needed in the first place in order to be able to hire the right people. We have been caught on the horns of this dilemma for twenty five years. Somehow the pump has to be primed so that we can start moving in an upward spiral. So far we have not been able to do it.

MM: Perhaps it can happen at the University of Arizona because they have a Chicano president. If the president makes a commitment to it, he will follow through because it is in his own best interest.

RP: You are raising an empirical question and I don't know the answer to it. I do know that the AACHE plan made the university itself responsible for implementing the recommendations. The plan also called for the creation of an advisory council made up of Chicanos from the university and the community to help the university implement the recommendations. At the time, given the lack of deployment of Chicanos throughout the organization, this was our best hope to follow through on the ideas contained in the AACHE plan. Viewed critically, the results were less than spectacular. So, change from the bottom up is not a cinch.

Chapter 7

On Rainbows and Coalitions

The Minority Advisory Council

The Minority Advisory Council to the president of Arizona State University was established as a direct result of the first institutional plan following the strategy of the Arizona Association of Chicanos for Higher Education. The institutional plan contained twenty-five recommendations for action that were aimed at improving the educational services that the university was providing the Chicano community. Recommendation twenty-five specifically called for the creation of a Chicano Advisory Council.

The president resisted the idea of a Chicano Advisory Council and instead suggested a Minority Advisory Council, which would include Chicanos, Blacks, American Indians, and Asian Americans in its membership. After some negotiations, the Minority Advisory Council was established with staff support to be provided by the newly created office of assistant vice president for academic affairs and director of minority affairs, which was occupied by Miguel Montiel.

The first chair of the council was a prominent Black from the community. He was followed by a Chicana activist, also from the community. The last and final chair also was a Black. The committee included representation both from the community and from the university. Raymond V. Padilla was a member of the council. Miguel Montiel staffed the council, which was disbanded by the university shortly after it submitted its final report.

The Meaning of Recommendation Twenty-five

MM: I suggest that as a framework for discussion we incorporate the university's point of view in the establishment of the Minority Advisory

Council as well as the appointment of the assistant vice president for academic affairs and director of minority affairs. We should take into account the rules of engagement between the university and Hispanics. Specifically, what expectations did the university have in entering into a working arrangement between minorities (including Hispanics) and university officials, including faculty?

Within this framework, we can then critique the events. For example, you have mentioned on several occasions that we as a council were misguided in going through the exercise of developing yet another action plan when, in fact, several plans had already been created.

RP: Here's my question: Why did the Minority Advisory Council begin its work by producing an action plan when already the Tri-university Committee on Student Recruitment and Retention (that you chaired) had submitted its plan of action to the Board of Regents? In starting out anew with the construction of an action plan, what was our thinking? What were we trying to accomplish by creating yet another plan of action?

MM: Well . . .

RP: Before you answer that question we need to take into account another piece of information. Remember that the recommendation to the president for an advisory council first appeared in the AACHE plan of 1984. It was recommendation twenty-five in the Arizona State University institutional plan. The rationale for this recommendation was that the preceding twenty-four recommendations required some mechanism for their implementation. So recommendation twenty-five requested that the president appoint a Chicano Advisory Council whose primary function would be to advise the president (and therefore the entire university) on ways and means to implement the twenty-four substantive recommendations contained in the institutional plan.

When I drafted recommendation twenty-five, I had in mind that the substantive recommendations might largely just remain on paper. There was no reason to believe that our recommendations would fare any better than similar recommendations that were issued by the Board of Regents through its Tri-university Committee. Making and receiving recommendations is largely a game for universities. Clearly there was no reason for us to presume that the twenty-four substantive recommendations would be self-implementing. So the Chicano Advisory Council was intended to exert continuous pressure on the university through the office of the president. From my perspective, the value of the council was its potential to provide political leverage for us in getting the university to engage our agenda. Through the council we could become more influential and pressure the university to accept greater ownership of the problems that we faced. We wanted the university to take specific steps to address the issues that were important to us. I also recognized at the time that it would not be feasible for us to get a large bureaucratic organization like the university to move against its own perceived interests. So we needed to find ways to get the people at various levels of the organization to buy into our proposals. The Chicano Advisory Council was designed to help us achieve those ends.

MM: It doesn't necessarily follow that our vision of the council would be similar to the university's. Remember that the argument has always been made by universities that if something is created for Chicanos, then the universities also must create the same thing for Blacks, Native Americans, women, and who knows what other groups. Interestingly, this argument is not made in reverse, that is, in places where there is a large concentration of Blacks. If we were at Wayne State University in Detroit, for example, and a so-called Minority Advisory Council were established, it would consist primarily of Blacks. There is no question about that.

Arizona's demographics are important to the point that I am making. It is significant that Arizona is about 20 percent Hispanic, 6 percent Native American, and 3 percent African American. You will recall a recent meeting with the provost where he talked about a "mistake" he had made at Wayne State University regarding this very idea. He mentioned that he had "learned" a lesson so that now he would never promote ideas like proportional representation of various ethnic groups on minority committees.

The Rules of Engagement

MM: Let me take you back to another conversation that you had with a different provost, Kinsinger. He wanted to make sure that the interests of minorities were congruent with the interests of the larger university community. It is also important to point out that Kinsinger wanted to decentralize authority and shift it from the central administration to the various colleges. He wanted to accomplish this in a principled way. One principle was that he would never appoint a committee whose charge went counter to the existing mission of the university. This put us in a very difficult situation. Specifically, this meant that whatever was done relative to minorities had to be congruent with the rhythm of the university. In other words, we could not have a contentious situation. Harmony was to be pursued.

But how could such harmony be achieved in our case? This is a key question. By definition we are outsiders. So how can our interests be harmonized with the interests of the university? That was the dilemma facing the Minority Advisory Council. It was a dilemma that in retrospect placed us in a trap because there was never any interest on the part of people in power to harmonize with our interests—it was always someone else's interests that prevailed. Nevertheless, this was the rule under which we engaged the university.

As an aside, I believe that the current provost has continued Kinsinger's decentralization philosophy, but this time without a definitive set of principles. It seems that the university, although it talks about improving undergraduate education, enhancing minority student participation, and improving its relations with the community, does not have the power or the leadership to implement these ideas. The deans do whatever the hell they want and nobody seems to be able to stop them. It is a very complicated situation that has everything to do with the fragmentation of our society and an absence of leadership at all levels: majority and minority, faculty and administration, business and government.

RP: I don't remember that conversation specifically, but I do remember some of those ideas. For many years my argument has been, first, that we did not get very far with the universities when we dealt with them as if they were our enemies. Second, when one looks at what universities say about themselves, as reflected in their catalogs, for example, their stated goals are in fact not antithetical to ours. We are both interested in the production of knowledge, the advancement of technology, the development of civic leaders, the critique of society, and so on.

MM: The issue is, are we included in the universities' mission? Ultimately, we also have to question whether the universities are serious about their mission statements; more and more I believe that this is not the case, at least not here at our university. We can touch on this later, but for now let's just stick to the question of whether we could be an integral part of the university.

RP: My point is that during the early period of Chicano campus activism, we presumed that there was something noxious about the universities that prevented us from coming together with them. My observation is simply that there is nothing inherently noxious about the universities in terms of what we want for ourselves.

MM: But the original confrontation that took place in 1964 involving the free speech movement at Berkeley and other elite campuses stemmed from the view that universities were noxious indeed. The students did believe that the universities were heading down the wrong path; that they were instruments of the defense department. The best example, of course, was the close connection with the Lawrence Radiation Laboratory up on the hill next to Tilden Park overlooking U.C. Berkeley. It is one beautifully blended landscape and many believed at the time that it was also one interlocking ideological panorama. I remember discussions at Cal, and you took part in some of them, where universities were characterized as instruments of oppression that needed to be changed.

RP: That is true enough. And yet, although the free speech movement was part and parcel of the early Chicano campus activism, it was not the main inspiration for our Chicano critique of the universities. That is a very important point.

MM: But the point is that to a certain extent we incorporated that rhetoric. At a political level it had to do with the role of the university in the war effort, the critique of the Vietnam War, the bombing of Cambodia, which, you will recall, created a major uprising on campus. I remember the uprising very well because I nearly got killed when a tear gas canister landed between my legs, and it took several hours for the sting in my eyes and face to subside. For a moment I thought that my voice would change permanently! Anyhow, at a social and cultural level, our struggle had to do with legitimating ethnic knowledge in the curriculum and reclaiming our history. Along the way we incorporated the rhetoric of race and racism as our own. I don't think this ever worked very well.

RP: It is true that during the sixties we borrowed some of that rhetoric. But over the years that is exactly what I have advocated that we move away from. Because it wasn't an authentic rhetoric from the point of view of the Chicano community.

When Chicanos first went to the universities during the sixties, it was in the context of the antiwar movement, the civil rights movement, and the counterculture movement. At the time, we adopted certain rhetorical devices and ideas from these movements that probably were not very useful in the context of our long-term interests. The most important issue for us during the late sixties was incorporation into the universities. We felt left out. Perhaps you are pointing to a profound contradiction. Why the hell would Chicanos seek incorporation into the universities if the universities were truly seen as noxious entities? I believe that it was really only a small faction of Chicanos who viewed the universities as noxious. Most Chicanos simply wanted in. And they used the antiuniversity rhetoric of the various movements to try to gain entry.

MM: Exactly. Those of us who found ourselves at Sather Gate [U.C. Berkeley] knew that we had an opportunity that could not be squandered by nonsense. It had taken us a good deal of studying to get there. Remember, I made it through the system before I was identified as a "minority." In those early days, there were no advantages, and many hidden disadvantages, to being a minority. I paid my way through undergraduate school. When I wasn't working I was studying in the library.

RP: Early on I saw the antiuniversity attitude as a contradiction and decided that it wouldn't take us very far in achieving our goals.

MM: That is a very important point. When you think about it, we have not yet dropped that rhetoric. You can hear it still among some Mechista student factions.

RP: Well, I'm not saying that the critique of the university by the counterculture movement and others was entirely off the mark either. I just question the fit between their critique and our own critique of the universities. It seems to me that our critique has to be grounded in a totally different perspective. Looking back to the sixties, what we wanted was to become active participants in the universities. We did not want to be passive participants. We wanted to have the power to change the universities so that our goals could be achieved.

MM: To adapt the universities to our needs. That is what I tried to get at during my tenure in the vice president's office. To determine the "fit" between the rhetoric of minorities and the minority programs that the university had established.

RP: That is the legacy of the radical critique that we appropriated. That is the shape that it has finally taken. But there are still quite a lot of people who haven't been able to work their way out of the original contradiction. So they still view the university antagonistically. By the early eighties, I had already worked through this contradiction. When we first met with President Nelson I advocated a ten-year Chicano action plan. It was to be a collaborative plan between us and the university. But it also was a strategy for us to reclaim rather than reject the university.

MM: The point is that when we offered a ten-year action plan the university responded by saying, "O.K., we think some of these ideas are good. We are going ahead with a council, but instead of a *Chicano* advisory council, we are going to establish a *minority* advisory council." That is what I mean when I talked about "the rules of engagement." Now let's talk about the purpose of the Minority Advisory Council.

RP: Well, first of all, why would the university not want a *Chicano* advisory council?

MM: That is precisely why I am trying to determine first the rules by which the university tried to engage us. Remember that the principal task of the Minority Advisory Council was to advise the president on all matters related to ethnic minority access and underrepresentation, and on the relationship between minorities and their respective communities. My job as the director of minority affairs was to facilitate the work of the council.

At least that is the rhetorical framework within which we and the university mutually engaged. By establishing a minority advisory council, the university was presumably following the recommendation of the AACHE plan, with some "minor" changes. The biggest change, of course, was to include all minority groups in the advisory council. That represents a rule of engagement from the point of view of the university.

An Offer the University Could Refuse
RP: All that is true enough. But let's pull back a step or two. In the first

instance, the university simply refused to consider a *Chicano* advisory council. There is a memo in our files from two assistant vice presidents that is basically a draft response to the AACHE plan. They advised the president not to establish a Chicano advisory council because, according to their perspective, the university then would have to create separate advisory councils for Indians and for Blacks.

MM: The vice president for business affairs made the same recommendation prior to that memorandum. That was particularly ironic when you realize that he was hired, so the story went, because the president thought that he was a Chicano! This was a very silly story, but it points out a profound truth, which is that affirmative action is a corrupt business where faces and names are more important than ideas and practices. Here we were trying to understand the role of Chicanos in the university, and the university was trying to hire people as Chicanos without even discussing it with the Chicanos on campus. This also should tell us something about the rules of engagement that I have been talking about. If this story is true, it should tell you something about the profound disrespect toward Chicanos, and, to put it delicately, our politeness.

RP: So the president got a staff recommendation that it would be unwise to create a specifically Chicano advisory council. And the rationale given for this recommendation was that creating a Chicano advisory council would lead inevitably to the need to create similar councils for other minority groups, particularly Blacks and Indians.

MM: Yes, exactly.

RP: The president simply parroted back to us the staff recommendation when he told us that he would support an ethnic minority advisory council instead of a Chicano advisory council.

MM: That's right.

RP: You will recall that at the time, I became quite agitated. I did so because I had become extremely sensitized to what I considered an absurd situation in Arizona: Whenever the university established a committee to deal with minority issues, it used what I labeled the "three-three-three plan." That is, the committee invariably consisted of three Chicanos, three Blacks, and three Indians.

MM: And a White as chair!

RP: Indeed. This was at a time when approximately 18 percent of the state's population was Chicano, 2.7 percent was Black, and about 6 percent was Indian. Yet, on these university committees the various ethnic groups would be equally represented.

As you know, I spent many years in Michigan where the Black population was the predominant minority. There I had always seen what I called the "ten-one-one plan": Committees would include ten Blacks, one

Chicano, and one Indian. That plan went on for a long time.

MM: It's still going on.

RP: No one really challenged it, certainly not the Whites. In Michigan I never saw an equal distribution of minorities on any committee.

MM: So why is it that the same administrators who operated under those rules over there came over here and were against the idea of proportional representation? All of a sudden they saw proportionality as an objectionable policy. Why the change? There are other examples of this apparent change of heart as administrators circulate around the country.

RP: To put it mildly, I was puzzled by this change of heart. Here I was in the middle of the Southwest and Chicanos apparently had allowed ethnic committees to be established on the three-three-three plan. I immediately challenged this concept, first among Chicanos. Why should we tolerate this situation? Such committees should have membership that is proportional to the actual ethnic populations in the state. That is the generous version. The stronger version was, why shouldn't Chicanos predominate in such committees? This would correspond to the Black situation in the Midwest. I urged the group to demand proportionality in all ethnic committees, especially the Minority Advisory Council.

The Superstructure of Black and White Relations

MM: The university's approach has historical roots. It goes back to the War on Poverty during the sixties. A key idea of that period was to include community participation and empowerment in all development projects. During the early development of those projects, there was a great deal of Black involvement nationally, but also in Phoenix. This created the illusion that there were a lot more Blacks in Phoenix than was the case. I think that the Black churches had a lot to do with organizing their people in very effective ways.

But it also has to do with the mind-set that people from the East and the Midwest have about minorities. Their image of minorities centers on Blacks. Many university administrators, particularly in those days, knew little about Chicanos, so they did not consider Chicanos in the overall scheme of things.

I suppose it also has to do with what Shelby Steele, the Black critic, has identified as the need for White folks to absolve their guilt regarding the so-called inferiority of Black folks. My personal opinion is that some Blacks have learned to exploit this situation very effectively and that people in power positions have learned how to keep us divided. We always seem to fall for it. This exploitation, I believe, often hurts not the power brokers who make the decisions, but those in the lower ranks. It helps explain much of the acrimonious relationship between Whites and Blacks and Jews and

Blacks, but primarily with the younger people who have been muzzled from discussing this situation in an open forum. I also think that it has to do with the poor political organization in the Chicano community. It is a festering problem in our society. It is a very complicated issue.

RP: At that time there must have been fewer than 3 percent Blacks in the Arizona population.

MM: Yes. But when you went to community meetings, there was lots of Black involvement. Some community people were actually designated as leaders by the people who ran the programs, usually Anglos. They always had one or two very prominent, and many not so prominent, community leaders. I recall when Phoenix had a charter government and the elites always selected a slate of candidates that provided equal representation to Blacks and Chicanos. So in Phoenix the illusion was created that there were a lot more Blacks than actually existed. In fact, if you look at the demographics of the city of Phoenix, for example whom they employ, you become aware of very significant participation by Blacks in many segments of city government. There are important city departments that lack any administrative representation by Chicanos. It is as if people operated on a zero-sum basis: that Black positions are allocated at the expense of Chicanos and vice versa. This is how both groups view the situation when there are hires involving Blacks and Chicanos. Time and time again you see fierce fights between Chicanos and Blacks for what are relatively unimportant posts, but little concern is shown when White males or females are hired for what are obviously high-power posts. It is a most interesting phenomenon. There has been a great deal of antagonism between minority groups that has really only helped the people who actually hold the power.

RP: During the Continental Congress, the Southerners and Northerners agreed that a Black would count three-fifths as much as a White. Now Chicanos count one-third as much as a Black. So in the eyes of an Anglo, Chicanos are one-fifth of a White. Is that what all this adds up to?

MM: Even though I am referring to local politics, the decision-making arena is on a national level on issues of affirmative action, housing, and other broad welfare and educational matters. It is important for people to understand this phenomenon. Chicanos are still basically invisible. Blacks have a lot more prominence in their relationship to people in power than we do. It's not a difficult idea to understand.

RP: What you are saying is that Anglos control the configuration of power. They decided to allocate equal power to both groups. In a sense, the national prominence of Black issues compensated for the much larger population of Chicanos in Arizona, so they all wound up equal.

MM: Present conditions often have their antecedents in decisions that were made years before. For example, when they started building public housing in Phoenix during the late forties, a decision was made that Blacks would live in Matthew Hansen, Chicanos in Marcos de Niza, and Whites in Duppa Villa, all segregated from one another and from the White middle class. So the basic configuration of which people would live where in Phoenix was determined by policies made years ago. Furthermore, although poverty is concentrated in both communities, the allocation of resources has generally focused on Blacks over Chicanos. For many years, for example, the majority of public housing in Phoenix went to Blacks even though they constituted a very small fraction of the population. These patterns have continued to the present.

RP: But the creators of those policies and patterns were never the Chicanos or the Blacks.

MM: Or Indians for that matter. So even though Blacks were not the initiators of the so-called equalizing policies that we see manifested in the universities, they often have been the beneficiaries. Just like we are. But in this case we seem to be a little bit more "victimized" than Blacks. The same applies to the Indians. The Indians get an even smaller slice of the pie.

The Rule of Proportionality

RP: So let's go back to the president's response to recommendation twenty-five. After we had conversed with the president and determined his resistance, we figured that he was not going to appoint a Chicano advisory council. So Chicanos made a political decision to go ahead and accept his idea of a minority advisory council. But there was one proviso: he had to agree that the minority advisory council would have proportional representation from the various minority groups. I was bound and determined to crack the historical three-three-three pattern.

At first the president wouldn't hear of it. That has always baffled me. You see, his reaction showed how entrenched in their consciousness was the pattern that you just described. When challenged to pay attention to the actual population demographics of the state, university administrators simply did not want to do it. It took a month or two before the president accepted the idea of proportionality. The president's letter in which he finally agreed to the idea is an incredible document. Essentially he accepted the idea of proportionality but added so many caveats that he actually rejected it. Sort of.

MM: So they accepted proportionality more or less.

RP: They wanted to have their cake and eat it at the same time. They more or less wanted to agree with us, but they did not want to make themselves vulnerable to pressure from other ethnic groups. I think that is what it all boils down to. In fact, they actually appointed council members in a proportional manner. But they were reluctant to develop a policy as such.

That incident illustrates the tenacity with which administrators hold the idea of treating all minorities as equals in a phony kind of equality. It is equality only in the sense of compressing things down to a very low common denominator. We can all get treated equally because we're all treated as basically worthless. Whatever any ethnic group gets within that calculus is of minute advantage and is obtained only through enormous effort because everything is compressed to virtually nothing in terms of political empowerment.

MM: Exactly. And the whole thing promotes animosity among the different groups over virtually nothing. I think that what we found out at the end of the process that created the Minority Advisory Council is that the prize was nothing.

RP: It is important to understand how the Minority Advisory Council evolved from our original idea to create a Chicano advisory council. Because this has implications for what was to follow. Remember that conceptually, the purpose of a Chicano advisory council was to follow up on the implementation of the twenty-four substantive recommendations in the institutional plan. But what would be the purpose of the Minority Advisory Council? This group could not seek to implement only a plan to help Chicanos. What I am saying is that the switch from a Chicano to minority advisory council was a very successful strategy to derail the Chicano plans for engaging the university. We were the only ethnic group that actually had an action plan.

MM: No, that's not quite true. The Indians had a plan—the Navajos had submitted a plan a long time before. The Blacks also had a plan.

RP: You can call them plans if you want to. But they were more like dream sheets. I saw them. I have them in the files. They did not have plans in the same way that we had a strategic plan. What they had were documents in which they asked the university to do this or that. These plans did not approach the sophistication of the AACHE plan.

MM: What difference does it make?

A Difference in Political Clout

RP: It makes a lot of difference, because the Blacks and the Indians had not yet gone through an internal political process, such as the one we went through, to develop a collective plan that actually was subscribed to by some identifiable group. If you look at the Black and the Indian plans, it is very difficult to determine their political status.

MM: Well, the Blacks, for instance had some kind of council. They met periodically with the president of the university. The group was made up of faculty, administrators, and community leaders. They are the ones who prepared the Black proposal.

RP: They were merely an internal referent group. Ours was a statewide association, which was much more sophisticated.

MM: But, I'm looking at this from the point of view of the university. The university says, "Oh, we have plans from everybody. We can't just respond to the AACHE plan." Remember, the university gets a lot more heat from Blacks than they do from Chicanos on political correctness.

RP: My point is that once we agreed to the Minority Advisory Council we were confronted with the problem that there did not exist an institutional or statewide plan for higher education that was crafted by minorities themselves. We were suddenly thrown together as minorities. Our individual group efforts were largely cast aside. What was the university to do? Logically, it decided that we needed a minority action plan.

But we as Chicanos had already learned a valuable lesson. In developing a statewide higher education plan, we had learned that the important thing was to approach each institution individually, to particularize things, as it were. Well, the same should have been obvious to us in the context of minority groups. We didn't really need a minority plan. What we needed to do was to particularize the needs of each ethnic group and determine how each group wanted to move forward.

MM: You will recall that one of the first things that we did when the Minority Advisory Council met was to develop a detailed set of principles by which we would operate. One of the principles was that all of the minority groups are different and have different needs. There are commonalities between the various groups, but each group has distinct needs. The Indians pushed strongly for this principle because they usually get ignored in multiethnic agreements. It will be interesting to see what will happen with Native Americans with their newly won economic power derived from gaming.

RP: Everybody supported that principle. I went along with it. From the very beginning, my position in all of this was that we as Chicanos had already identified what we wanted. But we needed to hear what the Blacks and the Indians wanted so that together we could form some kind of coalition. That was my instinct in terms of how things should go.

But the Blacks did not come forward with a list of things they wanted, and neither did the Indians. If you remember correctly, or if you look at the record, it was you, an administrator, who pulled out the so-called plans of the Blacks and the Indians that you have alluded to. In a sense, you declared what it was that the Indians and Blacks wanted.

That's not the process that I was expecting from this group. I was expecting that the Indians would step forward and make some kind of structured, rational statement about what it was that they wanted; same thing for the Blacks. Why didn't that happen?

In fact, the Blacks and the Indians had not gone through a political process of consensus building within their own communities. To be able to say to the higher education system of Arizona, in a political way, "Here is what we want you to do for our communities," requires such a process of consensus building. We had actually engaged such a process, and thus I contend that the AACHE plan had a very different political status from the so-called plans of the other two groups that you mentioned.

MM: Maybe for Blacks it wasn't important to do that.

RP: If that is true, then it was a great political mistake to throw them in with us. We should have resisted it.

MM: It was as important to the Blacks as it was to us. The point is that they needed to get some of the resources that were to be allocated.

RP: But not automatically. That's not the way I was playing the game. At that time I was insisting that there had to be political support for a statewide initiative from each ethnic group. If this were so, the Blacks would be able to say what they wanted and have some kind of political muscle behind it. Same thing with the Indians. But neither of these groups was organized, or had paid enough attention to the issues, to develop such a plan. When I understood this situation, I saw a large distance between the level of preparation of the Chicano group and the other two main groups, the Blacks and the Indians.

MM: That is true.

RP: Given this asymmetry of political preparation between the various ethnic groups, the key issue for me was how to get them to coalesce. Somehow we needed to bring along the other two groups as quickly as possible if there was going to be a quality effort. I was keenly aware of the fact that it is not possible to have a coalition if the various parties do not bring something credible to the table. For coalitions to work with these minority groups, they have to come to the table as equals. And they have to be clean about what they put on the table. We brought to the table the AACHE plan. But I think that this was overwhelming for the Blacks. Not only were there more Chicanos on the council, because of the proportionality principle, we also brought forward a sophisticated agenda. They came to the table as you've described: as the perennial representatives from the Black community. Isn't that true?

MM: Yeah, representatives from the Black community have been effective in advocating their interests. We have seen this when the university tried to move against Black administrators. They also have been effective in developing a power base. They have a powerful Black university system and they have been successful in electing public officials.

RP: Individuals like them don't necessarily have any particular expertise in higher education. Moreover, they were not in a position to do quickly what had taken us years to accomplish, that is, construction of the AACHE plan. Nor did they have the necessary political infrastructure in place state wide. I immediately noticed all these things and concluded that we were going to be in really bad trouble.

In this context, when you administratively brought forward the existing minority plans, I thought that it was kind of ingenious. But I also thought that it was kind of ironic that you should take the lead on behalf of the other ethnic groups because they were not coming to the table prepared for the give and take of coalition politics. How could we negotiate with them for a joint effort if they couldn't operate at the same level that we were?

After you brought to the table the "plans" for the Blacks and the Indians, then you tried to articulate the commonalities that existed between all three documents. On top of that, you also brought to the table the relevant committee reports from the Arizona Board of Regents, who also had dealt with issues related to minorities.

MM: That was our mandate. Remember what I said earlier about the provost's need to find congruence between minority interests and those of the university.

RP: I always understood these actions as your attempt to shape things in a certain way.

MM: Remember that the policy of the Board of Regents was our guide. That was the mandate that the provost had given. As an administrator, you're always safe if you stick with the policies of the Board of Regents.

RP: But the regental policies were always ahead of the universities.

MM: Yes.

RP: So you wouldn't necessarily be safe there. The regents were pressing ahead while the university administration was resisting change. But I understand the political point that he was making: namely, that administrative action is best expressed when it is consistent with board policy. In general, I agree with that principle. But in the concrete case that we are discussing, invoking this principle meant that we would have to spend considerable effort to fit together the various plans that had been produced by the various minority groups and the Board of Regents. In the end, that process consumed us and we ended up simply producing a document.

MM: Exactly.

Putting a Black in Charge

RP: It took us a couple of years to do it. In the meantime, the council witnessed all kinds of side shows that conditioned the work of the group. For example, initially you chose to put a Black in charge of the council. Right? That's very interesting politics.

MM: That was Alton Washington.

RP: A very good person to work with. Nevertheless, as a participant observer I saw that Chicanos had pressured the university for a Chicano advisory council, only to be forced into accepting a minority advisory council with proportional representation, and then a Black got appointed as chair.

MM: No, he got elected by the committee.

RP: O.K., so you finessed it!

MM: I don't think so. You know why he got elected? Because he has very strong ties to the Chicano community. He also has strong ties to the Black community. He is respected and trusted by the Chicanos as if he were a Chicano. Why? Because he has always conducted himself in a very upright manner. He has always been fair minded. So I think that the council did a very smart thing by selecting him as chair.

RP: Well, I don't know. This is the sort of thing that I questioned because I knew that something like that was highly unlikely to be seen in, say, Detroit, if the Blacks there had undertaken a major political initiative as we were doing in Arizona.

MM: Exactly.

RP: I can't see Blacks there appointing a Chicano to head it. I just can't imagine it.

MM: Well, why did it happen then?

RP: *Pues, yo creo que por babosos* [Well, I guess because we were foolish]. But you are my friend and I don't wish to insult you.

At the time I believed, and I think that I still do, that the Chicanos were uneasy because we dominated the council in terms of membership. So consciously or unconsciously we were being overly defensive. In effect, we were saying something like, "Since we have proportional representation on the council, we have the lion's share of the membership. However, we're going to be fair and put a Black in charge." If this is true, then I am going to add something to your earlier analysis. Not only were the Anglos controlling the configuration of power among the minorities, it seems that Chicanos introjected these patterns and reproduced them even when they didn't have to. Their political consciousness had been overdetermined by their environment.

MM: There is a reluctance among Chicanos to take charge of things. I'll give you an example that is very interesting. You recall that we had a search for the director of the Chicano studies program. There was a lot of conflict between the men and the women. The women basically were distrustful of the men. I was brought in to set up the selection of the search committee. I negotiated with the dean to appoint the committee.

My intention, of course, was to facilitate the process and encourage women to control this thing. So I went in with the idea that I would let them know up front that whatever they wanted that's what they were going to get. They were going to control the search committee. When we sat down with the dean, no one there was willing to become chair of the committee. As a result, the dean thought it okay to appoint as chair a faculty member who is a very respected person with someone in her past who came from Spain, but who does not necessarily identify with our aspirations.

A lot of people think back and say, "How come they chose so and so as chair of the committee? This is a Chicano committee." But I talked to a lot of other people and basically they refused to accept being the chair of the search committee. That forced the dean to select the respected professor, thinking, you see, that the person was acceptable to us, and nobody said anything. Is that your point?

Subtle Politics

RP: Yes. How do you explain that reluctance? I have already brought forward the hypothesis that Chicano political consciousness has been overdetermined by the environment. But I think that there's more to it than that. Chicanos are fairly sophisticated politically. So there is the possibility for a rival hypothesis. One has to notice that Chicano politics are very subtle. They're much more subtle, let's say, than Anglo, and certainly than Black, politics. Maybe they're more akin to Indian politics; they also operate with subtlety. In the case of the Minority Advisory Council, the Chicanos may have been trying to maintain a political balance in order to prevent things from blowing up. We had taken a great political risk in joining the other minority groups instead of going it alone. Whatever made us think that we could get the three groups and everyone else to come together?

MM: I was very reluctant to take on that challenge. It's very difficult. There was enormous potential for an explosion, and also to make the university look bad. I think I was also afraid of the possibility of the other groups walking out on the process. I had a great respect for the people on that committee — Alton Washington for one, and John Lewis, the head of the Intertribal Council. A blowup would have insulted the president, and would have resulted in a loss of face for everyone. A failed project as it was, I think it was important for us to work together.

RP: To make everyone look bad. So maybe the chicanada were acting very sophisticated when they selected the Black chair. Perhaps that was your point earlier. But I'm also trying to look at this thing from other perspectives. Perhaps it was a sophisticated and even overly sophisticated move at the same time. What I mean is that in the real political world the chicanada simply have got to take charge if we are going to move an agenda. We needed to come up with other ways to work out the power differentials with the other minorities. Putting a Black in charge was not a particularly good solution.

In spite of all this, I still thought that there was potential for the council to shape an action agenda. Since I had inferred from your behavior that the basic task of the council was to devise an action plan, I did not think that it mattered very much who chaired the group. Well, it wouldn't matter a whole lot, unless the chair became mischievous.

It's Risky Betting on Rainbows

MM: In fact, during the third year, when another Black took over the council, the situation became untenable. It did so precisely because the new chair did a lot of underhanded things. For instance, when the council agreed to push Project PRIME, several Blacks went and had a discussion with the provost about what we were doing, thus undermining the council, which one of them chaired. I read a letter that the chair wrote to the provost wanting to know about Project PRIME, and why it wasn't addressing Black concerns. It was, of course. But we went ahead and hired a White woman to direct the program so that Blacks would not be upset at a Chicano directing the project. This is another case where Chicanos folded to the unethical behavior of the chair. No one called him on it, and people operated as if nothing important had happened. Think about the consequences of this type of behavior multiplied many times over in interactions between Blacks and Whites. It is the kind of politics that has always been difficult for me to understand. In all fairness, I have seen Chicanos on campus playing this same game.

RP: That's exactly the kind of risk that we were running by appointing a non-Chicano to chair the council.

MM: At that point Chicanos decided to do away with the council. It was disbanded because I saw that there were a lot of things that were going to happen that would be detrimental, not only to the few things that we managed to accomplish, but to the interests of the university, to my interests as assistant vice president, and, of course, ultimately to the interests of my boss.

RP: By then the potential instability of the ethnic troika had begun to show. Once we started with a Black as chair, we had to continue that pattern until the potential for destructiveness was actualized. Then the only alternative was to discontinue the council. During the several years that it existed, the council only managed to come up with yet another plan. But the real lesson that came out of that experience, something that the university should have learned but didn't, is that issues faced by various minority groups cannot be properly addressed by lumping them all together.

MM: I think that you might be making a terrible assumption in thinking that the university doesn't know what it's doing!

RP: Are you saying that the university was using this as a strategy?

No Room for Whites

MM: No. I don't think that there was bad faith in the sense that the president didn't have good intentions. I think the president in fact had good intentions. One issue that I wonder about, in this instance, is why there weren't any Whites on the council? This is a very important point that Richardson addressed in a letter to me. He argued for the inclusion of other players, particularly those with power, who were sympathetic and could help move forward the agenda. He was right.

RP: Fine. But there are two aspects to this. Richardson essentially was asking the question, "Why didn't you set up an advisory council on minority affairs, rather then a minority advisory council?"

MM: It's a very good point, and one doesn't negate the other.

RP: Clearly that was an option. But, you see, Richardson didn't know the history of the Minority Advisory Council. He did not know that we originally had asked for a Chicano advisory council, which had an even narrower focus. Against that backdrop, it would have been very difficult for us to agree to a council on minority affairs. Such a vehicle would not have been responsive to our needs.

MM: His point was that a more diverse council would be more effective, given the politics of the university, in moving the agenda. I think he made a good point.

RP: I disagree because, as I have stated, in the first instance there was no minority agenda as such.

MM: There was an agenda. I just read through the agenda.

RP: What? To come up with a plan?

MM: No. To work with community leaders, with the vice president for student affairs, and with the university management and staff to make the university more accountable to the community. Also to advise on the implementation of all plans related to the underrepresentation of minority groups at the university.

RP: Those are mostly political goals. There's no substantive agenda.

MM: The point is that there has been implementation of some specific programs, for example, expanding the representation of minority groups. We have gone through all that.

RP: I agree with that part.

MM: It's not like there wasn't any agenda.

RP: There was no agenda in the sense that the various minority groups could not articulate what each group wanted and then develop a cohesive plan of action that had political clout. Instead, we had a collection of documents from sundry sources with questionable political support. And the biggest problem is that of all the recommendations in all those plans not a single one originated from the office or department that would be charged with implementing it.

The Council's Accomplishments

MM: A lot of things emerged from this council. Let me give you just two very important examples. One is that we pushed the idea of including minorities in the procurement process. The university now had to consider minorities in its business dealings. The point is that the council pushed the administration and it picked up the ball. Another important point is that several of us from the council met with the president and pushed hard on the Martin Luther King, Jr., commemoration. Alton pushed the president very hard and we supported him. Out of that exercise emerged a dialogue. This was way before the decision was finally made to honor Martin Luther King, Jr. That's a very important accomplishment.

Finally, the most important thing is that we were instrumental in instituting the twenty-one-point Action Now program. This program involved every department in the university on issues of affirmative action. There were weekly meetings to monitor the situation and to discuss how to implement the twenty-one-point strategy. That didn't last long. It ended when the president resigned. But the point is that the Minority Advisory Council was involved substantively.

RP: What you have described is a sundry set of activities that came out of the Council.

MM: Except for the twenty-one-point point Action Now program. That was a real strategic plan with teeth.

RP: We'll deal with the twenty-one-point Action Now plan later. The other things you talked about are just a sundry list of what came out of the council. Sure, something was bound to come out of that council. But if you read between the lines in what you just said, what really came out for the Blacks on the council was not an action plan. They used the council as a vehicle to get something for themselves, namely the commemoration of Martin Luther King, Jr. You see what I'm saying? Their strategy had very little to do with developing a coalition for action on higher education issues.

MM: We did not set up a coalition. As much as we tried.

RP: The group was disorganized politically; there was no organic coalition. That's because there was no prior history of working with the university from a multiethnic perspective.

MM: Another point that we ought to make clear is that organizational change is not linear. Whatever happened cannot be attributed to any one event like the Minority Advisory Council. There were many other things going on. It was an epoch in the politics of the Board of Regents like no other with regard to minority concerns. At that time there were five, perhaps six, regents who were outspoken advocates of minority issues (two regents were Chicanos). It is understandable why university officials were promoting minority programs. It is quite a different situation now where there is very little interest in these types of issues. The Minority Advisory Council may not have been the single independent variable that created any particular change. It was one of many factors that contributed to subsequent events.

RP: I saw myself as a participant in all of this chaos. As I said, I quickly concluded that the Blacks and the Indians were not coming to the table with an action plan equivalent to ours. So substantial coalition building was not really going to be possible. It was going to be a matter of waiting to see what they were going to want to get out of the situation. That was fine with me, so I left it alone.

But I don't like to waste my time. So I began to figure out what we could really get out of this thing. Here's what I concluded: First, as we have noted, the university claimed to be doing many things already on behalf of minorities. These activities had been stimulated by the tri-university report and similar pressures. These activities were trotted out in various reports by the university whenever it wanted to show that it already was addressing the needs of minorities. As I thought about this, I realized that the university was indeed involved in dozens of activities putatively aimed at meeting the needs of minority students and so forth. But in a way, these activities were totally subterranean, totally invisible, and unaccountable to anybody, including ourselves. Even though we had the most interest in these programs, we had the least control over them.

MM: I think that it's instructive to realize how these reports are put together. Every year the Board of Regents required a report on the status of minorities. Each of the vice presidents issued a memorandum asking everybody down the chain of command to submit reports about everything having to do with minority programs. Bureaucratically, all programs have to justify themselves. So whether or not they are dealing with minority issues, they all claim to have a minority component. What you get back is a stack of reports that is forwarded to the person who writes the annual report (usually that was me). The person who prepares the annual report simply takes the unit reports and puts them together. It is no more than an ad hoc approach to paste together a favorable report about what is going on at the university; the real situation is more fragmented than what appears in the annual reports. What you are saying is that there is no coherence to minority programs.

RP: So I wanted to turn the situation upside down. Remember, my strategy had always been to try to influence what goes on at the unit level where minority programs are operated. That was the purpose of the Chicano advisory council that we originally proposed. We needed to influence unit-level operations even though we did not have a network of our people placed in the various units. That really was the whole point of establishing an advisory council in the first place. If we had already had our own people in the various units, we could have just talked to them about our interests. But there was no such network. We had little or no control over programs because people sympathetic to our interests had not been hired. So, for me the problem was to find ways to influence the behavior of the people who in fact were in charge of programs. That is what the game was about and I was racking my brain to figure out a way to get the Minority Advisory Council to engage this agenda.

MM: That's right.

A Workable Strategy

RP: I came up with a very simple solution. Why didn't we take the university at its own word? Let's say that the university is doing a lot for minorities, maybe even more than it knows about. You see I was pushing the logic to the extreme. Perhaps no one really knows what is going on. So I suggested that the Minority Advisory Council ask the university to provide an exhaustive list of all programs that were serving minorities. If you think about it, this was a first step in making the university accountable. Of course, no one really knew how many programs the university operated in the name of minorities. In the one-hundred-year history of the university, no one had bothered to list every program that the university claimed addressed the needs of minorities.

MM: Remember that you and Alfredo de los Santos, from the Maricopa County Community College System, also requested an evaluation of all minority programs? It was not simply an enumeration.

RP: That was the second point I was going to make.

MM: That's the key. I mean, the enumeration was always there.

RP: Not really. Nobody knew for sure what was going on. So my strategy was to get the Minority Advisory Council to ask two simple questions: First, can we get from the university an exhaustive list of minority programs? Second, how effective is each program in meeting its goals?

These questions implied that after identifying all of the minority programs, we needed to evaluate them for effectiveness. We also needed to determine how resources were being applied to operate these programs, including dollars, of course. This strategy would have given us a clear understanding of what efforts were under way, how much they cost, and what we were getting out of them.

So what happened? After about three years, when the council was about to go out of business, we finally got a list of minority programs from the university. For a long time, the university absolutely resisted the idea of enumerating all of the minority programs.

MM: No, it didn't resist it; it just didn't know how to go about doing it. I'm serious. They had no idea what was going on. What was resisted was the evaluation. That's what was resisted, not the listing of programs. As a matter of fact, the yearly reports on minority activities that went to the Board of Regents were essentially an uncritical description of these activities. But the evaluation was really resisted.

RP: Let's be clear here. The enumeration was resisted, but after three years it got done. The evaluation was resisted forever; it has never been done.

MM: It has yet to be done.

RP: Indeed. So you can see how I tried to steer the Minority Advisory Council. At least I tried to find out what the university was doing to help minorities. That was intended to identify the various points at which we potentially could engage the university politically. This could be done through the mechanism of program evaluation. If the Council could become involved in those evaluations, that would give the council significant influence throughout the various layers of the university.

MM: The university resisted examination of its own performance on minority issues because such an examination would raise a contradiction between the university's presentation of itself—as a rational institution seeking truth and avoiding waste—and the reality that in many ways it is an irrational process that refuses to look at itself on any level. It refuses to ask itself whether what it's doing is effective or not.

Remember the one important concession by the university to minorities to increase the number of minority students by 10 percent per year. When you think about it, it's a very weak goal. Because the real issue in increasing minority participation has to do with the university taking responsibility for organizing the other levels of education to be more effective in educating minority students. In other words, that's one of the things that the university will not take on because it's just too hard. The point is that evaluating itself also is one of those very difficult things for a university to do. If it were to do so, the university would expose itself to the constituencies that it has neglected.

RP: But in its reports to the regents the university was claiming just the opposite, that minorities were not being neglected. It claimed to have dozens of programs in operation to address their needs.

MM: But it has to say this. Otherwise it exposes itself, not only to minorities, but to the larger community. The message would be: "Look, we're spending millions and we're getting nothing." The cost-effectiveness argument, the essence of the rationalist process, is where the contradiction lies.

RP: In that sense, the minorities also would be risking criticism. I wasn't naive about this. But I was willing to take the risk because I wanted to attack the university argument that we talked about earlier, namely that in responding to the regental directive to do more regarding minority programs, the university simply provided a list of all the things that it was already doing and then said that it could do more of the same if it got more resources. I wanted to be able to challenge the university program by program. In other words, we should not simply accept the claims of the university that it was already doing good things. In the best academic tradition, it had to warrant its claims.

I believe that the Minority Advisory Council could have been successful with this strategy. My problem was that the group didn't seem to understand what I was doing politically. Or maybe it didn't care for such a strategy. The only risk to us that I could see was that taking inventory of all minority programs at the university might show that the university was spending lots of money on minority issues. In such a case, it would be very reasonable for our opponents to say, "What the hell more do you people want? Look at all we're already doing!" I was willing to risk that outcome. I was pretty certain that the reports on minority programs were greatly exaggerated.

It is important to point out that once the university had inventoried its minority programs I intended to have the council select a few of them, say five or ten, and visit them. The council could then become a kind of board of visitors or auditors. Through this program auditing process we could begin to have an impact on the university. That was the strategy that I was pushing. You see, it had very little to do with writing up a new plan.

MM: Part of the problem was that the council didn't have the energy to undertake those activities, even though it understood their importance. How are you going to get busy people to take the time to do something like that? We had a hell of a time just getting people to the meetings. Remember that one of the problems with these councils is that it is always the same people who are asked to join a dozen or so such groups. That's always part of the problem with community groups. It is hard to keep them on course, but it is also hard to keep them energized.

RP: That's a very good insight. And that is precisely one reason why we didn't really want that kind of advisory council in the first place. The Chicano advisory council that we originally asked for was to be constituted by people who would be willing to do what we just talked about. Knowing all this you can see why I felt that we had lost it all when we couldn't get the university to agree to a Chicano advisory council. Such a group would have had much narrower interests and could have been carefully appointed to be more of an activist group.

At any rate, when the official list of minority programs did come out, I was shocked at the claims that the university was making.

MM: It's unreal. There were something like two hundred programs and millions of dollars. However, if one were to take the time to investigate the paper flow, one would find that this list is consistent with the reports that went to the Arizona Board of Regents. I know, I wrote most of them. Nevertheless, it was hard to believe those reports.

The University's Response

RP: And nobody challenged the list! Moreover, our idea about evaluating minority programs did not die either. Instead it was transmogrified through bureaucratic processes. After the council had already been disbanded, the university hired three external consultants to report on minority programming on campus. One consultant came from the University of Texas, another one from Colorado, and the third from somewhere else. They were three famous White guys who came to evaluate our minority programs. That is how the university implemented the council's recommendation to evaluate all minority programs!

MM: It's just another example of how one idea turns into another. One objective of the evaluation was to look at the campus climate. I've got the report someplace.

RP: But none of the external evaluators were minority persons, not to say Chicanos. They all were Anglos who came from the outside and knew nothing about the history of what was going on.

MM: Worse yet, they didn't even bother to talk to me or to you for that matter. That's the way business is done in the university. This is not unique to minorities. You set up a pilot program and something else emerges, and whoever does it has no connection to the originator of the pilot program. There is no real continuity of ideas so that they can gain power. There are just separate chunks of activities.

It is also a testimonial to the lack of power of Chicanos because programs that allegedly have something to do with us are instituted without our advice and certainly without our consent. Many of these efforts are more cosmetic than substantive. There are many examples in our conversation of this problem. My feeling is that the culture of the university, with its fragmented goals and constant striving for recognition among various groups and individuals, encourages this type of antidialogical activity.

RP: There is a constant repetition and whirling around of things. My point is that the university could not totally ignore the council's exhortation to evaluate its minority programs. So the university took my strategy and reversed it. Whereas I had proposed a very simple yet powerful strategy to allow us to be more active within the university, by bringing in outside consultants the university successfully deflected our efforts. The idea of evaluating minority programs was so threatening to the university that it couldn't simply ignore it; it had to be actively short-circuited.

MM: Did you take part in any of those reviews?

RP: Of course not. Politically I knew exactly what was going on.

MM: I did. I guess because I had to. This is yet another instance where a decision was made and the people who pushed for the original idea didn't get brought into the discussion. It is a statement more about our status and lack of power than anything else.

RP: Well, if you had to! I did read each of the three reports. They were hilarious.

MM: Because the reports were written in limbo; they had no connection to the world. In collaboration with one of my students, I just finished a paper that tried to fathom the reasons for the lack of connection between the realities of the university vis-à-vis minorities and the type of reports that are written. We argue that there are a set of interrelated assumptions that portray an unrealistic vision of the university. For example, university officials categorize all minorities from what they understand to be a Black perspective because this is the vision that fits with their experience and quite frankly with their career opportunities. Obviously they are not all the same and what one group needs and wants clearly is different from what other groups want. The Minority Advisory Council taught us that. Another assumption has to do with the idea that institutions act in a benevolent and rational manner in their approaches to the problems of minorities, and we know that our experiences indicate otherwise. Often people act at best in manipulative ways toward one another, and groups with relatively less power are more easily manipulated and denied the benefits of the institution.

RP: The reports presented a kind of virtual reality, to use a bit of technobabble. They had no grounding in anything real to us. They constructed vignettes of virtual reality. Of course, the consultants made good money, I am sure. Did any one of those reports have an impact on anything? Did they change anything? No. They represented a political response by the university to the activities of the Minority Advisory Council.

But they served additional purposes. Remember that at about the same time then-governor Mecham was demanding that the universities become more efficient. In fact, I think that the key words that were bandied about were "effectiveness" and "efficiency." These reports were used as part of a larger strategy to derail the Mecham evaluation initiative. How ironic. If Mecham had only known that his ideas on this score were essentially consistent with those of ethnic minorities! He should have called for evaluation of minority programs and sided with the Minority Advisory Council. That would have been a case of strange bedfellows indeed!

MM: You can imagine how the university would fare on the issue of cost-effectiveness alone. Herein lies one of the reasons why university officials as well as minorities are reluctant to examine the issue of integrating programs. These types of redundancies would expose what would be perceived as waste. I rarely detected an interest in coordinating programs. What I did observe, however, was an agreement among program directors that their particular programs were effective, and that they should be left alone to pursue their own interests. It is sad to say also that most of them thought that all of the programs, save their own, were of little use.

RP: This is a function of the way that the university is organized. With minorities, however, it may be worse because we have a lower status.

MM: That's true. Let me give you an example of the redundancy of university activities related to minorities. As an assistant vice president, and later as a codirector of Project PRIME, I visited many schools. I recall a school administrator, a friend of mine, telling me that they had hosted eleven separate visitors from eleven separate units from the university. None of these people appeared to know about one another's visits. They were all recruiting, but not all of them were interested in minority students. The point is that the university is a very wasteful place. It has too many people doing the same thing. So an evaluation is really quite threatening, particularly if you have a governor who is an enemy of the university. It is not too difficult to envision how the university could be streamlined in dramatic ways.

RP: Such a streamlined university also might be a different *kind* of university. I mean the logic of efficiency could lead in many different directions, not all of them palatable.

MM: The point is that Governor Mecham would have looked at it in that fashion, as efficiency. In many staff functions the issue of efficiency is very legitimate. This certainly is the case with recruitment in the high schools. There could be better coordination of these types of activities.

RP: To reemphasize my point, a weakness of the university is in the evaluation of its efforts. That is precisely the weakness that I tried to exploit as a means to empower us and the Minority Advisory Council. I think that it was a very powerful political strategy. In spite of our discussion, it still puzzles me that the council didn't exploit this strategy. We were in a position to make it go.

MM: It's not that the Minority Advisory Council was against it.

RP: It just couldn't do it for the reasons you described. From my point of view, implementing this strategy was the most that we could have achieved with that particular Minority Advisory Council. The ideal, of course, would have been the formation of an ethnic coalition where together we could have approached the university with a comprehensive agenda that had political clout. Instead, the university was very effective in shielding its vulnerable points. It effectively protected itself from evaluation by minorities, the governor, and the Board of Regents. It protects itself against all comers, let alone our group. For the university, we must have been just a sort of Dirty Dozen.

I am not naive, however, to think that efficiency is the overall objective of these endeavors. The university is part of the vast welfare state. It is a place not only where knowledge is created and where people are educated, but also a place that creates jobs for people. The fight over the welfare state in this country is not only or even primarily about lazy people who work or fathers who won't support their children. It is about a system of interlocking bureaucracies that support the welfare system — judges, social workers, probation officers, eligibility workers, and farmers. The analysis depends on what slice of reality you are looking at.

MM: This conversation reminds me of an experience I had just a couple of weeks ago when I was asked to attend a strategy session on how some Chicanos from the community and the community colleges should approach the chancellor. My basic pitch was to tell them about our experience with the Minority Advisory Council, and the idea that as long as you ask for meetings and plans university officials will always agree because it buys them time, makes them out to look like good guys, and they don't really have to do anything. They don't have to allocate any resources. The important issue, it seemed to me, was to get a commitment on resources and on actions that will move forward an agenda. I hope that they learned from our experience.

Chapter 8

Intellectual Space

Getting People Involved

RP: In some ways, the creation of the Hispanic Research Center was a fluke, in the sense that I can't recall any particular moment when I, or people around me, decided that it was important to have a center as such. It was more like a collection of ideas, misgivings, and longings that were felt by the group and that eventually were expressed through the establishment of the Hispanic Research Center. What got me involved in these activities, as I explained before, was my interest in identifying some projects that could serve as a focal point for examining ourselves, for organizing ourselves, and for developing strategies that could help us change for the better the institutions around us, particularly the university.

So I was looking for opportunities to get people involved. I had learned along the way, since my days as an activist student, that in order to get people to participate in activities related to Chicanos, one must first find ideas and projects that other people are interested in and then work one's own ideas through them. I have found it extraordinarily difficult to get other people to buy into something that I just think about abstractly. There has to be a specific project or program. It's not easy to get other people to agree that you have a great idea and then commit themselves to it. It is even less likely that they will devote a substantial amount of time to implement the idea. It just doesn't work that way. This difficult problem of getting people interested and involved may explain why some individuals "go it alone." You see what I'm saying?

MM: I'm not sure what you mean by a "fluke." If by that you mean an accident, I don't think that was so. In a general sort of way, we have always talked about setting up a consulting firm, or a research institute, that would begin to actualize much of what we started with Romano at U.C. Berkeley. The important idea was that we needed to explain our own history and our circumstances from our point of view, and a research center, I think, was always in the back of our minds. So I don't think it was a fluke.

What made the concept difficult to implement was that we did not have the wherewithal to implement our ideas. For example, I remember when Senator Gutierrez first got into the legislature. We had talked about setting up a consulting firm but we had no idea what to do. Now Gutierrez has a consulting firm that is real. But remember, what does it mean to set up a consulting firm in his fashion? It means basically that you work for the interests of the people who have money. So Gutierrez has become a wealthy man, but it's around protecting the interests of people who have money and who want more money out of the public trough.

I understood the contradiction of why we couldn't pull off our ideas. We were too closely tied, you see, to our own ideology. There's no way that you are going to get money based on an ideology that operates out of protecting the interests of Chicanos. This is a dilemma that we faced in the recent controversy we had related to Motorola. Students pointed out the contradiction by letting us know that if we took money from Motorola we were in effect taking "blood" money and acquiescing to the corporation's pattern of polluting the environment. This is the same issue that students raised about the University of California and its research efforts under the sponsorship of the defense and energy departments. At some point, when we set up the research center, we either ignored these issues or we just went forward on our path, a path that was defined by the abstract idea of seeking knowledge for its own sake.

RP: Because we were in a university setting, such an idea could gain support.

MM: At some point we needed to develop skills to maneuver within and outside the university in order to garner some of the political power that's out there, even if the development of a center was a minor concession.

RP: You have touched upon the idea that I'm trying to express. My point is that it didn't have to be a center. We needed to undertake some large project to demonstrate to ourselves and the university that we had sufficient skills and political resources to address the needs of Chicanos. But as the process started, I wasn't overly confident that we could pull it off. Had Chicanos reached the point where we could get a large project through? Remember the notorious meeting that we had with the president when he said, "For the first time, a Chicano legislator has had a significant impact on the budget of the university."

MM: That was truly a remarkable thing for him to say.

RP: And then he added that he wasn't sure if this kind of influence could be sustained. You see, there was plenty of reason to doubt the robustness of that influence, even among ourselves. Could we really prosecute a Chicano agenda within the university?

So when the idea to get something going first arose, it wasn't about a center at all. I agree with you that we all knew that centers were possible and that perhaps we should be creating one. But the original idea was to establish a Chicano studies program. At that time there was a glaring omission at the university, namely the absence of Chicano studies, even though we were well into the eighties.

MM: But there was an activity resembling a Chicanos studies center at the university that had started when I first arrived in the midseventies.

RP: That resulted in establishing the Chicano studies collection in the library.

MM: It was called American Studies, and it was organized by Manuel Servín, an historian from the University of Southern California whom everyone remembers for his book, *The Awakening Minority*. He later went to edit the *Rocky Mountain Journal* at the University of New Mexico and died shortly thereafter. The last time I talked with him was at Monty's Restaurant where he interviewed me about the now-famous Laundry Strike that took place at the university in 1968. The university had been conducting business with a laundry company that was hiring Mexican workers at below minimum wage and without benefits. At the time, I was working as a research assistant. A group of students, mostly Mexicans but not exclusively, led initially by Arturo Rosales and later by Alfredo Gutierrez, organized a march on the president of the university to protest what they felt was an unethical alliance with the company.

It was a moment of great triumph for Chicano students. They marched right into the president's office; there were over one hundred students. We marched in an orderly fashion, and some of the administrators quite frankly did not know how to handle it. I recall having a discussion with one of the vice presidents who seemed to be losing his cool : "How dare these punks!" I walked up to him, told him he was overreacting and that he was making the situation worse by his behavior. Years later, as he left for another university to take another post, he told me that if there was anything he could do for me to just let him know.

I recall many of the students. Although scared, they were nevertheless triumphant because they were involved in an event that transcended their own personal concerns. For many of them it was their first meaningful confrontation with an institution that seemed impervious to their concerns. Anyhow, Servín made one of the early efforts at organizing Chicanos in an effort to address Chicano knowledge and to develop a Chicano studies program.

I recall that David Maciel, who later went to the University of New Mexico, also was involved in this early effort. I think that there were some courses taught. This is a good example of early efforts to establish a Chicano studies program. But the fact is that we did not achieve a recognizable Chicano studies program.

Testing the New Vice President

RP: We did gain a pretty decent Chicano studies collection in the library out of these early efforts, thanks largely to the efforts of Christine Marín, now an archivist. But in the early eighties, it was Arturo Rosales from the History Department who came forward and said that we needed to develop a Chicano studies program at the university. His suggestion coincided with the arrival of a new vice president for academic affairs. Some members of the Chicano Faculty and Staff Association (CFSA) wanted to meet with the vice president to test him, to see how supportive he would be, and so on. Hearing that there was some support among the CFSA for the creation of Chicano studies, I recommended to the group that we meet with the vice president for lunch and have only one item on the agenda. The agenda item would be the Chicano studies program; we would ask the vice president if he would support it. We did in fact have lunch with the vice president. I expected that he would simply be polite to us. Much to my surprise, he actually agreed with the suggestion and said that he would support Chicano studies. Given the events that followed, I think that he probably stuck his neck out more than he wanted or perhaps more than what he felt comfortable with later on.

MM: Because he was new.

RP: Because he was new and didn't quite understand what was going on. Remember, it was his first time in the Southwest. He came from the Midwest and really had no idea about what he was doing with chicanada. So after that luncheon meeting, the idea of creating Chicano studies gained momentum.

Testing Ourselves

RP: My strategy then became one of not just supporting but pressing the idea. Chicano studies was going to be a test case to see if we could undertake an initiative and move it forward successfully to a conclusion. Such an initiative would require both rationality and politics, the two things that I thought were very important for Chicanos to manipulate effectively.

So I drafted a follow-up letter to the luncheon meeting with the vice president. I don't know what would have happened if I had let things go of their own accord. I am saying that after that luncheon meeting there were different possible paths into the future. I took the initiative to follow up on behalf of the group and with their support. My strategy was to put to good use the enthusiasm of the group that was generated by the positive response of the vice president. The purpose of the follow-up letter was to test our ability to engage the university in a rationalist mode. Through the follow-up letter, we simply reaffirmed our desire to develop a Chicano studies program, acknowledged the vice president's support for the idea, and asked him to suggest the steps that needed to be taken to advance the idea further.

A Recalcitrant President

RP: Indeed, some further steps were taken with Rosales as the titular head of this initiative. In fact, we had a meeting soon thereafter with the president of the university. His response was unequivocal. He said two things: first that he did not support a Chicano studies program, and second that he would be willing to consider a research center of some kind. I have no idea why he took that position.

MM: Well, I'll tell you. I knew that he would take such a position because, as you will recall, you and I, and perhaps others, had met with Gutierrez. He told us in no uncertain terms that there would be no way that the president would support Chicano studies. When the president served as an administrator at the University of Colorado at Boulder, the Chicano studies effort over there blew up in his face. He had a very bad experience with Corky González and the students in Colorado. I guess that he didn't want to go through the experience of having to deal with militant students, and with professors who used classes as lobbying points for activism—Mau-Mauing is what it was called. There were instances of violent or at least threatening behavior on the part of students.

It is also important to point out that during the Vietnam War, a professor named Starsky was fired by the Arizona Board of Regents for canceling classes so that he and perhaps also his students could take time to demonstrate against the war. Someone, I am sure, had reminded the president of this incident. It is a very sad story since Starsky from that day on always had difficulty finding a decent academic job, and, according to some of the professors who have been here a long time, was left with a broken heart. Anyhow, there were compelling reasons, from an administrative viewpoint, why the president did not want difficulties with a Chicano studies program. Perhaps it was an overreaction to an earlier experience.

RP: Whatever the reasons, we now had a very interesting situation.

The vice president had said that he was going to support Chicano studies. The president essentially vetoed the idea. That could easily have killed everything, right? What did we have to go on? Clearly, it was the research center. So we latched on to that idea. Personally I also was not totally certain that we wanted to establish a traditional Chicano studies program. Many of us had experience with earlier Chicano studies programs and it wasn't always good.

Critique of Chicano Studies

MM: You wrote a pretty negative paper about Chicano studies. Would it be honest to say that it was negative?

RP: I guess you could say that it was negative. More to the point, I would say that it points out many of the deficiencies and failures of the early Chicano studies programs. Based on such a critique, I had concluded that a research center might be a very effective way to engage the issues important to Chicanos. You will recall that we framed those issues in terms of generating new knowledge through research that emanated from us and that related to our concerns. We were also concerned that such knowledge not be misapplied to our community. I also figured that instructional programs dealing with Chicano studies could always be implemented at some later date. So I developed and then promoted the idea, among those individuals interested in Chicano studies, that we could reach our ends by creating a research center. That's how the idea of the Hispanic Research Center took shape.

Implementing Strategy

RP: By agreeing to a research center, we had both the vice president for academic affairs and the president lined up in support. The challenge then was to develop a step-by-step process to get the center approved by the university. So we created a Chicano faculty committee whose job was to carry out the necessary politicking and bureaucratic maneuvering. Such a committee also was consistent with the idea of involving more and more people in the process. As you recall, we elected two untenured professors to cochair what we called the Ad Hoc Committee for Chicano Faculty Development. I suppose that we could have used the CFSA itself as the leadership group, but that would not have provided the kind of faculty legitimacy that we really needed. The new committee focused strictly on faculty concerns about research.

Creating the ad hoc committee provided us more flexibility in building a rationale for the center. We focused on the idea that we did not have enough Chicano faculty in the university to produce the kind of research about Chicanos that we were interested in. Therefore, more Chicano faculty were needed along with more Chicano faculty development. In the political context of the moment, this idea made a lot of sense.

One of the things that I noticed upon arriving at the university was that many Chicano faculty were leaving the university after four or five years. The pattern seemed to be that Chicano faculty were hired and then fired at the point of tenure review. It was a very regular pattern. In fact, we fought a couple of battles along those lines to "save" some professors who found themselves in exactly that situation. When I looked at the vitae of these professors, and noticed the reasons they were being denied tenure, almost exclusively the problem was in their failure to produce enough publications. Or at least that was the conclusion of the review committees.

Difficulties with Tenure

MM: That wasn't true in all cases. In some cases, it was just pure and simple politics at the departmental level that had little to do with performance. Let me give you some examples. There was a Chicano professor in the school of social work who was let go because of his publication record. However, when you compare his work with other professors in better standing you can see that his record stood up in comparison with other tenured professors. He didn't have a lot of publications, but the ones that he did have were of high quality. The artist Eugene Quesada is another example. I served on the tenure and promotion committee when Eugene's tenure came up. They wanted to shift him from one department that appreciated and needed his type of work to, I think, agriculture where they had different sorts of expectations. The chair of his department had changed the rules of the game and because Eugene did not fit the new requirements, they wanted to get rid of him. They wanted to do this not on his record of past performance or his talent as an art teacher, which I understood to be excellent, but on the basis of new criteria. They claimed that he hadn't done any research or exhibitions, however they judge people in his field.

I wanted to impress on the committee the unfairness of changing the rules. My only recourse was to abstain from the vote. I wrote a minority report to the provost. The provost granted him tenure. I don't know if his decision had anything to do with my letter, but the point that I want to make is that there are many instances of injustice involving Chicanos that cost us a great deal of effort to rectify.

Jim J. is another case in point. He was let go partly because of his record, but mostly because of the dean who, although he was Black, was very antiMexican. I think the dean had a strategy to get rid of all the Chicanos. In fact, he got rid of most of them, but also hired very few Blacks. Jim never learned how to maneuver in the institution. He failed to submit his papers properly, and he really did not know how to negotiate. He would take the assaults against him as personal assaults, you see. So he just never found out, or never learned, how to fight back. I cannot explain to you just why that is the case. But it seems to be the case with quite a few Chicanos.

RP: I agree with you that the tenure process is multifaceted, and that it isn't always what it's cracked up to be. But what I'm trying to say is that, as a political strategy, I used the received view of the institution. The official view was that Chicanos just weren't productive enough in research and publications.

MM: I agree with that.

RP: So I simply used that view and turned it around to our benefit. My logic was simple. If Chicano professors have a problem with research and publications, why don't we do something about it? That turned out to be a compelling argument. But we needed a specific solution. So I suggested that we create an intellectual space, a research center, to support Chicano faculty in their research and publication efforts.

To support this idea I argued that Chicano faculty were too isolated, and that there was little or no respect for the kind of ethnically based research that many of them wanted or felt compelled to do. But all of this made sense only by accepting the basic premise that Chicano faculty were not sufficiently productive in the ways that the university expected. Of course, as you pointed out, this was not the whole story. But it was easier for me to build an argument for the center based on accepted institutional views.

MM: In spite of how the decisions were made on many tenure cases, I think that publications and research were, and still are, legitimate issues. There has to be productivity.

Turning Liabilities into Advantages

RP: What I'm trying to say is that, as a general political strategy, you must be able to turn in your favor arguments and ideas that are used against you. In this case, we even had to accept temporarily some of the unfair treatment that we were receiving. We also had to develop specific mechanisms that would help us to implement our strategy. That is why we created something like the Ad Hoc Committee for Chicano Faculty Development.

This committee allowed us to repackage old ideas into a new form that would benefit us. Moreover, the committee provided us with an instrument for gaining approval for the center. But here we had a really difficult structural problem. Quite simply, the committee had no standing within the university. Normally, a department or some other academic unit decides that they want a center. Then they talk to the dean and gain his or her support. There are standard operating procedures to get approval all the way up through the university governance structure and eventually to the Board of Regents. At that point, the proposal is either approved or not. In our case, we had a group of faculty from all over campus who were proposing the center. There was no department chair or dean who was shepherding our proposal through the normal approval process. That was a tremendous problem.

No Support

MM: We had no support, beyond ourselves.

RP: That's right. And even among ourselves, who could you really count on?

MM: Well, we could get people together to talk.

RP: So implementing the center became a test of ourselves.

MM: Another issue is whether or not we knew what to do. Even if we had the will, knowing what to do was problematic. It's not so problematic any more, but it was at the time when you and I first started trying to create the center.

RP: Establishing the ad hoc committee was part of the answer. But from an organizational point of view the ad hoc committee was problematic. It stood out and called attention to itself because it was not part of the regular administrative process. Having the ad hoc committee in charge of our proposal meant that the proposal was being inserted into the university more or less sideways. This meant that our proposal could not be treated routinely by the university; everything had to be ad hoc.

At the same time, we had to build support for the proposal within ourselves. Success depended on establishing a very strong consensus among us. How else were we going to push the proposal sideways through the organization? That's why it was essential to enlarge the circle of participation and we brought in people like Alberto Ríos, who was very well respected even then before he got tenure. We involved nontenured professors in key positions and then supported them so that they learned as they went along.

The whole exercise was inductive. We got them to understand the general ideas with which we were working, but I don't think that they, or we for that matter, knew exactly how to successfully maneuver through the approval process. In retrospect, we organized ourselves, redefined approval procedures to some extent, and actually gained approval for the center all at the same time.

Forming a Technical Team

RP: Another problem with the ad hoc committee was that it really was not an effective mechanism for engaging in administrative actions or sustained technical work. Our solution to this problem was to suggest to the vice president that he appoint a "technical team" of faculty so that they could actually put together a proposal that was administratively actionable. The technical team, which would receive stipends and other support, could actually do a feasibility study and out of that design a standard proposal for the center. In the end, you and I and a graduate student wound up being the technical team. As part of that effort, we created the Office to Establish a Chicano Studies Research Center. From an organizational point of view, the office represented an ad hoc solution to the absence of a department that normally would have moved forward our proposal. Thus, the office gave us both technical capability and organizational standing. The ad hoc faculty committee then became a political lever that we could use to support our efforts.

MM: That was during the 1982–83 academic year.

RP: As part of the technical team, you and I visited existing centers and programs at other universities. That was part of our rationalist approach to designing the proposal. Once we had a draft of the proposal, we sent it to the vice president and asked for his comments. He basically agreed with what we had prepared.

The Noxious in the Innocuous

RP: What is interesting about the approval process is the kinds of questions that are raised that seem innocuous but that can easily derail the whole process. For example, where to locate the center organizationally became a critical question. Surprisingly, and perhaps curiously, the vice president suggested that maybe we didn't need to create a new center. We could take an existing center, retool it to suit our needs, and in a sense take it over. From the very beginning I thought that this was a very bizarre idea. I couldn't imagine how something like that would work politically.

MM: Remember that the Southwest Studies Center was facing disestablishment. By then it had only a skeleton staff. That strategy would have resulted in an altercation that would have derailed us into other pursuits. That center had an agenda different from ours. It was not an Hispanic or Chicano agenda. I think that the vice president suggested this because it would have been a lot easier for him and also less expensive. I don't know how much money had been committed by the legislative agreement to our efforts. But the vice president could have used it to revive the Southwest Studies Center and we probably would have been left with nothing.

RP: I agree with you, but I also think that it was an attempt to dilute the ethnic focus of the proposed Chicano studies center by mixing it with general concerns that were not primarily ethnically based. I think that this has been a consistent strategy by university administrators. They deflect our efforts either by mixing us with other ethnic groups or by incorporating us into other activities that do not have an ethnic focus. The general strategy is to blend things so that the sharp focus that we want to put on certain issues becomes blurred and our concerns become confused and obscured. *En otras palabras, nos la barajean* [In other words, they double deal].

MM: We have discussed the Minority Advisory Council as a good case in point.

RP: Exactly. The vice president's suggestion reflected the same strategy with a slight twist to it. *El mismo gato nomás revolcado* [A repeat of the same thing with insignificant changes]. Had we fallen for that ploy, it would have kept you and me busy for a long time trying to disentangle the political skeins of that situation.

MM: I never took that suggestion seriously, though. I would have preferred to do anything rather than go into such an abyss. It would not have worked. So I for one never really saw that as a threat; I never would have participated in that. I don't think you would have either.

RP: No. But the point is that politically we had to respond to the suggestion because it came from the vice president himself.

MM: In all fairness to him, he was not adamant about it. He just kind of threw it out. He really didn't push it. He was kind of testing the waters. We have seen similar behavior from the current provost who tried to persuade us not to push for departmental status for the current effort to establish Chicano studies. When the vice president saw what a strong reaction we had to his takeover suggestion, he pulled back.

Intellectual Displaying

RP: He did. My point is that politically we had to handle it as if it were a serious suggestion. We gave it the academic discussion that it merited and then sent our reaction back to the vice president. So we only gave the idea mock consideration. And we couched our negative response in very diplomatic, rationalist language. In other words, we were Mau-Mauing intellectually the way that academics do when they want to justify a conclusion that they have already reached. What we were really doing was displaying our ability to engage the institution on its own terms to get what we wanted. Clearly, if he had insisted on the takeover strategy, it probably would have killed the effort right there.

But there was also something else that struck me about the approval process. The vice president told us almost immediately that there was no money to create the center. He said it straight out: There is no funding. Remember that in the early eighties we were in a steady-state-or-declining budget for a number of years. In fact, for over a decade the universities were either in a steady-state-or-declining budget!

MM: But the steady-state budget was merely rhetoric. It was budget talk, in the sense that the university always plans its budget on a base plus inflation. So when they talk about a decrease in the budget, they are always talking about a decrease in the increase. It's the same kind of rhetoric that is going on in terms of the national deficit; it's decreasing the rate of the deficit. It's the same kind of mumbo jumbo. Until about two or three years ago when in fact the university's base budget was reduced.

RP: At that time it was mostly rhetoric. I think that the budgets were flat. But he was very unconditional. No doubt about it. That surprised me because we were going to ask for very modest funding. We're talking about a hundred and fifty thousand dollars on a budget of several hundred million dollars. That's a ridiculously small sum of money. So it surprised me how categorical and direct he was. He struck me like Mother Hubbard with no food in the cupboard.

MM: The point is that he didn't want to use his discretionary money for this activity. I don't know how much discretionary money he had. The way in which the vice president's office was run at that time was to tax every department. They would tax 2 percent of each department's budget. That was the discretionary money that would be used by the vice president's office in case there were budget revertments, which was almost always the case. The money also was used to fund little projects, say to help some faculty member go to Europe or something. Anyway, this was the vice president's slush fund.

RP: For our part, we made it very clear in our proposal that the research center was going to be a long-term, ongoing effort and that the university needed to use state funds to maintain its operations into the foreseeable future. So we were not really asking for slush fund money. I think he understood that.

MM: That's true.

No Room at the Inn

RP: So his categorical assertion that there were no resources was a real challenge to us. I picked up the signal and became even more adamant in insisting that unless the university was willing to fund the center at a level that would assure its financial success, we shouldn't even attempt it. We became hard-liners on this point.

The message that we were getting from the vice president was no different from what we had heard before many times throughout the years. Whenever Chicanos asked for something, the university's response was always the same: no money. For us there was never any room at the inn. So

I decided to take on this issue and insisted that we were going to have state funding for the center. My worst nightmare was that we would get the center approved and then get only twenty thousand dollars a year, or some small amount, to run it. We would end up only with a license to hunt for extramural funding. I thought that would be a terrible mistake.

So we had to develop a plan to finesse the vice president. We did it by accepting the received view that there was no money. Then we proposed two alternatives to the vice president. The first alternative said in effect, "Don't worry about the funding. Approve the idea and let us worry about the funding, but assume that we will get state funds. We will go to our friends in the legislature, present our ideas, and ask for their support." New money would be added to the university's base budget for the center. In effect, with this option we were saying to the university: "You don't have enough money. Fine. Keep your money. Just agree to the concept and go on record that there is no money to fund it. Otherwise we can't go ask for money. We'll take our chances with the legislature. If we succeed, we succeed; if we don't, we don't."

The second option was for the university to fund the center through internal resource reallocation. That can be done. For a year or two, the university might carry the center through reallocation, but eventually it could be included in the base budget and funded directly by the legislature. That is doing things the quiet way.

Clearly, the first option could potentially become very high profile. The legislators were likely to ask why we were going to them with a one hundred fifty thousand dollar proposal. Why couldn't the university just take care of it? I knew that, and everybody else did too, so I was pretty sure which option the vice president would choose.

MM: The administration had also warned us that there would be no way that the legislature would fund an ethnic-specific center. Although they did do it for the University of Arizona, namely, the Mexican American Studies and Research Center.

RP: Right. They tried to dissuade us from pursuing the first option.

MM: Here again we see a consistent pattern. Anything that's ethnic specific is deflected.

RP: Actually, we didn't have to argue the point too much. We simply said that either option was acceptable to us. Of course, I really wasn't eager to take our proposal to our friends in the legislature. The administration's warning wasn't totally baseless.

MM: Off-budget funding would have required a separate decision package.

Horse Trading in the Legislature
RP: We were not even talking about that. Ours, in effect, would be a

renegade decision package. There was a well-established process in the university for approving official decision package submissions. We didn't have any intention of using that process.

MM: That's my point. Such a renegade decision package would have been difficult to pull off in the legislature. This involves a different type of politics that we rarely get to play. The university's pet projects are identified and ranked, usually by the president's council and the lobbyist. The projects are funded separately and apart from the base budget. If you look at the university's budgets over the years, you appreciate where the priorities of the university lie.

RP: But it also would have been a great embarrassment to the university had we attempted it. The finesse move was to see whether the university was willing to risk political embarrassment or simply give us the lousy hundred and fifty thousand dollars and move on. I was pretty confident that the vice president would just give us the money. Which he did. My major point is that the funding issue was also a major trap that could have derailed our efforts.

MM: You know why we got the money, right?

RP: Why?

MM: That was one of the items that Senator Gutierrez put into the pot when the horse-trading took place on the university budget in the legislature.

RP: Yes, it was part of the wheeling and dealing.

MM: It was part of the last-minute horse-trading that goes on in the appropriations committee. For the university it was very little, but for us it was quite a bit.

RP: It was everything. We had no other Chicano programs.

MM: I think the first year we got a hundred thousand.

RP: What you are saying is that we still had to use political muscle to implement the second option; it was deal making. But it wasn't as high a political profile, or as risky, as the first initiative might have turned out to be.

MM: There wasn't a separate appropriation.

RP: And we still had to use our political capital to get the money reallocated internally. Without political influence, we might not have been successful in getting the university to reallocate funds. Our implied threat to go directly to the legislature might not have been enough to persuade the vice president. The fact that we had political resources outside of the university did help us out.

Avoiding Little Mistakes

MM: Do you recall a meeting we had with Senator Gutierrez about this issue?

RP: I don't think I was there.

MM: It's a very interesting story. Loui Olivas, who was serving as the president of the Chicano Faculty and Staff Association, and a bunch of us met with Gutierrez, who at the time was serving as majority leader of the Arizona state senate. Loui, our spokesman, walks into Gutierrez's office, shakes hands with him, and hands him a list saying, "Alfredo, here is what we would like you to cover in the appropriations meeting." Gutierrez looks him straight in the eye and tells him, "I don't need you telling me what to do in appropriations." If Gutierrez hadn't been a friend, the center would have been dead right there.

RP: Another potential trap!

MM: It is important to avoid little mistakes because they can turn out to be major disasters. We all have to learn how to deal with politicians, to stroke them. So Gutierrez went into a big tirade. He did not like people telling him what to do. He knew how to take care of his business, and hoped that we knew how to take care of ours. I think, however, that he was more amused than angry with us. I should add, in my defense, that Loui never told me that he was going to hand a set of instructions to Gutierrez. The important point here is to appreciate the importance of organizing a strategy before acting. It was difficult for us because we were always working outside the institutional framework. As you have discussed, we rarely have the support of colleges or our departments. If you look at the decision packages that have been funded over the years, they have had the full support of the departments and the vice president's office. It is their projects that they fund. Those projects are seen as important; not so with most of our efforts.

RP: Fortunately, we managed to get the university to relent on its belief that there was no money for the center. And we got the proposal through the entire bureaucratic process with a combination of the technical team, the Ad Hoc Committee for Chicano Faculty Development, and our political friends. Explaining that process alone would be quite a story in itself.

MM: I think that the proposal was good, and not just because we wrote it. It had good ideas that are still vital, that still have meaning today. I recall how hard we worked to get it done. But do you think that the quality of the proposal made any difference in this political process? I mean, is there a connection between the quality of the ideas and the fact that the proposal got funded?

RP: I don't really think so.

MM: It's kind of sad, huh?

Struggling with Ourselves

RP: Yeah. But you have to remember that we were struggling with two very different processes simultaneously. The one that we have been talking about is bureaucratic, it's the university process. We were also struggling with ourselves. It's very difficult to maintain continuing interest in a project such as the one we are talking about. The whole thing went on for about three years. Our little ad hoc committee was little more than a bunch of professors who got together whenever they could. Getting them to agree to anything was not easy. It requires you to think things through. They are really the ones that you have to sell the ideas to. I was trying to promote the concept of a second-generation Chicano studies program. That's the label that I used to help us think through what we were trying to do. Most of us had experience with the first generation of Chicano studies programs. Since the late seventies, Chicano studies programs throughout the country were in a period of decline. So it was time to revitalize those programs.

MM: The "Berserkeley" model is the best example. In all fairness these efforts were started by students and young academics without rank, power, or status. It is no different from many of the things that you and I have been involved in over the years.

RP: It was true all over California.

MM: Did I ever tell you the story about my experience with the Chicano studies people at Berkeley? I was an assistant professor at the time. One day I got a call from some activists in the Chicano studies program telling me that they wanted to interview me. I said, "You want to interview me for what?"

"Well, we want to interview you to see if you're going to be on the faculty of Chicano studies." I told them that I already had a faculty position, and that I was not interested in a position in Chicano studies. I guess some Chicanos in the program took it upon themselves to license any Chicano professor on campus. That's the only thing I could figure out. They insisted on interviewing me, so I agreed. I couldn't get the guy to understand that I already had a job on campus.

RP: They had to approve you, is that what you're saying? To see if you were politically correct, as the current expression goes?

MM: Exactly. I walked to their building and got "interviewed." There were a lot of people at the interview. After the interview they let me know that I had not gotten the job. I had not passed muster because I was too intellectual, and probably because I was not radical enough.

RP: That's the time when they didn't want to be intellectuals. I remember that. Maybe it had something to do with Chairman Mao.

MM: It reminds me of the last time that I got interviewed. I was interviewed two years ago by the provost for the deanship of the School of Social Work. The provost said, "I have to interview you for that job." I said, "I'm not interested in the job." He said, "Well, will you come talk to me?" So I went to talk to him. Then he called me and said, "You didn't get the dean's job." I said, "I wasn't looking for a job." In this case, the provost was using me to legitimize whatever decision they had already made to hire this other guy as interim dean.

RP: Of course.

MM: But you're demeaned as a human being, both by the chicanada and by the people whose job it is apparently to demean you.

Avoiding a Sham Program

RP: Along the same lines, I was very conscious of the fact that if the university wanted to be smart, and there was no reason to believe that it didn't have such a desire, they would just Mau-Mau and give us a sham program. A center or something else that wouldn't really make any difference, that would have no substance, and that later would be judged as such. The whole thing could have been reduced to a political ploy to short-circuit us. That was another potential trap. The fact is that the ideas that we were proposing really had merit. And the proposal was prepared professionally and with a lot of care. We wanted to convince our own faculty, and the faculty at large, that we had worthwhile ideas. This was our only defense to prevent the university from creating a politically moti-vated, low-class program whose only real purpose would have been to shield the university from political attacks by Chicanos. Remember, I wrote my critique of Chicano studies at about this time. I noted that some programs were being maintained by universities merely as a safety shield against political attacks by the Chicano community.

MM: The paper you presented in El Paso?

RP: I originally presented it in southern California; then it was published by the University of Texas at El Paso. One of the criticisms that I made was that some Chicano studies programs had deteriorated into a situation in which they were actually needed by universities. The univer-sities wouldn't get rid of them because they had become politically useful, but the programs weren't really doing much good for the Chicano commu-nity.

MM: It's not that they deteriorated. They had never really developed. Again it has to do with being marginal to the concerns of the university. You can't do much without resources, without support. Remember that much of what we do comes out of our hides; we pay professionally for much of what we do to promote the general good.

RP: That's true too. But in some sense Chicano studies had high ideals at one point and even those had deteriorated over time. The universities had always dealt with these programs politically by establishing low quality, low-resource programs from which they expected little, if anything, that was academically worthy. But the universities ended up trapping themselves into maintaining the programs because politically they couldn't get rid of them. So eventually there was an odd sort of accommodation. The faculties in those programs weren't very productive, but they couldn't be fired. On the other hand, when the universities had to deal with pressure from Chicano communities, they would trot out their Chicano studies faculty. So it became a cozy coalition of odd bedfellows. In designing a second generation of Chicano studies, I wanted to move away from this unsavory situation. To avoid the trap, the proposal had to be of high quality. We needed to convince ourselves that we could design quality programs that the university wouldn't be able to use against us. I am not claiming that the university will never use the center against us. I am just saying that I was very conscious of the fact that our own initiatives could be used against us, and that we had to guard against this possibility.

Extraordinary Self-Consciousness

MM: The thing is that we are extraordinarily conscious of our presence in the university.

RP: That's true.

MM: Self-conscious to the fact that a lot of people think we don't belong there. It's real clear, every time you turn around, you sense it. It is very interesting to observe. Part of the reason is that we are perceived as pushing against the grain, as nonconformists. Our projects are not viewed as important and our advocacy is seen as a nuisance to the mainline academics. If we want to work with our communities, it is not viewed as a legitimate academic endeavor. I guess one could conform and gain favor with one's department. It is a very difficult line to toe because it is important to get rewarded. We have to maintain a balance, but often it is difficult. Over the years I come in and out. In my department, for example, I served as a program director for a couple of years, but now I have the need to work out in the community and I have been trying to do that. If your timing is off and you don't have the support, you can get hurt. I think this is happening to me now.

RP: I'm also beginning to see that sometimes even Chicanos and Chicanas themselves think that they don't want to be there.

MM: What do you mean by that?

RP: Some Chicano professors of high intellectual quality look at the universities and say, "This is a sham! I shouldn't want to be here." And they opt to leave the university. This is a very interesting development. The whole thing has gone full circle.

MM: I don't understand.

RP: You're saying that chicanada are acutely conscious of the fact that they are not wanted and that they are seen as not belonging in the universities. You see?

MM: That's why they try to do so well.

RP: Because they're not wanted. First they struggle. Then they overcorrect. What I am saying is that one of these hypercorrections is when some Chicano and Chicana faculty say, "To hell with you! I don't need to be here."

MM: But who said that, for instance?

RP: Cristina G. is the most recent example. She didn't have to leave. Delfi M. is another example. Basically she had the capacity to do the research that was required of her. But instead of doing it, she was running around Latin America working on various political causes. It was her choice and she refused to change what she wanted to do to adapt to the requirements of the university setting. I see evidence of two distinct reactions by Chicano faculty: In one case we are very sensitive to our presence in the university and how others react to us; in the other case, we simply say "screw you" to the university.

MM: It is understandable that some Chicanos take that route. It is difficult to prepare materials about everything that you have done to get tenured or promoted. From what I have seen, Chicanos don't do well with those endeavors. It's pretty self-serving. And it is difficult to expose yourself.

Feet to the Fire

RP: It's very dehumanizing for certain individuals. It goes beyond what they're ready to do. Recently Richard R. (a White professor) recalled that as an assistant professor "my ass was put to the fire, like anybody else." He mentioned this in the context that some professors came to the department already tenured. What you are talking about is the way in which untenured professors get their feet put to the fire, to paraphrase Richard's felicitous expression. Some people find this experience demeaning.

MM: Because it's so dirty. It creates an illusion of one thing, but it's really something else. First of all, it's a secret process, and it's very dehumanizing to find out how people go after each other with hidden agendas and political agendas. An illusion is maintained that the process is about merit and performance, but in many instances it has very little to do with a professor's academic performance.

RP: That's the dark and hidden side of academia.

Faculty Criticisms

RP: Returning to our center proposal, it went through, I think, because it had a lot of merit. The university, in its rationalist mode, had very weak defenses against such a thoughtfully constructed proposal. The only way they could attack it was politically. And the only real opposition came from the Academic Affairs Committee of the Faculty Senate. That's because your opponents from social work had an opportunity to critique it.

MM: There was no real critique; it was actually a harassment tactic from some of the committee members who asked me to attach resumes to the proposal—that was really the extent of the attack.

RP: They also said that there were contradictions, and questioned the kind of knowledge that was going to be produced by the center.

MM: Real lightweight stuff.

RP: It wasn't very difficult to deflect. Actually, I simply outmaneuvered them parliamentarily. But they did represent another kind of trap that we had to avoid, only this was not an administrative trap, but a faculty trap. I was on the Academic Affairs Committee when the center proposal was reviewed. When the subcommittee presented its review and recommendations to the full committee, I basically said, "Look, we accept these criticisms and we'll respond to them." Like you, I took the position that the criticisms were not lethal. Using very diplomatic language, I suggested to the committee that they permit us to respond to the criticisms, but instead of bringing a revised proposal back to the Academic Affairs Committee, we should simply present the revised proposal to the vice president, who also sat on the Academic Affairs Committee. If the vice president agreed with our amendments, then the proposal would need no further committee action. I did all this as a substitute motion to the original report of the subcommittee and it was approved. That's how we avoided the faculty trap.

MM: Otherwise they could have kept us in committee for another year.

RP: Easily.

Extravagant Use of Time

RP: A curious thing is that by the time the committee approved our proposal, we had invested about three years of effort to create the center. You and I had never intended to devote that kind of time to any one project. As I have explained before, my agenda was to start a number of projects that would promote broad Chicano activism. Any time you concentrate on one project or activity it limits your ability to engage in a larger set of activities. It turns out that I was involved with the center project for ten years. To be honest, when we started this project, I did not envision that it would take such a long time.

MM: But you knew that it was going to be a major effort.

RP: Yes, but I didn't really intend to be the one to set up the center.

MM: Well, who was going to do it? Remember, in addition to the time we spent putting this thing together, I spent one year as the interim director.

RP: As I saw it, we had about fifty faculty on the ad hoc committee. There was plenty of talent, so there was no need for me to devote my energy to running the center. I wanted to operate more generally as an activist. For me the center project was a vehicle to test some ideas about how to organize Chicanos in higher education.

By the way, when the proposal was actually approved by the Board of Regents it was approved as a consensus item. There wasn't even a vote.

MM: Many such items, once they actually reach the regents, are acted upon pro forma.

RP: So the real battles were internal within the institution.

MM: It has to do with the president approving it. All these decisions were made before the fact. Regents rarely involve themselves in details of this type. In January of 1996 a new epoch begins for the regents. Most of the people who supported minority initiatives will be gone, and a new group of more conservative regents will assume power. They will surely challenge much of what goes on in the university — set-asides, affirmative action, and minority (and even perhaps) women's issues will be challenged. We will have to change the way in which we operate. I don't think this is altogether a bad thing.

The Dog That Caught the Volkswagen

RP: After we got the center proposal approved, we were like the dog that finally caught the Volkswagen. Remember that ours was a kind of renegade proposal in the sense that it didn't go through a regular academic department. The whole thing was ad hoc. So after its approval, there was no visible support anywhere to implement it. Funding was provided at the vice president's level, and that leaves you very vulnerable within the university bureaucracy.

MM: When we got the money during the first year, it just came all of a sudden. We were not prepared; we had no infrastructure. Is this what you are saying? In a sense, the money came as a surprise. You see what I'm saying? We didn't anticipate the money when it came. That's when I became the interim director.

RP: Structurally we were handicapped because normally, if a proposal like ours gets accepted, the department chair and faculty, along with the dean, would move the project along. We didn't have any of these support structures.

MM: That's the point. It became our job to set up an infrastructure to operate the center.

RP: At least that became our strategy.

MM: We needed to create linkages with the appropriate departments. That's more or less the same thing that's going on right now with the efforts to establish a Chicano studies department.

RP: I'm saying that under normal administrative circumstances we would not have had to create a special office.

MM: We didn't have support. Our first task was to begin negotiations with the appropriate deans to set up the infrastructure. Next, we needed to gain the goodwill of the larger faculty. To be real crass about it, a hundred thousand dollars could buy you a lot of goodwill. I managed to fund a lot of little projects to get a lot of support and at least the illusion of activity.

RP: That is the strategy that you implemented.

MM: There was actually no way to implement a sustained program while trying to negotiate with a college. There were a lot of people sniping.

RP: So you bought off a lot of people.

MM: I wouldn't say that I bought off people. We started a lot of initiatives that could not have been monitored.

RP: I understand.

MM: Some of those debts you had to pay later.

RP: The point is that the special office was created due to the lack of support infrastructure; we used the office as a leverage point.

Doing Things Sideways

RP: Let me ask you this: why did we have to do all these things sideways? Why didn't the president, once the regents had approved the center, simply tell a dean, "Implement this." Presidents do have that kind of power.

MM: The fact is that we did not have support within the institution for the center. Even with the small budget that we had, we still had to negotiate our way into a college. Also, rarely have I seen the provost or the president really engage the deans, department chairs, or the faculty to promote and support Chicano activities. They stand off on Chicano issues and let us figure out how to do things without any kind of support. I think that many department chairs feel that administrators often try to push issues related to minorities down their throats without really involving them.

RP: Yet, we've concluded just the opposite. I never felt that the president really supported us.

MM: It's a dual thing. Faculty set-asides are a good example. The administration throws money into the departments, but the departments feel that they are being imposed upon. Even though there is no support for Chicano hiring, the departments feel that somebody is imposing on them. That explains why some departments actually refuse the set-aside money. The Hispanic Research Center was not seen differently from the faculty set-aside. The regular faculty see these things as political concessions to the Chicanos who are outside the academy. I have noticed, however, that this is not necessarily the case with women candidates, provided they are white. Departments are not so resentful when women candidates are involved. Faculty also exhibit a greater sense of obligation or guilt with Black candidates. The important point is that these decisions are usually either/or—the tendency is to pit one group against the other. It is a zero-sum game. Whatever you get is at the expense of someone else. We always seem to fall into the trap.

RP: But the center proposal was approved by everyone, including the faculty senate. Still it had little legitimacy.

A License to Root Around

MM: I have been thinking about the idea of legitimacy. What is legitimacy? Legitimacy includes the notion that resources are put into particular endeavors. When money is put into a particular endeavor, it tells you where the heart of the institution is. We're talking about a hundred thousand dollars for the center; there's no heart there. There's no real commitment for these kinds of activities. The university never really supported us. We were always outsiders. In spite of all those committees that we went to, there was no real support other than from us.

RP: But don't you think that people outside of academia would find all this very strange? Here you have a proposal that started from the bottom, worked its way up the organization, gaining approval all along, including the Board of Regents. The center even gets funded. But the CEO of the organization doesn't tell the troopers to implement it. Instead, they left us to negotiate.

I see a pattern here. Top -level administrators simply gave us a license to root around in the organization and get whatever we could. They put a few dollars in our hands and turned us loose to see what we could do with it. But you are right, it wasn't all that much money. The college deans might well have laughed at it.

The only thing that tempered this strange process is the university's fear that things might blow up politically. That would have been negative for everyone. So there must have been some concessions here and there. For example, the vice president must have twisted the dean's arm to convince him that the center should be housed in the liberal arts college. I don't think that we would have found a home otherwise. In other words, I don't think that the money we had would have been sufficient to wheel and deal. A million bucks, maybe. What strikes me is the attitude of top management to let these things just float.

MM: But it is the same thing with many other activities, not just ours.

RP: I suppose that it is comforting to know that we are not being singled out in this respect.

MM: Our problem is that we don't have people in high-level positions to support us.

Tiny Footholds of Power

RP: In fairness, there is another side to this story that we shouldn't overlook. I don't think that it would have worked if the president had said to us, "Go talk to dean so and so. You are going to be in his college and the dean has agreed to oversee this project." I think that we or someone in the group would have resisted it. We might have been suspicious of the president or thought that we had lost control of the project.

Universities tend to work that way. People are very jealous of maintaining tiny little footholds of power, influence, and control. You see what I'm saying? So the university administration might have seen things in this light. They might have thought, leave those guys alone. If you try to tell them what to do, they're going to bounce all over the place. Let them flounder around and do whatever they want. They'll be happier if it's their own floundering. See what I'm saying? The university is a strange world in which autonomy, control, influence, and power are exercised in unusual ways.

Anyway, we managed to get the center housed in the College of Liberal Arts and Sciences. That allowed us to move forward with the search for the permanent director. At this point we had a problem because you weren't interested in the position, nor was I. A few people on the periphery expressed some interest, but they could not muster support from the group. Here was another potential trap: Finding a director who could move forward with a difficult agenda.

Finding a Director

MM: Weren't you the head of the first search committee?

RP: Yes. It was important to hire a permanent director. It was an unusual search because, although it was conducted impeccably, it produced absolutely no results; an almost perfect process with zero product. One has to ponder that.

MM: I've thought about it. The top candidate really was using us for his own ends. He was not serious about coming to ASU. Some faculty members are experts at applying for positions so that they can get their salaries matched at their home institution. It seems like such a dishonest ploy. It works if you are a member of the "good old boy" network.

RP: I think so, too. But the dean also was angling for his own interests; he saw an opportunity to get another faculty member and wanted to make sure that he got a faculty member who was acceptable to one of his departments. I think the dean wanted a candidate that he wouldn't have to fight about with a department. At any rate, at the end of the first search the committee gave the nod to a finalist, but since he wasn't all that interested in us, the whole thing fell through.

Chicanos Had Bailed Out

RP: There is one more thing about the first search for a director. By the time that we were looking for a director during the middle eighties, many Chicano professors had bailed out of Chicano studies. Successful professors had made it largely by going into the regular disciplines. The smart professors, if you will, had recognized that you don't build a career in academia through Chicano studies. Even if you have interests in Chicano studies, you pursue them in other departments. That didn't really surprise me, but it was sad.

MM: That's not sad; that makes sense. Given the structure of the university, that's the only way to survive.

RP: It was sad to me because we were promoting Chicano studies and there were no takers. We had a legitimate position, we were serious, we had spent a lot of energy, yet most everybody had concluded that these things were not serious anymore. It wasn't a good foundation for building a serious scholarly career. Of course, we also were an unknown quantity. Who knew about our university at the national level regarding Chicano studies? We had no record to speak of. So nobody wanted to take a chance. It was too risky. We got all kinds of strange candidates applying for the position. Quite a few were clearly not qualified.

The message that I got from this situation was very unsettling. It showed how far Chicano studies had deteriorated as a field. Here we had a very good job, a tenured full professorship at a significant university with a very reasonable salary and the pool of candidates numbered no more than twenty or twenty-five. I have been involved in many searches and know that a position like that in other departments might have drawn a hundred applicants or more. To me it was hurtful because we had spent so much time and energy to get as far as we had gotten. The idea that we could invest so much effort and then not get taken seriously just smarted a bit. This isn't to say anything negative about the candidates who applied. I thought that some very good people applied. We just did not have the range of choices that we should have had.

Padilla's Candidacy

RP: Anyway, the process broke down. That put you on the spot because now you were looking into possibly a second year as interim director. We had to do the search over again, and that's when you guys pulled out the long knives to make me a candidate. That was the farthest thing from my mind. And I had good reasons. First, I didn't want to be tied down to any one project. I had a larger agenda. Second, I have always believed in the principle that if you go around rocking institutions, don't expect to be the one who is going to be rewarded by those institutions. That just seems common sense to me. Someone else has given this principle a name: the *piñata* principle.

MM: Absolutely, and neither one of us ever approach it in that light.

RP: I never even thought of asking for anything that even smacked of personal advantage.

MM: Remember that the second time around we did get some good candidates.

RP: Also, the dean had fully awakened and by then had a definite agenda about whom he wanted to bring on board. We were really in danger of having, not the president nor the provost, but the dean decide who should head the center. Another potential trap!

The dean manipulated the second search committee by appointing his own chair who would see after the dean's interests. That's the political problem that we were facing. I saw that clearly and it certainly didn't encourage me to become a candidate under those circumstances. But I also recognized the danger that after all our hard work we were going to lose the whole thing.

There were two issues that had to be resolved before I would seriously entertain becoming a candidate. First, there had to be political support from outside the university. I did not think that the college was going to give strong support to the center. Second, I was very concerned that my own career was going to be put on hold for a number of years. I was an associate professor, hoping to get full professor. I didn't want to mortgage my career.

You all managed to allay my fears on the first count, and my worst fears turned into reality on the second one. It took me ten years to get promoted to full professor in part as a result of taking the center directorship. However, looking back upon it, I don't regret making that decision. The work was significant, but it does prove the point again that getting involved in these kinds of activities has implications for individual careers. I think that we can see from the behavior of Chicano academics that they are only too conscious of this situation.

MM: In the second search one of the candidates who was interviewed was a personal friend of the dean of the college of liberal arts and sciences. I am not sure if he was interested in coming. There were two additional candidates, however, who were clearly interested in coming and who also were interviewed. By that time I was in the vice president's office. As I recall, there was a deal struck that truly benefitted us. There was an agreement with the president, the vice president, and the dean to hire several finalists, no matter who got hired as director.

RP: Yes. Three people were hired on that round.

MM: When Gary Keller came I did not know him. But I told him that we were not going to support him. That we couldn't. That we were committed to you. I was up front. But I also told him that if he was interested, we would love to have him as a faculty member at the center. No bull, he was very supportive about that.

RP: He was a great asset to the center.

MM: Absolutely. A great asset to the university. There's no question about it.

It is also quite interesting that one of our faculty colleagues took great exception to your candidacy. I had a long conversation with him, where he basically agreed to support you. Then I remember that at one meeting he kind of reversed himself. I have no idea why or what precipitated it. I called him on it in front of the group and that strained our relationship. But I have no idea what turned him around. These efforts are very difficult because they create great divisions, and we don't seem to know how to avoid them. There was, however, great support for your candidacy on the search committee; Barbara Flores and Allan Matheson, the law professor, really championed your candidacy.

Avoiding the Dean's Trap

RP: Once I became head of the center, I felt that I had to do several things. One was to find an accommodation with the college. I understood that it wasn't their idea to put us there. We needed an accommodation so that we wouldn't be constantly at each other's throats. Things didn't start very well, but it wasn't because of me. I had better sense than to start things in a bad way. When I stepped into the director's job, I already had a lot of experience in administration. This experience helped me quite a bit. For example, the dean tried to do something odd. He wanted to keep control of the center's budget in his office. Obviously that's administrative non-sense. If I had not been a seasoned administrator, this could have been yet another trap for the center. Can you imagine having a line unit in which the dean's office controls the unit's budget?

When I met with the dean for the first time as center director, I simply said, "I understand that you want to keep control of the center's budget.

That's fine. We'll spend money. But if you're going to exercise control from here, I will not take any responsibility for the expenditures or for keeping the books straight." I also asked him if he also controlled the budgets for all other research centers. Of course, the dean was smart enough to understand my message so that the next day I had control of the center's budget.

There were many petty battles like that. I don't know if it was because of me personally or because of the center as such. I knew at the time that it wasn't going to be an easy life. The best that I could hope for was some kind of accommodation. An uneasy truce.

Chapter 9

The Elusive Community of Scholars

Creating an Intellectual Space

RP: We need to talk about the ideological framework within which we designed and tried to operate the Hispanic Research Center. There were certain results and relationships that we expected both of ourselves and other Chicano professors who were participants in the center. If you consider our arguments at that time, one of the fundamental ideas was that Chicanos working within universities needed an intellectual space in which we could conduct our work that focused on Chicano issues. We felt that within the traditional departments we lacked the freedom to engage, in an unrestricted manner, the salient issues that required academic attention: who we were, where we had come from, where we were going, the critique of existing knowledge paradigms, and so on. The absence of such an intellectual space penalized us because when we did engage concerns such as these the results often were not well received by our colleagues in the regular departments. Our thinking at the time was that this failure to connect our intellectual concerns with the academic organization caused many of us to be ejected from the university, typically as part of the tenure review process, if not earlier.

MM: Let's examine the premise that academic departments are not appreciative of our intellectual products. What evidence do you have for this? They could argue, with some justification, that we were creating very few intellectual products or that our intellectual products were not of high quality. Therefore, from their perspective, the issue is not the thematic content but the quality of the intellectual material.

On the other hand, you do have a point that minority content has not always been an acknowledged area of study in academia. This, however, is not dissimilar to other areas of study that have had to wait their turn as it were. For example, only a few years ago the study of gerontology or aging was not viewed as an area worthy of study, and the people in this area had to fight hard to get accepted. The same probably applies to women's studies and I suppose eventually we will be saying the same thing for gay studies.

There are many instances that I can cite where the intellectual productions were meager. I can cite the example of one of our colleagues who was denied tenure on the basis that he didn't have quality intellectual production. As an experiment, I had a disinterested friend examine his documentation, including his grievance against the university. I asked her whether she thought that we had a case. Her conclusion was that the department was justified in denying him tenure. Her conclusion was based not on whether he was a Chicano or not, but simply on the quantity and the quality of his work.

The hypocrisy in this decision, however, is that if you match the performance of at least four faculty members that I know in that department, his intellectual products are quite comparable to their products. There is much that we can say about that situation. I am sure the same issues exist in the College of Education. I am sure that you will agree that these are very complex issues.

Quality and Presence

RP: These issues are all interrelated. You may recall that in the sixties the chief concern of Chicanos in the universities was that we could not find ourselves within the existing intellectual spaces of the universities. We were invisible because the existing academics had never thought it interesting or useful to focus on the kinds of concerns that Chicanos felt were important to us. So to begin with, we did not start from a premise of quality; we started from an existential situation in which we found ourselves in an academic world in which we basically didn't count; our basic identity, our basic existence was not even factored into the nature of things. That is where we began.

MM: But why is it that we didn't count?

RP: It appeared to us that we didn't count because when we looked around the academic world its intellectual productions did not reflect or resonate with our own experiences. For example, when Romano reviewed the anthropological literature on Chicanos that was produced largely by Anglos, their interpretations didn't seem to square with our experienced reality of Chicano life. Historical accounts by non-Chicanos also did not seem to square with our own view of our history; the same could be said about social science in general. So at that moment we challenged Anglo intellectual productions in these areas.

We began to look critically at the existing knowledge base on Chicanos and noted how it constituted a very small part of the academic world. In all important areas of academic concern, science, literature, history, culture, and so on, we were noticeably absent. That became the first point of our challenge.

As a counterpoint, we were challenged to point to the Chicano intellectual products of abiding importance. Take literature, for example. We were asked something like, "What have you people produced that is worthy of being included in the canon of American literature, not to mention world literature?" In response, our first impulse was to scramble to see if in fact we had some great unknown novelist somewhere whom nobody had paid attention to. The point is that at a certain historic moment there was a confrontation between ourselves and the university because we did not see ourselves included in the academic world.

MM: So Chicano intellectual productions didn't have legitimacy in the universities.

RP: That is true. But beyond that, at that point we did not even have many active scholars. So it wasn't even a question of good or bad scholarship; there simply wasn't enough of it, good or bad. So you see, for us it was essentially a question of presence.

MM: So this is a central issue with which the Hispanic Research Center was to struggle. But, as a matter of fact, by the time the center entered the struggle, there were already many Chicano studies programs in existence.

RP: Such programs had already been around for ten or fifteen years.

MM: So what we were trying to do at the university was to get legitimacy for our intellectual enterprise. The question is, what is legitimacy? Would you accept that this is what we were trying to do?

RP: I wouldn't pose it strictly in terms of legitimacy; in this case, legitimacy is part of it, but it is not central . . .

MM: But you just said that we were excluded.

RP: There are many reasons for being excluded, not just legitimacy. We were being excluded because we were considered academically uninteresting or unimportant; legitimacy carries more of a political connotation.

Around 1969, when Chicanos began to arrive at American universities in significant numbers, the basic issue was that we could not find ourselves in the academic environment; we were strangers in a strange land. We belonged to the same society but our experiences, our culture, our lives, our very selves were absent from academic discourse. To the extent that we had a presence, ideas about us were filtered through the eyes of the Anglos. We were seen as strange or quaint. That was a troubling situation that we felt needed to be challenged.

MM: Our existence in the United States is paradoxical. On the one hand, Mexican people were the original settlers. They settled the Southwest when Americans were not yet interested in this part of the country. The Anglo expansionist philosophy led to the Mexican War and the Mexican people were quickly disenfranchised from their land. Since the Mexican Revolution, however, we have been seeing the gradual immigration of Mexicans into the United States. Now we are literally seeing an invasion of Mexicans into this country. Even middle-class Mexican people are clamoring to enter. We see the reaction to this "invasion" through the politics of Governor Wilson in California. The original Mexican settlers still exist, of course. They live in New Mexican, in Southern Texas, and perhaps in parts of California where they are generally integrated into the larger population. Here we must point to an interesting phenomenon: many of these so-called original settlers are really *genízaros* or simply detribalized Indians. The composition of Chicanos in this county is a complex matter. There was a very strong culture in the Southwest. We need to explain what happened to it.

Reviving the Community of Scholars

RP: What you're saying is that we could have looked at our existential situation in academia and asked, "How did we ever get into this pickle?" And I suppose that the answer to that question could have been given in terms of politics, history, and ideology. There could be many ways to explain the situation.

My point is that we collectively recognized the situation that we were in, and we wanted to do something about it. And one of the strategies that we came up with was to create an intellectual space that would facilitate our intellectual productions. What such an intellectual space presupposes and requires, though, is the existence of a community of scholars. In fact, such a Chicano community of scholars did not exist. That is really what accounts for the lack of Chicano intellectual productions.

MM: Relatively speaking we seem to lack such a community. A couple of years ago, Felipe Ortego and I wrote a paper on the idea of change and the Chicano community. We referred to community as simply a group of people sharing like interests and goals. Warren refers to community as action organized to "afford people daily local access to those broad areas of activity which are necessary in day-to-day living." In day-to-day parlance, we talk of towns as communities even though the residents may not share common goals. In large terms, one talks about the "Los Angeles community" or the "Phoenix community." Nisbet, however, is more on target when it comes to the issues we are talking about. He argues that community provides the legitimacy that is needed with respect to such things as authority, function, membership, and loyalty.

RP: So the Hispanic Research Center was designed to create a support infrastructure that would allow and foster the productions of a Chicano community of scholars. Such a community would have a physical and sociological presence on campus. A physical presence means the allocation of resources, while a sociological presence implies scholars who work together rather than individually. So the center represented both a pragmatic and an idealistic moment at the same time. Pragmatically, if we wanted to create an intellectual presence on campus, we needed to establish the necessary organizational infrastructure. Idealistically, we saw ourselves as holding up the traditional idea of a community of scholars, even though that idea had long vanished from the American academic landscape to be replaced by the competitive and entrepreneurial academic.

Originally, I had it in mind that we would be given the opportunity to hire a certain number of professors who collectively would carry on their work on Chicano issues. I think that this is where we had our first serious problem in pushing forward the center's agenda.

As you will recall, at the beginning we got money for a director, a secretary, and two visiting professors. Obviously, this was not going to go very far in establishing a Chicano community of scholars. At that time, the only other possibility was to affiliate with the center Chicano professors who were already at the university. But even that strategy had its limitations because there were so few Chicano professors at the university to begin with.

As a result of this situation, the first order of business for the center was to bring to the university as many Chicano professors as we could and then try to entice them to join the center and thus begin to form the community of scholars that we desired. We went down this slippery road of recruitment innocently enough by asking the university president to allocate two faculty lines to the center, which would be used to recruit jointly with other academic departments. Under this arrangement, the new recruits would be given released time to the center.

One reason that we used this particular strategy is that the center was not a tenure-granting unit. The center was constructed specifically under that condition, so we were dependent on the regular academic departments to hire the faculty that we hoped to enlist in creating the Chicano community of scholars. That turned out to be a weak strategy.

MM: You're saying that we really didn't have the power or the authority to hire our own people. We were partners but not equal partners with the departments. They had veto power.

RP: At the outset, we did not have the wherewithal politically or economically to recruit the people that we needed to create the community of scholars. We had some power and some of the resources, but we had to hire collaboratively with other departments, which means that we really had no autonomy.

MM: Why did we recruit collaboratively?

RP: Because politically it was the only way that we could move our agenda. Remember my axiomatic belief that we can only gain as much power or resources on campus as we can leverage from political pressure that is applied on the university by Chicano community groups or individuals. The resource configuration available to the center was a direct reflection of the pressure that was put by our community on the university. That was as much as we could get.

MM: I can't recall if at that time there were positions for academic professionals.

RP: There were.

MM: In retrospect, it seems to me that hiring two academic professionals, rather than joint professor appointments, would have been more productive for the center, at least in the initial stages. Since academic professionals would have been full-time employees of the center, they would have been in a better position to prosecute the objectives of the center. They, unlike faculty, would have not had dual loyalties. We could have had more control over who came, and it would have been easier to pursue a research agenda through such ideas as the Community Documentation Program.

RP: That's possible.

MM: It is easy to criticize oneself in hindsight. But I think that we were naive politically in not appreciating those kinds of positions, or, to be perfectly frank, not even knowing about them. I'll tell you honestly that if I had been aware of that option, we could have at least had a chance to discuss it.

RP: We didn't discuss it because at that time our framework was that we needed many more professors at the university. I certainly was following the idea that to change the university meant that we needed to hire more Chicano faculty. Academic professionals don't have the same status as professors.

MM: My point is that we didn't even consider the option because it wasn't part of our worldview. And quite frankly when you look back and assess the contributions, commitment, and passion of many of the professors that were hired, I'm not sure that a mistake was not made. Academic professionals were not part of what was accessible to us because we didn't know about it. In other words, I am talking about our political naïveté in carrying out some of our ideas.

RP: I don't think that it was just naïveté. We had analyzed the university and recognized that the power of the university was in the faculty. We had learned that lesson from the academic struggles of the late sixties and early seventies. We lost many battles because it was students who exerted the majority of the effort. They went as far as they could go, but often it was not far enough. The real power was in the hands of full professors.

MM: Absolutely, I agree.

RP: So we went for the jugular. Whatever other possibilities might have existed, we simply cast them aside, we didn't even bother looking because we understood at that moment that it was the faculty—the right faculty—who would make it possible to change the university in the long run. The real question then became, who are the right faculty? After a while, this turned out to be a very important question.

Remember that by the early to mid eighties, many Chicanos had more or less bailed out of Chicano studies. It was questionable whether we would be able to find people who would be willing to reconnect with the original ideas of the Chicano movement. We simply had to move ahead as there was no other choice. As director, I tried to fill the two faculty lines collaboratively with other departments and protected our interests as much as I could.

The Role of Community Influentials

MM: Tell me about those lines.

RP: When I was approached to become a candidate for the center director, I insisted that at least a couple of faculty lines had to be allocated to the center. In addition, I didn't want to take a bath in my professional career; I feared that I would have to put it on hold.

MM: In fact, you did take a bath.

RP: Yes, but it was temporary. At least I have to look at it that way.

MM: The context in which all this came about is that we had very few people apply during the initial search for the director. There was José Angel Gutiérrez from Texas. Along with people like Corky González and Reies López Tijerina, he was one of the leading figures in the Chicano movement. But he became a very controversial figure. He was even mentioned in the Watergate scandals. Many Chicanos accused him of being bought off by the Republicans.

When he came to interview, we knew, or at least I knew, that there was no way he would get hired. The dean was from Texas, and I know that he had many interactions with Alfredo Gutierrez whose endorsement would be needed to get the directorship. Alfredo had told me that there was no way that this guy would get hired at the university. I told Alfredo that he had the responsibility to tell José Angel to his face about the situation. I told Alfredo that José Angel was coming to my house the next evening at seven o'clock and that he and José Angel were going to go at it. That is how the concerns between them were aired.

The first concern was that José Angel did not have the requisite academic credentials. His vita indicated that most of his activities were political. But in all honesty that shouldn't detract from a man who has great brilliance and organizational skills. Many men from his generation got burned because they were real activists, and in a sense many from the next generation—leaders in waiting—profited from their activism. This had been one of Alfredo Gutierrez's criticisms of many Chicano leaders operating out of Washington, D.C., who just waited around playing it safe and then profiting from the activism of other Chicanos. Anyhow, José Angel is a victim of his earlier activism. He was shunted aside for safer kinds of people—he couldn't buy a job.

The other basic charge that Alfredo Gutierrez made to José Angel was that because of his history and ideology he would have great difficulties working with other groups. Ernie Cortéz, a McArthur Fellow and long-time activist, has referred to these guys as "ethnically exclusive."

The important issue, however, is that we simply did not have a wide enough range of choices among the finalists. That's what led to our decision to encourage you to apply for the job. To that end, we held a meeting in which Alfredo was present. What did he tell you at that meeting?

RP: He basically indicated that he would provide political support. Without such support, I knew that a bid for the directorship on my part would be stupid. But if someone like Alfredo was behind it, and if all my colleagues who mattered were behind it, then the most that I was likely to sacrifice was my own professional career. I was quite committed to the ideas that we were working with, and had been for some fifteen years, so I figured that if I did have to endure a fall it would be a relative fall and I could recover from it.

MM: It wasn't the fall of Adam in other words.

RP: It was going to be Padilla's fall! I figured that I would take the job for two or three years until things stabilized. It actually took a little longer. But it still worked the way that I had anticipated. It never was my intention to become director and retire off that position. That's the usual course, you know. These appointments become almost proprietary.

I mentioned to Alfredo the importance of gaining access to at least a couple of faculty positions because I was unnerved by the idea of being the director of a center that had no faculty and thus no ongoing research. That is why I bargained for the two faculty lines.

The Role of Campus Administrators

MM: In retrospect, do you think that the president's refusal to support a Chicano studies department was an effort to deny us the power that comes with a department? Did we get duped by that strategy?

RP: At that time I don't believe that anyone seriously considered the departmental option. We didn't get far enough in the political process to engage the issue of departmental status. I believe that the university president reacted more on a personal level as you suggested.

MM: I don't know. It's a bit like the current provost extending into three years the ongoing efforts to establish a Chicano studies department. In three years he'll be gone! We have gone through similar situations numerous times. An administrator will promise to deliver on this or that agenda, but it is done way into the future. In the meantime we think we have won a victory because the interim agreement is to set up a committee to plan for this or that event. However, when you analyze the situation you find that the promise is merely a delaying tactic and we fall for it. It is partly our lack of power, and our desire to think that we are involved in moving an agenda. It is also connected to our naïveté and lack of experience. How can you rely on an institution that has had twelve provosts in a period of ten years? Didn't we get duped by the end of the process?

RP: We worked as skillfully as we could within the existing political limitations. I wasn't shy about challenging anything. Yet, I didn't challenge the president on his lack of support for Chicano studies. I didn't particularly want a traditional Chicano studies program. So I didn't challenge the president because I had already personally decided to develop a Chicano studies research operation. At that time, I still had vivid memories of how the faculty, the administrators, and the students in the Chicano studies program at Berkeley could not get along. That's what my dissertation is about. I was dead set against re-creating the Berkeley dynamics. So actually I used the president's reluctance to support a traditional Chicano studies program as a leverage point to establish a strictly research-oriented center.

MM: I was in agreement, too. It's not that I was against the idea of Chicano studies. I was concerned with infrastructure so that we could have more control over the operation.

RP: A year or two before, we could have created a center capable of housing tenured faculty positions. But it just happened that at about the time the center was created, the vice president for academic affairs was on a major campaign to remove tenured faculty from organized research units. He wanted to make a sharp distinction between academic departments and organized research units. In fact, he was quite successful in this effort. By the time we created the center, university policy prohibited the assignment of tenured faculty to research centers. So our inability to hire tenured faculty through the center was basically a historical accident.

MM: Maybe.

The Advantages of Ambiguity

RP: So that is when we moved into collaborative hires between the center and other academic departments. What is significant here is that the original two faculty positions that were available to the center were supposed to be the beginning of the Chicano community of scholars.

Actually, as part of my being hired as director, two other finalists, a male and a female, also were hired as joint appointments between their respective departments and the center. To be honest with you, I always took these two faculty hires to mean that the president had come through on the deal to allocate two faculty lines to the center. However, the situation was fairly ambiguous, in large part because the deal was made behind the scenes. No one in the university administration had ever told me straight out that I had two faculty lines for the center. But I knew about the understanding, so the male and female finalists *could* have counted as the two promised faculty lines. But remember that I was not directly involved in their hiring. So things were fuzzy enough that I was able to pretend that those two hires didn't count against the promised lines.

MM: The women on campus, including the search committee chair, wanted the female finalist hired. They were willing to put pressure on the vice president. So in a sense there was no cost to Chicanos to bring her in. This was a women's hire. She had an outstanding record and I felt that she would make an important contribution to the Hispanic Research Center. Our main ally in this effort was the professor in women's studies who later served on the search committee for the HRC director. I guess what I said earlier about how she did not fit our aspirations was wrong. It also proves that we need to learn to connect in more effective ways with other groups on campus. The male finalist had an impressive record, but there was no way that we could support him given the commitment that had been made to you. I didn't know him from Adam, but I decided to play my chips and level with him. I told him that we were impressed with his record and excited about what he could bring to the university: grants, an exceptional academic record, and an active publishing organization. I honestly told him that we had decided to go with you but was wondering if he would be willing to come to the center with you being the director. I also remember asking you if you thought you could work with him. I was happy to see that both of you agreed to the terms of this informal agreement. He came as part of the package. That was a win-win situation all the way around: for women, for Chicanos, for those of us who had committed to you as center director, and for the vice president because it made it possible for him to strengthen his hand with the Chicanos.

RP: But you can see that all these things went on outside formal channels and largely before I was hired as director. So that by the time I was ready to come around asking for my two faculty lines the answer could have been simply that the center had already gotten the two promised lines. So I had to finesse things a bit. I did this by waiting a decent interval before saying anything about hiring faculty.

When I finally was ready to hire faculty, I wasn't quite sure how to go about it, given that tenured faculty could not be hired directly by the center. It may sound strange but the person who gave me a significant clue was the dean of the College of Business. We did not necessarily consider him friendly on issues of importance to us.

The Influence of College Deans

RP: How it happened is that I decided to talk to various deans. My basic approach was to say something like, "I've got a faculty line. Do you want to hire somebody?" It was quite a naive approach. I thought that I had two lines and that by offering one or two deans a line each I could hire the two people that I needed. I figured that each hire would be assigned 50 or 60 percent to the center and I'd give the rest of the time to the hiring department. According to my reckoning, this approach would increase staff to a total of four faculty, plus myself, at the center.

I first talked to the dean of the College of Public Programs, who gave me some very interesting counsel.

Before I continue, there is one additional detail I need to relate that turned out to be very important. Before approaching the deans, I had approached the vice president asking for the two promised faculty lines for the center. He basically responded with something like, "Sure, you can have two faculty lines, but we have already allocated all faculty lines to the departments for this year." In other words, the cupboard was bare!

I wasn't too happy about this, so he retreated a bit. He retreated by saying something like, "The deans have faculty lines that they are going to fill anyway. Why don't you go talk to the deans to see if they're willing to hire people collaboratively with you from their allocated faculty lines. I'll write a memo to the deans approving these collaborative hires."

MM: Did he write a memo?

RP: He did. And that is the way that the vice president wanted to handle the commitment for the two faculty. In other words, at that point I was royally screwed; there seemed to be no hope.

Nevertheless, I did follow the vice president's suggestion and that is how I wound up talking with the dean of the College of Public Programs. At that time, the dean was on his way out. He had quit in disgust, so he was extraordinarily frank in our brief conversation.

When I showed him the vice president's memo, you could see the fire in the dean's eyes. He laughed out loud. He didn't laugh in a mean way; he simply laughed at the organizational dynamics, at the position in which I had been placed. Perhaps he saw in my cornered position something that resonated with his own experience as dean. He said something like, "Well, Ray, what you have here is a license to hunt!" That's how he said it. "Good luck," he told me.

MM: Laughing at you.

RP: Yeah. Or maybe himself, or the vice president. Who knows? But he also said that what I really needed were some lines that I could leverage with departments. That was the end of the conversation. But I thought about what he had said and exclaimed to myself, "He's right!"

Of course, I never liked the vice president's approach in the first place. Yet, notice that when I asked the vice president for the two faculty lines he did not say that we had already hired two faculty. He instead took the position that all faculty lines had already been allocated to the colleges and there were no other lines to draw from.

So after talking with the dean I sent a memo to the vice president objecting strenuously to his approach. I told him that the approach was not going to work, and that we needed to have the two faculty positions assigned directly to the center, not to the deans. I sent a copy of the memo to the president. So in organizational terms I misbehaved. My claim was that two lines had been promised. This put the vice president in a very difficult position.

Clearly the president was aware of the two-line commitment, which my memo brought back to light. So the president basically directed the vice president to allocate two lines to the center. Remember that at that point the vice president was about to leave the university. This made the vice president's position very unstable.

The bottom line is that I refused to accept the vice president's deal. I went over his head, reminded the president about the two lines, and the president literally told the vice president to implement the commitment. Naturally, the vice president was unhappy because he had been overruled.

MM: I think that this type of communication between administrators is the cause of many of the problems in the university. The game playing that goes on, as in this case, includes tactics to delay decisions, sending one on wild-goose chases, and exploiting people's ignorance of the bureaucracy. It is as if all of us did not work together and wanted the best for one another. I know this is idealistic, but it hits at some of the difficulties in creating a community of scholars, which, as you already mentioned, was lost many years ago in academia. Did he tell you anything?

RP: What can I say? Of course the vice president could not say no to the president. But you know how it is when administrators dissimulate. I mean, they're going to do what they've been told to do, but they're not going to help to move things along in any way. That is what happened. I just kind of played dumb for a little bit. I knew the vice president was hurt, but I also knew that the faculty lines were going to be there, since the president had spoken.

So in a roundabout way I got a lot of help from the dean of the College of Public Programs. As a result of our interaction, I wrote a very powerful memo to the vice president that was actually intended for the president. And that is how I finessed the vice president.

Once I had clearance on the two faculty lines, I continued my rounds with the deans. I next met with the dean of the College of Business. I explained to him in general terms what I was up to and that I had two faculty lines. I didn't say anything to him explicit about how those lines might be used, but in my mind I assumed that if he wanted a line, I would simply give it to him. Remember that at the time I was real keen on hiring an economist because you and I had decided that Hispanic entrepreneurship was to be an important research emphasis of the center. Since the Economics Department was housed in the College of Business, that is why I targeted that dean in my early visits.

The dean's remarks were to the point and very productive. He said something like, "Look, I'll take you up on this, and here's what I'll do. I will give you half a line if you give me half a line. Then I will go to the departments and encourage them to look for people. I can't tell you what the departments will do, because I can't order the departments to hire anyone. But I will open it up to them, tell them that this is desirable. So if you give me half a line I'll do the rest. If you give me two half lines I'll try to go for two professors."

This conversation hit me like a lightning bolt, just like the previous one with the dean of the College of Public Programs. What struck me this time was that the guy was leveraging. He didn't know that I would have given him one of my two lines straight out. You see, he just wasn't used to working in that kind of world. In his world, you leverage everything and so he simply assumed that I was working within the same paradigm. Luckily I had been conservative enough not to tell him right off that he had a line if he wanted it. Instead, I simply invited him to entertain the idea of recruiting collaboratively. He simply took that to mean that an even break would be acceptable to me, which, of course, it was.

What's important is that his behavior changed my paradigm. After our conversation, I no longer saw myself as having resources to hire two people. Clearly, I could leverage my two lines to hire four people. Actually, there could have been any number of people because I could have divided my two full-time lines into, say, quarter lines. But at that moment I was simply enthralled at the possibility that I could hire four faculty for the center. Since I already had two, I could wind up with six faculty members working at the center half time or more each. So I am oddly grateful to this dean whom we had never perceived as being particularly helpful to us.

The Influence of Vice Presidents

RP: As I mentioned, all this was going on while the vice president was on his way out of the job. In fact, the vice president did leave, and Roland Haden, the dean of the College of Engineering, was appointed as interim vice president. I immediately made an appointment to see Haden to talk to him about what was going on with these faculty appointments. It wasn't clear to me how the actual appointments were going to be made.

Haden's style was totally different from Kinsinger's. Whereas Kinsinger had been very difficult to work with, constantly resisting everything, Haden immediately saw what I was up to and understood my problem. Perhaps I benefited from his having been dean before being appointed interim vice president.

MM: Let me tell you about both of them because I worked for both. Kinsinger operated out of a set of administrative principles based on decentralizing the decision-making authority, including the budgeting process. So each dean made decisions about his or her own budget. They also had discretion over most administrative matters.

Kinsinger maintained his power by "taxing" each college for a fixed percentage of its budget: 1 or 2 percent. This served as his discretionary pool of money that he used for bargaining when demands were made on his office. He would use this money to settle his commitments and bought and sold favors in the university.

He also was not open about his decision making. If it was convenient for him to tell you that he was going to do something, he would actually tell you so or imply it. So that he set people up, particularly if you were ignorant of how the university operated. Afterward people would try to navigate through the bureaucratic maze of the university and eventually come back to him bewildered because nothing had been done. This tactic would allow him to buy time on certain issues.

Haden was a totally different kind of administrator. He was clear on decisions. I remember a big fight over two hundred thousand dollars that had been allocated for minority programs to the vice president for student affairs. I argued that it was a mistake to allocate the money to student affairs because at the time I believed that money for minority programs should go directly to academic departments. This would serve to make the departments directly accountable for the performance of students. Student affairs programs were more oriented toward social and cultural activities.

I wanted the money placed in the Mathematics Department where the failure rate of students was astronomical. So I began negotiations with the Mathematics Department, which, along with the dean's office, agreed to use the money to fund a mathematics program that would be supplemented with an English component. An agreement was reached by all parties and outlined in a letter. It is interesting to note that the math department did not keep its word about including an English component. Also, it disenfranchised a community organization that had originally come up with the idea for the program.

There seems to be a pattern where ideas that are developed by the community later are usurped by the university. Two issues are important here: one is the usurpation of community projects, which serves to break community power, the very thing that we profess to be promoting, and the other is the manner in which many minorities begin to see these supplementary programs as proprietary. So they use the programs to leverage personal power, particularly against people they don't like, including students. I have seen this not only in the math project but with some of the people at the financial aid office who discriminate against some of the kids and favor others, and also, in the Hispanic convocation that originally started as a student program and now has been converted to a personal project to promote this or that politician. The consequences of this behavior on our young people are quite serious. It sets a bad example.

At any rate, Haden said, "If you're with me on this one, lets take on this fight." In other words, he was willing to take on the vice president for student affairs. "But you've got to do your part; you've got to take the crap that is going to come with it." So he went with it. I mean, he went to the president. Obviously this action aggravated the already strained relationship that the vice president for student affairs had with Chicanos. You have already told the story about her resentment to your comments about minority recruitment and retention.

The point is that he was straight. He was clear in terms of what he wanted. When he told you something, either yes or no, it was clear. You didn't have to guess and play games with him. That's why I had such great respect for Haden. Vice President Kinsinger was more difficult to read, and it resulted in many difficulties in getting things done, at least the things we wanted to do. He got many other important things done while he was here at ASU so he knew what he was doing.

RP: It's true that Kinsinger strung us out for four or five years. We could have accomplished what we did within a year or two, but he strung us out for half a decade. When I went to see Haden about the faculty lines, I wanted to make sure that I had my bases covered. It took only about ten minutes to take care of business. He actually told me what to do. He gave me a blueprint as to how I could do the collaborative faculty hires, plus he prepared an implementing memorandum, which he sent to me and all the deans. As a result of Haden's work, I literally succeeded in transforming my earlier license to hunt into a license to deal. And thanks to the business college dean I knew exactly how to deal: leverage.

MM: I was included in many of the decisions that affected minorities. In other words, we had a voice inside of Haden's administration. We could make suggestions; we were a part of the process. We at least had a voice even though it was not always heeded.

With Kinsinger, even though I was there, and even though I was allowed to say things, there was less openness in the process. He clearly did not trust one of the vice presidents in his staff whom he felt was always working against him. That guy later left. He had a different style. Kinsinger also seemed to be less knowledgeable about Chicanos in the Southwest. He decidedly had a more Midwestern orientation toward Chicanos. In fairness, however, he did try to hire a Hispanic dean in the College of Education, but thanks mostly to the bungling and in-fighting among Chicanos in the college we lost the opportunity.

The Power to Leverage

RP: So that's how the first cadre of faculty at the center were recruited. That would have placed our level of effort at about six professors. It took a couple of years to do all of these hirings. Just as this cycle of hirings was coming to an end, various pressures on the university, of which we have already spoken, converged in such a way that the university decided to establish a twenty-one-point Action Now program.

The heart of the Action Now plan was a set-aside of faculty lines at the vice president's level. These lines were to be allocated to those deans and departments who were willing to diversify their faculties. This was a very important initiative. When the program was announced, I immediately noted its significance. By then there was a new interim vice president for academic affairs.

MM: Yes, it was an important initiative. And the Minority Advisory Council should have gotten some credit for pushing it with the president of the university. It is interesting, however, that the council was not represented in the deliberations that took place in developing the plan, which involved all the top officers of the university. The language of the twenty-one-point plan does incorporate the ideas of the Minority Advisory Council, but it did not include the individuals. I wonder why there is never any acknowledgment for minority efforts in this regard. Anyhow, the new vice president was serving in an acting capacity.

RP: I met with the vice president once again and said to him that it was great that the university had the Action Now program. I pointed out that we had been very successful at the center in doing collaborative hires with departments. I explained that I worked with only those departments that were interested in collaborating. In other words, I gave him to understand that we were soft-pedaling the hiring of Chicano faculty. Given our success, we could help out in the Action Now initiative. In order to do so, we would need to find a way to make the set-aside lines available to the center. Once again, I used the rationale that by being affiliated with the center, the new faculty would be advantaged when it came time for tenure review.

As a practical mechanism, I recommended that for every hire under the set-aside, a proportion of the faculty member's time could be assigned to the center if all parties agreed to it. We dickered back and forth as to exactly what portion of the faculty member's time would be assigned to the center. I'm pretty sure that it was the academic vice president who decided this issue. At any rate, it was decided that the maximum portion of time assignable to the center would be 25 percent.

Since the original set-aside was eight positions, this agreement opened up the possibility that I could add up to eight new faculty to the center with one quarter released time each. And it was expected that the program would continue for several years, each year with a new allocation of positions. Here at long last was the resource base that had eluded us when we first proposed the center.

There was only one problem in all of this. Like a worm inside a perfect apple, the problem resulted from the very rationale that I had used to convince the vice president to allow the center access to the set-aside positions. All of our faculty recruitment had been done through collaborative agreements with various departments. The new hires from the set-aside lines were to be done exactly the same way. To put it simply, the center would not have control over who would be hired. At best, we could have strong influence.

In practice, the collaborative hires required a very field-sensitive process. I think of it as a very elaborate dance between the center and a collaborating department. Using this approach we were very successful in increasing the number of faculty who joined the center. But we had limited control in terms of recruiting specific individuals who possessed the views and skills that we needed.

For a while, the center was more of an affirmative action operation for the university than anything else. I'm using affirmative action here in its true historic sense. What was sacrificed was developing the faculty resources that could be harnessed to carry out a truly sophisticated research agenda related to Chicanos. I went along with this program because I reasoned that it would be impossible to conduct significant research without a strong Chicano faculty base.

There is only one other part to the story of faculty hires for the center. It has to do with the new branch campus of the university. The branch campus was hiring quite a few new faculty. But it was not doing a very good job of hiring Chicanos. To the extent that it did hire Chicano faculty, I noticed a potential bureaucratic contradiction, if you will. On the main campus we were hiring Chicano faculty who had the option to be assigned to the center. This was intended to give them a leg up on getting tenured and promoted. At the same time, the branch campus was hiring similar faculty but not providing them with the same advantage. When I figured it all out, I brought this problem to the attention of the dean of faculty at the branch campus. First I met with her, then I followed up our meeting with a memorandum in which I basically argued that the university was leaving itself vulnerable to future litigation. Say a Chicano faculty member at the branch campus would be denied tenure a few years down the road. That faculty member could argue that he or she was not treated fairly, because similarly situated colleagues on the main campus had been given an opportunity to make tenure by being released to the center. There were several other arguments, but this was the key argument.

The dean of the faculty reacted very favorably to my arguments. In a way she said, "Well, we don't want that!" So it was decided to make it possible for new faculty hires at the branch campus to become affiliated with the center on the main campus on the same basis as the Action Now program. Technically, that created a very large pool of potential hires for the center. That's how we began to recruit a significant number of Chicano faculty to the branch campus who also had an affiliation with the center. To this day, faculty from the branch campus have a very strong presence in the center.

MM: They are almost half of the faculty.

RP: These various initiatives made it possible for the center to hire about twenty-two faculty who were assigned to the center for some portion of their time, from 25 percent on up.

Not a Community of Scholars

RP: The important question is, was this the way to build a Chicano community of scholars?

MM: The question is whether in fact we have a Chicano community of scholars.

RP: My question implied the answer: no.

MM: Let me ask you this: What do you mean by a community of scholars? I think that this is a more fundamental question than whether we have one.

RP: A community of scholars was supposed to be a cadre of dedicated Chicano academics who would create intellectual productions such that a Chicano presence on campus would be manifested. Remember that we originally launched the center project as a reaction to our absence from academic discourse and our invisibility on campus. The center was supposed to establish an intellectual space in which a Chicano community of scholars could live and thrive. Over time these scholars were to produce intellectual products of sufficient quality and quantity so that the legitimacy issue would simply become irrelevant.

The community of scholars was supposed to be populated by Chicano academics who shared in this vision and who were willing to work hard to realize it. Logically, we should have been able to design an appropriate organizational structure, acquire a resource base, and hire into the unit exactly the kind of people who fitted into the agenda that I just mentioned. But as I have explained in detail during this conversation, we never really gained unencumbered resources or the autonomy to control the hiring process. For example, early on we tried to hire an economist, but we could never get the Economics Department to agree on someone who seemed appropriate to us. I used to say half in jest, "There isn't a Chicano economist whom they think is qualified or whom they like." In effect, we could not target our hires to the areas that we thought were important. Our hiring was driven by which departments were willing to collaborate and which candidates the departments thought were most attractive.

Remember that you and I agreed on four areas of emphasis for the center: Hispanic entrepreneurship, science and technology, the Hispanic polity, and the arts. These focal areas should have driven our faculty recruitment.

MM: But we had some hand in the recruiting.

RP: It was a strong hand, but not nearly strong enough. We had a strong hand in the sense that the lines were allocated to us through the vice president's office. And no department could hire against these lines without our support. But our hand also was weak because we could not hire anyone without the support and consent of some department. It was a perfect implementation of the classic checks and balances theory without any thought given to the substantive programming issues. This is something that I have noticed often about Chicano concerns. The university deals with them almost totally from a political perspective and neglects the substantive issues.

MM: Weren't we on the search committees?

RP: I was a member of virtually every search committee for the collaborative hires. So how did I play my hand? That is the key to all of this, you see. I could have been very high-handed. I could have approached a department and said, "We want so and so, and we'll take no one else." Technically, we had the power to do so. But I think that such a stance would have resulted in very few hires, and a very bad reputation for the center.

MM: Yeah, that's a bad way to play your hand.

RP: So obviously I didn't play that hand. In fact, I played my hand in exactly the opposite way. My power to veto was left as an implicit threat. I allowed the departments to name their own search committees and to prepare the job descriptions. I reviewed the latter and made brief comments, but, for the most part, I did not get very involved in this part of the hiring process. I participated in the candidate interviews with great care and diligence. The departments knew that I could veto the final selection. So there was a lot of dancing going on to determine which candidate would get the nod. In some cases I agreed fully with the department's choice. In other cases, I felt that the choices would not lead to coherent staffing at the center, but if the individual was a strong scholar or seemed to have promise, I usually went along with the departmental choice anyway.

One of the implications of this modus operandi is that we were not able to assemble research teams when hiring center faculty. This meant that the center's research agenda would not be prosecuted on the basis of research teams but on the collective works of individual researchers. I didn't start out with this staffing strategy. It just turned out that way given the organizational constraints imposed upon us.

To make the individualistic approach feasible, I gave center faculty maximum autonomy to define their own individual research programs. This put collective effort at a disadvantage, even though I was trying to encourage it as best I could. But the individualistic approach kept the faculty happy. In effect, I had a large group of faculty from very disparate fields who were allowed to do their own thing. To keep some accountability in place, I worked diligently to develop an evaluation system. Every year, faculty were required to report on their activities and justify their continuing assignment to the center. Do you see what I'm saying?

MM: I see what you are saying, and it explains many of the problems with the center. Two issues come to mind. First, the question of loyalty. The faculty never saw themselves as being hired by the center, therefore they didn't feel accountable to the center. The second issue, I think a far more dramatic one in its impact, is that while we had developed an analysis of what needed to be done to prosecute a research agenda—focusing on entrepreneurship, science and technology, the Hispanic polity, and the arts—when it came down to implementing this research program it was totally ignored. The theory did not connect with the practice. How would you assess the faculty's academic productions in terms of quantity and quality, and whether they helped in the tenure review process?

RP: The senior faculty were in an excellent position to take advantage of the situation. Since they already had well-defined research agendas and were well published, they mostly concentrated on getting extramural funding through grants and contracts. So the individualist approach worked very well for the senior faculty.

The real problem occurred with the young, untenured professors. First, almost immediately they came under intense pressure from their departments. In other words, the departments did not enter into the collaborative hiring regime in good faith. The departments played games with the released time arrangement. On paper, they would claim to be giving a professor the promised released time, but in reality, they were pressuring the professor to devote full time to the department. This put the faculty in a squeeze because, as I just mentioned, I also moved aggressively to establish accountability mechanisms at the center.

These kinds of pressures proved lethal to quite a few of the assistant professors. We lost a number of them. And even though we continued to hire to replace some of the casualties, eventually we were losing as many people as we were hiring. Moreover, we were losing faculty under very unhappy and unfair circumstances. In a real sense, the center was not able to protect the junior faculty from the departments. We had hoped and expected that it would.

MM: That's been a continuing problem. But you haven't answered my question about what a community of scholars is.

RP: I'm building up to it. Part of the idea of building a community of scholars was to provide a safe haven where the kind of intellectual work that we have been talking about could be encouraged, produced, and respected. Unfortunately, besides the political difficulties that I just mentioned with our untenured faculty, we also developed internally a maternalistic orientation toward them. I don't know exactly how things got out of hand. It all started with the reasonable idea that junior faculty had to be "protected" from the political and bureaucratic assaults that many of us had experienced earlier in our careers.

For example, junior faculty should be protected from being put on too many committees. Minority faculty are put on too many committees as part of affirmative action window dressing, but when it comes time for tenure review, such service counts for almost nothing. As another example, junior faculty should be protected from being overly involved in community service, which usually does not result in publications. Along the same lines, junior faculty should limit their involvement in student advising, recruitment and retention efforts, and generally in dealing with the many problems that universities encounter when addressing Chicano and minority issues. The idea was that the senior faculty should become a protective buffer for the untenured faculty.

On the other hand, the idea also was to give untenured faculty every opportunity to conduct research and to publish in peer-reviewed journals. This was all part of the "protection" idea.

What resulted from this maternalistic protection scheme truly amazed me. After a while, I detected a most conservative bent in the untenured faculty. They would not take risks with anyone, including one another. They were not open to new ideas, or to accepting new people freely into the organization. Their typical response to things was, "I can't do this, I can't do that, I shouldn't volunteer for this." Either they said it themselves or someone else said it for them. In effect, we had unwittingly removed the trial period that is so necessary in academia to filter out the good faculty from the mediocre.

The maternalistic protectionism that we inflicted on the junior faculty steered the center in an overly conservative direction, in my opinion. Whereas the center should have been a very lively intellectual place, with people working together on projects of mutual interest and relevance to our concerns, people were mostly looking out for themselves and their own narrowly defined interests. Through good intentions, it seems that we wound up shooting ourselves in the foot.

The Gender Issue

RP: Part of our problem is that we were not able to handle very well the gender issues that began to surface in the center. It wasn't just an issue of dealing with junior professors, but of dealing with untenured Chicano and *Chicana* professors. In a sense, it was easier to be overly protective than to risk potential criticisms of gender bias. My point in all of this is that these kinds of organizational dynamics at the center were deadly when it came to the notion of creating a community of scholars.

MM: While all this was going on, were the faculty producing?

RP: Most of them were producing, but they were producing as individuals. This did not materially contribute to defining the center as an intellectual space. Too often, the faculty would use the time and the resources of the center to please their departments or to please themselves. Faculty who were interested in Chicano or Chicana issues simply did their work and found academic outlets for it.

MM: But there were no cooperative ventures. Part of the reason this happened is that there is a contradiction in the approach. Remember that we were trying to build a community of scholars and this required that people pull together not only with one another but with the community that we at least should be accountable to. There was an argument, however, that we should protect untenured faculty so that they could get on with their careers, and that they would participate in a meaningful way at some future date. It seems that everything was upside down. The paradigm needed to be shifted.

RP: That's right, in large measure.

MM: I attended four or five meetings at the center. One of the things that I noticed is what I would describe as a "heavy" atmosphere. I would say even acrimonious where anything that was said could and often was questioned as suspect or insulting to someone. Let me give an example of what I am talking about. One time we were discussing I don't know what and one of our female colleagues was making a point. By way of clarification, I said to the group, "What I think she is saying . . ." Abruptly, she interrupted me saying that she did not need anyone to reinterpret what she was saying. That she was clear on what she meant. I have heard countless people in meetings say exactly what I said, and never have I heard anyone come back at someone the way she came back at me. My intent was to support her position. My interpretation of this incident is that there was bad faith among the members of the group.

I also remember an instance when another female colleague said to the group that her interest in interacting with the group was strictly "instrumental." In other words, not as collegial but to serve one's own ends. This happened when you were trying to install the accountability system.

I think that she was basically telling the truth about her view of the world and the view of many of the people involved with the center at the time. "What can it do for me?" was the central question. Another way of putting it is that the center was not viewed as a place that would fulfill the need for community, which all of us have. It again goes back to the issue of legitimacy and the implied notions of authority, function, and membership that the center was designed to provide, but somehow did not. Somehow, Chicanas and Chicanos forgot or never knew about the connection between their jobs and the efforts of the Minority Advisory Council and the twenty-one-point plan, which you helped implement. The loyalty to the center one could have expected simply did not materialize.

It is fundamental to realize that the perspective of the center as "instrumental" flows only one way. While it was viewed as a place to get released time, it was not viewed as a place of protection that demanded loyalty. I think much of this lies with the university officials not acknowledging the contributions of the Chicanos who participated in the creation of the minority infrastructure, weak though it is. Anyhow, the "instrumental" remark told much about our situation.

RP: I remember the incident very well. But recall that the junior faculty also were under tremendous pressures from the departments to essentially sabotage their center connections. How she reacted to these pressures is interesting. For a year or two she tried to deny that she was being pressured by her department. Of course, I knew better. But she kept saying how great she was being treated by her department and so on. In fact, she was under enormous pressure to retrench back into the department. If you watched her behavior closely, at center meetings, when various things were proposed to bring people closer into the center, or to make them more committed and accountable, she resisted them.

For example, in one case she argued that she didn't have to do any Chicano work per se in order to be doing her job at the center. Everything that she did was by definition Chicano. That's because she was a Chicana. What kind of position is that?

From the very beginning, I interpreted this behavior to mean that she wanted to reduce her commitment and accountability to the center so that she could pull back into her department. But she, and others like her, should have been more clearheaded and forthright. She should have come to me and said, "I am being crapped on. I can't survive this arrangement with my department. I need help." Instead, she tried to fake it.

It reminds me a little bit of the analogous critique that has been made of Chicano and Black students. It seems that even though our students have a great deal of academic difficulty, particularly in rough courses like math and science, they won't study together in groups. I certainly didn't participate in study groups when I was an undergraduate or even a graduate student. We all went into our little corners and tried to tough things out. We were Lone Rangers while the Asians were studying in groups all over the place and just tearing up the university. Meanwhile, the Chicanos and the Blacks were dying in their little cubicles.

Something like this happened to the junior professors that we brought into the center. Instead of saying, "This is a crappy life. I'm hurting. Help!" they tried to tough it out. It's as if they were going through a test of their intelligence, and if they were going to fail they wanted to do it alone, away from public scrutiny. They couldn't ask for help.

MM: Part of the issue has to do with pride. We are a very proud people and it is difficult to confront the idea that we are outsiders and that by and large we are not appreciated. With respect to the center, it seems that many of the younger faculty view it as a crash pad; you live there but you put nothing into it.

It is most difficult to build a community within the walls of an impersonal university. I spent a whole year working on the idea of trying to build a campus community. I got the impression that people went along with the idea but that the idea of a collective effort to pull it off was missing. Clearly part of the problem is that the infrastructure to do it is missing. You cannot build community where there is nothing but competition. You cannot build community where you have so many departments competing with one another; where the budget structure actually works against the idea of collaboration. The end result of the so-called campus community is now a bunch of ethnic enclaves, which will probably end up isolated from one another and from the university.

The Importance of Reciprocity

MM: When I first came to ASU, and for many years thereafter, I actively reached out to people. One of the things that always intrigued me was that there were very few instances of reciprocity. I could never figure out why that was so. Why is there no reciprocity on a social level, and little on a professional level?

RP: The academy is a very lonesome place. University life is incredibly isolated. It's essentially a world of ideas, and people are really possessive of their ideas. So they almost don't want to talk about them for fear of losing ownership. Earlier I told you about a book that I want to write. Most professors wouldn't do that. They would figure that you might steal the idea and write a book or article based on it. Partly, it's just the way the university is set up. So people are very possessive about their ideas.

What I just said is also true of Chicano academics, since they must live in the same academic world. But I also think that the chicanada are possessed of a great sense of pride. Remember that we are talking about Chicano professors who are the survivors of a brutal educational system. Perhaps they were an A-plus student throughout their entire lives. They're supposed to be good. They beat tremendous odds in the educational system only to find themselves as professors in a system that is not particularly fair to them. In fact, it is trying to get them. When they understand this and realize that there is a real potential for failure, I think that they become terrified, as most of us would.

That's the way that I saw the situation. So I never became angry at these professors for doing what they were doing. I simply tried to cope with it. I was trying to build a community of scholars, and some of the tendencies that they exhibited would have taken us in the wrong direction.

I don't mean to say that it was just the junior professors who were culpable for not building a better community of scholars. I think that the senior professors were just as culpable. But their culpability lay in a different area. They didn't do enough of what you just said: reaching out. Of course, I am not dismissing the possibility that they might have lost heart if they tried to reach out and were rebuffed. I cannot begin to tell you how many times I tried to reach out to professors of all ranks and how cruelly and insultingly I was sometimes treated in return.

MM: I think that the difficulties are due at least in part to the man/ woman relationships that exist in academia. Chicanos are not immune from the acrimonious environment where more often than not statements about gender get misinterpreted simply because there is a great deal of bad faith. For instance, if you say something that can be misinterpreted often you will be attacked rather than asked what it is that you meant. It has happened to me on several occasions, and the inclination is simply not to say anything or to distance yourself from potentially uncomfortable inter-actions.

There is another important issue to consider: Depending on our circumstances, people have different perspectives on the world. Will Durant, who wrote about philosophers, always argued that an individual's philosophy is determined not only by the times, but by their personal lives as well. In part, this is how he interpreted the somber views of Schopenhauer and Nietzsche. I think that the acrimonious relationships between many Chicano men and women have to do with the negative manner in which women were treated in their homes. It comes out in serious moments of reflection. Furthermore, I have been told by Chicanas that they don't feel that they are included in important decisions; that Chicanos often exclude them and don't take them seriously. If you take such forces into account, it is not difficult to understand the view that women hold toward men. The danger is that some women are so angry that the behavior is generalized toward all men. This is also true of many men. It is something that all of us need to work on.

RP: It's amazing the suspicions that people sometimes have when you reach out. They do not assume that you have lofty motives.

The Lack of Civility

MM: Let me give you another anecdote about the lack of civility. I was at a meeting at the center and there happened to be a pile of sweet bread so I began digging into it. I ate two pieces of bread quickly. One of the professors jumped on me out of nowhere wanting to know how many pieces of bread I had eaten. "How many pieces did you eat?" she says. It's frightening stuff. I said, "Well, I don't know, two." "*Two!*" There's something wrong. I mean with that kind of interaction. It's brutal. I shudder when I think of those interactions.

When I became an assistant professor at U.C. Berkeley, there were only two minority professors, a Black woman and myself. The rest of the professors at Haviland Hall, the School of Social Welfare, were all Jewish, except for one Irishman. We had meetings, sometimes at various homes, and I remember being invited on several occasions to stay for dinner or even to stay overnight when it got late. I lived in San Jose and it was a long drive home. There was a whole different tone to the interactions. I'm not Jewish, but it was clear that I was part of the faculty.

You were treated with such respect and dignity. The cultural revolution was going on, and there were ethnic wars raging, but I'm telling you that those Jewish professors treated me like a colleague. I got used to that. I even got used to being a professor. Then I came here and tried to extend myself and expected that same kind of reciprocity, but it's not there among our people. That kind of, I don't know what it is, grace or openness, that I saw in the Jewish professors.

RP: Some of that grace comes from being in positions of power.

MM: They were assistant professors like me.

RP: Really?

MM: See, these are the guys I used to fight with. They're renown people in the field now.

RP: Part of the turmoil was created by the gender issue. It was very difficult to deal with.

MM: It's still there.

RP: But it's been moderated, partly because of the way things have developed. At a certain point, some individuals wanted to push the gender agenda within the center. But as we have noted, the center's culture was totally individualistic. Thus it was difficult to download onto the center any particular large agenda, including gender. So the attempt to bring in the gender agenda took on a negative aspect. As in any other political or ideological confrontation, it isn't always the guilty who get chastised, sometimes the innocent get chastised as well. Certainly confrontational behavior tends to break down the sense of civility and grace that you're talking about.

The Importance of Chicana Leadership

RP: I felt that I had to deal with the gender situation very cautiously. I didn't want to antagonize a potentially volatile situation. My own assessment was that the gender project was being prosecuted in a very unsophisticated way. This was due largely to the lack of senior leadership among the Chicanas. There were not enough Chicanas experienced in university politics. So from the very early skirmishes I concluded that it was imperative to recruit some senior Chicanas into the faculty. Remember that in the very first draft of the center proposal we had argued for hiring more Chicana professors. At that time there were very few Chicanas in the faculty at any rank. As it turned out, we were the ones who were responsible for actually recruiting the Chicana faculty, and ironically later we were facing the consequences of a gender-sensitized environment.

We were not opposed to the gender project, but there was no sophisticated leadership in the group. That's what led me to the conclusion that as a top priority we needed to recruit senior Chicanas to the faculty. Notice that we did recruit at least two senior Chicanas who became very important in providing leadership for the gender agenda and other important issues of general concern. As a result of these hires, the leadership for the Chicanas changed dramatically. The senior Chicanas brought experience and political sophistication to the university. They're a delight to work with, and their contributions have been very important.

MM: You are correct. This idea of mentoring is a most important element in creating a community of scholars. It seems that in many ways it has eluded our university. I think that it is partly a result of the times where young people don't seem to think that they have much to learn from older folks, and older folks don't seem to see it as their responsibility to help younger folks. We need to examine ways of creating more formal mentoring opportunities. There is another reason for the acrimonious relationship between Chicano men and women, and it goes beyond mentoring. It has to do with what many interpret as the *machista* behavior of Chicano men toward women. It is a most complex issue to understand. It is partly a result of our family backgrounds and women responding to an authoritarian environment. It is also, I think, that many of us simply fail to listen to one another. It has to do with many women doing the work and men taking the credit. I have seen this in many situations. Is the current director having a better time than you did with these kinds of issues?

Future Work

RP: It's hard to say. I don't talk very much with him because I don't want to taint his administration with the old agendas. I'm sure that he has had difficulties with individuals. My guess is that he may have some difficulties with the individualistic dynamics that we talked about. He's an experienced group researcher and needs group research. He probably was surprised when he came to the center and discovered that there was no collective research agenda.

MM: That's why I see the potential merger with the newly proposed Chicano studies department as a very important next step. Otherwise the collective part of the research agenda is doomed. The structural issues need to be addressed. Listening to the discussion on the merger last week made me appreciate the difficulties you have encountered in developing a community of scholars. When the merger was raised as an idea, the first thing out of one of the faculty's mouth was typical of what has occurred: "What's in it for me?"

RP: That's the way that the center faculty have been socialized; that's the culture they've developed.

MM: That's my point.

RP: Now multiply that point of view by twenty or more faculty and you see what you might get into.

MM: It's terribly destructive.

RP: It's a nonstarter for building the Chicano community of scholars.

MM: It's anticommunity.

RP: It is so with respect to the original vision of the center that you and I had. But you and I realized that problem long ago. I remember our conversation because you said that at some point the center would have to go through a winnowing process and eliminate from the center those people who were not really willing to realize the center's loftier purposes. But this is easier said than done. Remember that this is a very democratic community, almost to a fault. The faculty are locked into their individual interests, and they reinforce each other. So the center has not yet been able to go through the winnowing process. Perhaps it will in the future.

Chapter 10

All for Some and Some for All

RP: Today we're going to talk about the Chicano Faculty and Staff Association (CFSA). One of the things that you wanted to discuss is what you call the "rules of engagement," which means how the chicanada and the university actually interact with each other. What are the boundaries for the interaction? What is the context and what are the conditions for the interaction?

MM: The other day I raised this issue with Jack Pfister who served on the Arizona Board of Regents and was instrumental in pushing many of the minority initiatives. Jack was also the CEO for Salt River Project (a major Arizona utility company), and now is a distinguished professor at the School of Public Affairs. His idea of engagement deals with diplomacy: To be effective in an institution, you have to practice what he refers to as "personal diplomacy." His is the view of a power person in the elite class. I don't know if the idea of personal diplomacy applies to our situation. In the aggressive and violent environment in which we live, where the people, including Chicanos as a group, are out of the decision-making process, it is often viewed as a weakness if we act diplomatically.

Some militant minorities don't interact diplomatically, but aggressively and often violently. People who interact in a passive, nonaggressive way are often discounted. In group discussions, it is not uncommon to observe women being discounted, unless they get aggressive, unless they start yelling.

The other day I was talking to my daughter about a class she took in high school, which happens to be a Jesuit school. She mentioned that it didn't take long to realize that not only did she have to stand up, but that she had to yell for the boys to take into account the three girls in the class. I don't think that Jack's "personal diplomacy" is applicable to individuals who are viewed as members of a group without power. The basic issue has to do with the fact that many university officials, including faculty, view us not as individuals, but as part of a group, and we, in turn, often acquiesce to this view of ourselves.

How does the university view us? How do we view ourselves? What are the results of our mutual interactions? This is what I mean by the rules of engagement, including the fact that we're viewed in the context of a powerless group.

RP: Let's go back to what Jack said about personal diplomacy. Certainly one can ask why it is that we need an organization such as the Chicano Faculty and Staff Association and similar groups. Wouldn't developing the skills of personal diplomacy be a better alternative, given the way things function in the university? Wouldn't we be better off following a diplomatic line of action and simply create mechanisms to make sure that all of us develop to the maximum the skills of personal diplomacy?

Clearly, historically we have not done that. So one has to wonder what drives us away from the model of personal diplomacy and into something that we call the Chicano Faculty and Staff Association. Here a couple of points seem important to me. For one, some Chicanos in fact do exactly what Jack advocates. They develop personal diplomacy and stay outside of group action so that their influence in the university is based strictly on personal action.

MM: Which is what most faculty do. It is individual action, but it may or may not be diplomatic. You have to learn how to act diplomatically. If you were raised in a lower-class home, and by this I don't necessarily mean poor, or in a community where people don't have respect for one another you will not know how to act diplomatically. You have to be around people like Jack to understand what it means to be diplomatic. Individually it never hurts to treat people with civility. I think many of our Chicano colleagues, although they were quite poor, were raised to behave in a civil and diplomatic fashion. Others, however, don't know the first thing about being diplomatic, and it shows in the manner in which they behave toward one another.

RP: Personal diplomacy is part of the paradigm of acting individually. What we have through the Chicano Faculty and Staff Association presumably is collective or group diplomacy. Some Chicanos prefer the individual paradigm, and they are put off by groups such as the Chicano Faculty and Staff Association. They try to distance themselves from such groups and their activities.

The second point has more to do with organizational dynamics. The bottom line is that a substantial proportion of Chicanos experience some kind of racism or discrimination on campus because of our ascriptive status as Chicanos. The discrimination may be very subtle or quite overt. Usually it is fairly subtle, say the difference between being a lecturer or a tenure track professor, between making tenure or being knocked out during the fifth-year review, between having a line of research that is respected or one that is viewed as an ethnic thing. There are many other such contrasts that signal to a person that there is an institutional bias. Further, the reaction to that kind of institutional discrimination is not individual diplomacy but group action.

The Ineffectiveness of Individual Action

RP: I'm going to digress here because I want to tell you a story on this very point. As an undergraduate I came to understand for the first time that there are institutional dynamics one must deal with if one wants to take action on certain things that are bothersome about the university. My initial reaction was simply to look at the problematic situation strictly in individualistic terms, as if it were me personally who had to resolve the situation by approaching alone a committee, a department, or even a high-level administrator. It turns out that doing things that way was very difficult. It also took a lot of courage for just one person to face a department, the admissions office, or whatever. The approach was ineffectual because when you presented your views, no matter how rational they were, the organizational structure that was being confronted had ways of deflecting my complaints by providing rational counterarguments. So working as a single person, no matter how just the cause or eloquent the arguments, produced very little in return. In other words, I didn't understand yet about politics, or that the issues I was dealing with were political in character, rather than simply rational or personal. I was personally trying to change organizations.

The insight that I gained from this early experience is that I had to organize. Chicanos have to approach the institutional power centers, not as individuals, but as a group, even if the group is not very substantial and largely a fiction. Instead of taking personal action to redress some particular problem, it was far better for me to organize four or five of us, give ourselves a group name, then make demands of some university administrator. I could then approach the university as a chairperson or as the spokesperson for the group. That was much more effective.

MM: I think we should clarify one point: even though one needs to pursue collective political action, it does not preclude acting diplomatically. At that time, it may have been so. You may have been the originator of the strategy of confronting university officials in the name of the "community" or as the spokesman for it.

RP: That tactic came later. The first steps were taken by us who were already in the university, mostly as students. For example, the first thing I ever organized, with help from another student, was six undergraduate students at the University of Michigan. Nobody knew that there were only six Chicanos at Michigan. And I don't think that the university would have admitted publicly that they enrolled only six Chicano students. So in a sense we all created a fiction. The six of us met as a new organization called Chicanos at Michigan. It was then that I quit acting alone. I quit trying to develop a personal diplomacy and instead tried to develop group diplomacy. After we had created the organization it was Chicanos at Michigan rather than me alone that took on the Spanish department to demand that they teach courses relevant to Chicano Spanish.

MM: "Chicanos at Michigan"! You could have been a bit more creative. When Gutierrez, Rosales, and a bunch of others got together we actually thought of calling ourselves MARY—Mexican American Radical Youth. We changed our minds and called ourselves MASO—Mexican American Student Organization. It was a change from the "Liga Panamericana" of which my wife was the president. This was in the midsixties.

I recall that when I first got to the university as a professor in the midseventies there was a secretary who treated Chicano students with disrespect. Chicano students would go up to her and she would be disdainful of them. She represented the ethos of the place. I got all the minority students together, all twenty-one minority students—Blacks, Chicanos, Indians—and called a meeting with the dean. At that time the university was not accustomed to that stuff. I didn't tell him that I was going to march in with all the students. I was an associate professor; it's not like I was a little kid. So in walk all these students into the dean's office and I simply told him that we were not going to tolerate people from his office disrespecting students. I told him that I knew that he did not believe in this kind of behavior, but that he was responsible for his staff, and that it had to stop. Anyway, there is power in collective action, but it has diminishing returns in terms of your own personal position in an institution. You see what I'm saying? It does not come without a price. In a sense it's low-tech power; it's Mau-Mauing.

Knowledge as Power

MM: If you look at the idea of power as envisioned by people like Alvin Toffler, it is not simply a matter of getting what you want, but of getting other people to agree with what you want. What does it take to really get what you want? At the lowest level it's violent action. This is used by youth gangs in the inner city, by the police, and by militant groups. There is that implied threat of power through violence. The second source of power is wealth. People in power can reward you. A university official can say, "Okay, Padilla, you're giving me trouble. Why don't I promote you? Why don't I give you a higher salary and keep you quiet?" It works quite effectively for most people in most circumstances. We see the City of Phoenix coopted continuously by wealthy people. Their wealth can buy off people or they buy people to buy off people. The third source of power, which can be our salvation, is knowledge.

In a so-called service society, certain kinds of knowledge can influence wealth and neutralize violence against us. We have to think about our situation. We don't have great wealth. We certainly don't exercise violence effectively; even in our Mau-Mauing we're not very effective. So all we're left with is the possibility of influencing knowledge in and through the university.

I don't know to what extent we have been successful at that. My guess is that we haven't really been successful because I think we're in fields that don't exert a lot of power. We're not in computers. We're not in business. We're in education. To what extent have we exerted influence or developed technology in education? In the social sciences it seems that knowledge is not quite as powerful as in other fields in terms of influencing the direction of social policy. There are factors that influence social policy other than knowledge because it's political. You see what I'm saying? How do we assess our collective power as Chicanos.

RP: What you're raising is the problematic situation of the Chicano intellectual. You raise a reasonable hypothesis about where our power may be, where we think it may be, even if we don't see it very clearly. The battles that we've seen in the last twenty-five years are largely based on the premise that knowledge is important to us. Many of the clashes that we have in the university are about knowledge, but not necessarily about technological knowledge.

MM: But isn't technological knowledge the power that counts right now?

RP: Maybe. But it may be so only within a limited temporal framework. What is really important knowledge in the long run? Is it the knowledge that drives technology? Is it the knowledge that drives science as a quest for understanding the material universe? Or is it that the really powerful knowledge is the knowledge that's going to help us as a society to last a thousand years? So it is possible for us to be the creators of knowledge that could enhance society. But that remains to be seen.

MM: I understand what you're saying. I think it's a very important point. One of the things that's clear is that we're not involved, as are the

Jews, with new technologies. Michael Milken, for example, came up with innovative ideas on the use of junk bonds and strategies to capitalize undercapitalized industries. He got caught in other things, but the point is that he was a great visionary. The same is true with people in biotechnology, foodstuffs, and in organizing new ways of delivering new products. It doesn't seem that we're involved in those kinds of endeavors. You now sound like an idealist, like Atencio who is always talking about the *oro del barrio* [the gold of the barrio] — the knowledge we have developed in interacting with one another in ways that prevent violence and that could possibly be applied to the control of nuclear arms. Is that what you're talking about?

RP: It's a possibility because the strength that we bring to academia is a challenge to the materialist mind-set. All the things that you mentioned are what's driving the world in the wrong direction according to many. They entail the voracious consumption of the natural environment, the massification of the human mind, the almost total loss of self-determination by human beings because each of us is just one small statistic in a sea of consumers.

Historically, we have not been a central part of all the things that seem to be going awry; all the things that glitter in the present but that seem to have a short time horizon before they get out of hand. We are not automatically part of that miasma. But it is interesting that we could become a part of that miasma as we enter the universities and the larger opportunity structure becomes available to us. Then we might become no different from the Jews, the Italians, or any other ethnic group. But to the extent that there's anything to being a Chicano, we bring with us another set of ideas, say the Bartolomé de las Casas tradition. While the other academics are conquering the universe we ask, "What about values? What about your soul?" That's a voice that still resonates in us. Not in everyone, of course. But it's the voice that defines the Chicano intellectual presence. This voice startles the campus because it has been driven away from the campus for some time now. But it's a voice that still exists in our community in its native form and that increasingly has no place in the university as an intellectual enterprise.

MM: Our community's knowledge is illegitimate in the academy. It's not systematized, and therein possibly lies one of our intellectual responsibilities: to systematize this knowledge that you say is out there. Wouldn't that be the case?

The Reconstitution of Chicano Knowledge
RP: That approach may have some benefits, but it seems too pedestrian. I see us more as struggling with the reconstitution of our native

knowledge. We must reconstitute our knowledge in the context of designing new forms of social organization that will revitalize the barrios, the rural areas of south Texas and New Mexico, all those locales where the Chicano community has deep roots.

The question is how do we reconstitute native knowledge so that we don't lose the values, the messages, and the voices that have given important meaning to those locales that I mentioned? A key problem is that the miasmic situation in the brave new world that we have entered is so overwhelming, so massive and so powerful, that we may not have a chance to graft onto it those things that might move it in a different direction. That's the nature of the intellectual tension with which we grapple. That's what drives much of our work and that creates many of our contradictions, schisms, arguments, and other weird things among ourselves and with the other people around us.

The reconstitution of native knowledge cannot possibly be accomplished in one generation. We simply don't know how to do it; we don't know what the answers are. In fact, collectively we haven't even begun to dialogue in a serious way about the issues. We need to begin by saying, "Here is where we are, and here are the issues."

So far we have only some intuitive understandings about the situation. As virtually the first generation of Chicanos in academia, we're still close enough to the community to recognize the ideas and values that are important to it and to us, but that community is rapidly receding into the horizon. At the same time, we can see where we are and what we're heading into. We are so positioned that we still have sight of both horizons, the past and the future. So that we at least wonder, wouldn't there be some value in bringing forward with us some of our past that is not so bad?

MM: But the new technology is not necessarily against those kinds of values. The new technology is not necessarily destructive to our particular form of life. As a matter of fact it could actually enhance the forms of life that we advocate. A tolerance for diversity for example, fits perfectly with the changes occurring in the information age.

RP: There is a great dilemma with all the current technologies. On the one hand we hear a great deal of rhetoric about how technology can be used to, shall we say, humanize life. On the other hand, that technological power seems to be constantly coopted by the controlling sectors of society who seem bent on pursuing dehumanizing tendencies. For example, look at the reaction of the right wing with respect to health care reform and similar social issues. Their opposition is framed in the rhetoric of "empowerment" of people, which was first coined by the leftists. Thus, the right wing appropriates the rhetoric of the Left in support of a conservative or even reactionary agenda. It wouldn't surprise me if I soon ran into the ideas of

Paulo Freire repackaged by the Right in pursuit of conservative agendas. My point is that words have very little meaning today. Words are all over the place. We are being bombarded with words, constantly and from every direction, by the media. So it doesn't even take much effort to put words together that imply a humanizing purpose to technology. We must somehow look deeper than the words if we are to discern the true possibilities for technology.

MM: I think, however, that it would be more appropriate to couch this issue not in terms of technology alone, but in the context of a new civilization, that is, the shift from an industrial age to an information age. The factory model based on rigid hierarchies, massified approaches that treat all individuals alike, and slow responding vertical structures no longer seem to apply. It is possible that there is knowledge within our communities that can be used to adapt to this new civilization. It is imperative that we attend to these issues.

The Power to Communicate

MM: But don't you appreciate the great power of the conservative capitalists? The insurance companies, for example, can actually get people to believe that there's something wrong with universal health coverage. So people come to believe that they will be ripped off by universal health coverage and that the enemies of society are the people on welfare. You have to be aware of that kind of awesome power.

RP: Their awesome power comes in part from their ability to get a message out to millions of people.

MM: And we're not getting any message out. We have no vehicles to get our message out or to counter other people's messages. There's no Chicano voice in this country. Ours is a very weak message, and often distorted.

RP: I agree to some extent. But don't forget that the Spanish-language media, such as television and radio, also have tremendous influence in this country. There's a lot of power in Spanish-language radio and TV. People sometimes forget how powerful those media can be. Then, of course, there's the potential of satellite and cable. I was in Detroit recently visiting relatives and when I walked in the door of their house, the radio was blaring the latest Chicano music. They have cable radio and apparently there are several stations on cable radio that broadcast entirely in Spanish. One can subscribe to these services in just about any major city in the country. So who knows how the technology will go.

But your essential point is well taken. Because Spanish-language media are just as centralized and narrow, in terms of perspective, as any other media. They don't necessarily promote the kinds of values or dialogue that we're talking about. Going beyond all that, we have to look at the situation realistically and simply acknowledge that indeed we don't control a significant spectrum of the airwaves or other mass media.

On the other hand, I think that maybe that's to our advantage. Many of the things that we lack can be advantages because if we had them they would simply be like veils in front of our eyes, and we would not be able to see our choices as clearly as we can now. Would it really do us any good to get our fifteen minutes of time on the afternoon talk shows and spout some inanities? The powerful ideas that we now understand and feel would become just so many disembodied words floating in space, which has become the word junkyard of the information society. Our words would not have the impact that's required to explain or to confront our situation. The words would not be able to convey the struggles with which we contend in our everyday lives.

Communicating through Action

RP: What we need is a more powerful way of communicating. I mean that we have to go beyond words and communicate directly through action. The proper reaction to the useless verbalism of our society is what Atencio has termed a "consciousness of action" and action itself. Our behavior must follow certain patterns so that one is defined not so much by what one says but by what one does. In Anglo society, the value of the word, particularly the spoken word, has been almost totally lost. In Anglo society, spoken words are used like perfume, which casts out scents and odors in order to snare somebody's nose. Marketers use words in the same way to snare your senses and get you to buy something. Afternoon talk shows use words to snare your sensibilities and as chewing gum for the mind. We cannot follow that path.

MM: But we're as vulnerable as any other consumer to that kind of propaganda. As a matter of fact, we may be more vulnerable because we may be less critical of our situation.

RP: We are at least as vulnerable as any other group. Moreover, it's a worldwide phenomenon. Pretty soon someone will be able to locate you anywhere on the globe. That says something about how things are moving. And it's all connected to the view that you and I are buyers and consumers. So sellers need to get to you and me to get us to buy their products.

Then there is the view that it doesn't matter what people say, that words don't count, and that they don't have serious meanings. If that's true, if in fact words have lost their primeval power to convey a sense of life and possibility, then they are left merely with the power to orient you in the direction of what to eat and drink and wear, including underwear, or of things that prevent you from dirtying your underwear. If we're going to get beyond that impoverished view of words, then we need to get beyond words themselves. So that's why I advocate for action, even if it is only resistance to the hegemony of disembodied words.

But we need to develop grander strategies so that people can use action in positive ways also. I don't think that we are at that point yet because we have not been able to think clearly through our situation. Perhaps the Chicano *movimiento* was our first ingenious invention that allowed us to express through action what we were about. When we look back at the *movimiento* we see an incredible multiplicity of positive acts. There was tremendous effervescence in the production of art, theater, literature, and so on, along with an enormous amount of social activism. That's what results when our behavior is driven by positive actions rather than mere verbalism.

A Legacy of Hierarchy

RP: Let's go back to the topic of our earlier conversation when we were discussing the contrast between individual diplomatic action and collective action. I told you the story of how I started out by approaching institutional problems as an individual and the lessons that I learned. One of the big insights that I had at the time was that I had been socialized as a Mexican. That is, traditionally in Mexico personal diplomacy tends to produce better results than group action. I reached this conclusion because it wasn't just me who was behaving individualistically. I observed that the chicanada in general tended to act individually. That's one reason why César Chávez was having such a hard time organizing farmworkers. The farmworkers were not accustomed to using collective action to redress their grievances. Of course, from my present perspective, I am not discounting the possibility that I was simply inexperienced in dealing with institutions.

MM: That observation has to be placed in the context of the social structure in Mexico. Mexico has had a hierarchical social structure. Our families too are organized in that hierarchic fashion. So if you're a farmworker or peon in Mexico, you're not accustomed to collective action. You're accustomed to taking orders. That doesn't mean that there haven't been revolts here and there, as in Chiapas. But fundamentally people act within the patrón system, what they call *personalismo*, and Chávez was up against those kinds of psychological barriers.

RP: Perhaps, as Freire might say, we all introjected those social arrangements to some degree. But it didn't take long for many of us to realize that we had to change. I learned my lessons about social action at a very young age, perhaps when I was only twenty-one or twenty-two years old. The main insight was that you don't approach institutions individually; we had to act collectively. However, that insight also opened up a whole new can of worms. It was far easier for me to determine individually what the problems were, and what strategies might work, and to employ my personal skills to resolve them. I could use my personal assets, including personal diplomacy, to try to win.

Working collectively opened up a new social space in which many things became problematic that before had been very straightforward when I was acting individually. For example, simply getting together a group agenda and executing it was far more difficult than I had imagined. Nevertheless, what I'm saying is that as a general principle the logical response by us to institutional problems was group action. So in a sense our environment dictated the direction in which we had to develop and direct our action. This resulted in a move away from individual action and toward group action. That's what accounts for the creation of organizations such as the Chicano Faculty and Staff Association.

MM: One of the common problems with groups is that individuals may try to pursue their own agendas at the expense of the group. Such individuals, for example, may maneuver to meet individually with the university president or vice president to promote a personal agenda. Sometimes the personal agenda is in contradiction to the group agenda. That's what makes possible the cooptation of the group. One of the things that I learned early on in Berkeley was never to go alone to a meeting with a university official because it's too seductive. You can get seduced, even if you're not crooked. By meeting with officials as a group, you learn how to structure a situation so you're forced to work in the context of the group and to avoid the seduction of personal agendas.

The Effectiveness of Volunteer Groups

RP: You're now raising a broad issue related to groups such as the Chicano Faculty and Staff Association, namely how effective are they? Which behaviors make the organization either effective or ineffective?

As I mentioned in one of our earlier conversations, when I first came to the university I had already been an activist in academia for many years. Based on that experience, I had learned the group analog of what Jack called personal diplomacy, which largely pertains to individuals. What Jack was really telling you when he mentioned personal diplomacy is that in order to be effective in an organization an individual must act rationally. One has to follow protocol, be orderly, and know the appropriate politics. In other words, there is a framework of rationality to behaving properly in any organization. I discovered that there were similar considerations that applied to group action.

MM: Before you go on, let me make one point about personal diplomacy. An official in the university only has the power that is given by superiors, that is, delegated authority. With delegated authority you can exercise power in the name of the people above you or in the name of the people in power. Remember, we as Chicanos are not usually part of the framework of power; we operate in contradiction to the people in power. Personal diplomacy and getting ahead means eventually operating from the top. Operating from the top is always to the disadvantage of the people at the bottom. And we are usually the people at the bottom. So the dilemma is that if you use personal diplomacy to get ahead and exercise power, it will most likely be done at the expense of the people without power. It's a very interesting contradiction in terms of personally getting ahead while at the same time pushing the group agenda in a certain direction.

RP: What I'm saying is that there is a group analog to the notion of personal diplomacy. The group must work within a framework of rationality, not only in terms of the rules of the game, but more specifically from the point of view of tactical and strategic actions. Although we learned quickly that group action was more effective than personal action when confronting institutions, it was far more difficult to master the art of developing effective group tactics and strategies. One of the problems is that we started by following the Black model of social action that came out of the civil rights struggle. So this power that you were talking about earlier that comes out of the sheer threat of violence, for example, didn't seem to work as well for us.

MM: The initial phases of the civil rights movement were based on nonviolent coalition tactics between Blacks and Jews and young people. It later emerged into a Black concern. What happened also is that the movement expanded to address the concerns of women, Hispanics, Asians, and most recently gays. Each group went its own way, and although there are common concerns, my feeling is that by and large it is not a cohesive movement. The groups operate at cross purposes, and rarely address a common negative force. My point is that the Black civil rights movement has dramatically changed from nonviolent coalitions to aggressive and often violent noncoalition confrontations with other groups. The threat of violence to a great extent is the power of the civil rights movement. This threat is a great divisive force in our society. We need to recognize, however, that it was the Black civil rights movement that got other groups involved in the civil rights struggle.

When you talk of social action, however, the element of rationality does not seem to hold even in the university. The idea of social action implies making your case to those in power, or even to those who oppose you, and they are willing to listen to your point of view and take it into consideration in their decisions. Certainly, this should be the case in the university where there is an appearance of deliberation and where suppos-edly anyone who wants to can be heard. This is the appearance that we try to portray.

But it's an illusion. We mistakenly think that rationality and civility are values that at least in part determine how people operate. In the past few years I have witnessed an increasingly less rational and ever more uncivil environment. Let me tell you about a recent incident in one of the departments that will illustrate what I mean.

In this department, a small group of faculty members not in tune with the decision that a search committee was about to make about the appoint-ment of the department chair decided to exercise their brand of "personal diplomacy." One of the faculty members wrote a memo charging "racism and sexism" against the White members of the search committee. He referred to them as a White clique or some such term. He claimed that this group had once again denied women and minorities, surely referring to himself, the opportunity of even applying for the position. He directly charged the chairman of the committee with racism, and, what is worse, accused him of conspiring with the faculty member who was about to be nominated for a promotion in exchange for the nomination.

Obviously everyone got into the mix. The university conducted a formal investigation, and as far as I know nothing became of it. What is interesting, however, is that once a neutral person was appointed as department chair, the individual who made the racism charge was pro-moted and awarded some type of administrative assignment. The appoint-ment was made by the new department chair. Others who were involved in making the racism charges also were rewarded.

The departmental faculty, however, voted for the faculty's promo-tion, and continued business as usual. Unfortunately, the person who was charged with racism, and the specific charge of making a deal, which at least constitutes unethical behavior, to my knowledge was never charged or exonerated.

Now we all know that there is a great deal of discrimination in many departments of the university. What is interesting is how departments buy off outlaw faculty members whom they fear will charge racism or sexism, and how once these people get bought off somehow the issue of racism or sexism no longer seems to exist. I should point out that the departmental faculty voiced their opposition to the promotion but by and large the faculty took no direct action either to charge the committee chair with racism and conspiracy or to exonerate him and prevent attacks on other faculty members. "As long as it doesn't apply to me, it is not happening," seems to be the motto of the day.

It is obvious that personal diplomacy was not operating in this instance, nor was there more rationality in the process. It was brutal force, fear, and administrators who were willing to let the incident blow by. The critical issue for me is that the departmental faculty let the chair of the committee and the faculty member who was alleged to have made the deal simply live with that dishonor. It was a serious charge but nothing happened. The man who had been dishonored was left alone. As far as I can tell, people are now operating as if nothing happened. The new department chair seems to be pursuing a strategy of giving the most outrageous individuals whatever they want. Earlier you talked about the bidding for power and control within certain boundaries. In the case of the department I am talking about, although the boundaries were transgressed, nothing was done. The behavior is that of irrational children who have no idea of personal diplomacy or civility in dealing with one another. These people created an environment where anything goes. I heard of people posting notes demeaning one another, of attacks where there was physical contact, of verbal brutality against secretaries, of sexual harassment. Yet nothing happened and one must ask why. This hardly seems like a rational place. It is administration by noninterference.

There is no direction other than personal advantage. There is no ethical stance. Now, where is the personal diplomacy in this type of behavior? Where is the rationality? What are the rules of engagement? It would seem to me that it would be very difficult to compete in this type of environment. The personal costs to the losers and the university are quite high and have impact on all of us. Perhaps the victors in these battles prove their will, but I think that this is not the type of politics that we should be involved in. It is a test of wills without compassion, civility, or love.

The Limits of Confrontation

RP: Remember that when Chicanos first came to the universities in significant numbers during the late sixties, the Black civil rights movement was already in transition from an ideology of pacifism to the more militant stance of Malcolm X and others. At the same time, there were uprisings in the cities, and more generally a culture of violence was becoming evident in the society as a whole.

MM: It started to happened while Martin Luther King, Jr., was still alive. When King started organizing in the North, the young Black groups there went against him because they thought that he was selling out. People try to forget that now, but Martin Luther King, Jr., was in a lot of turmoil because the groups in the North did not want to follow the strategy of coalition building and nonviolence. That's when the Blacks and the Jews started to fall apart. The Jewish community is now more to the right on civil rights issues. It is referred to as the neoconservatives.

RP: As Chicanos finally began to arrive at the campus gates, Martin Luther King, Jr., was assassinated and the Black civil rights movement started to turn violent. So our initial group actions were influenced by the environment around us. Moreover, it appeared at the time that the universities were responding to certain kinds of confrontational tactics that were used by Blacks and us as well. But the universities were quick to develop strong defenses against those kinds of tactics. So by the early eighties I was keenly aware that we were not going to go much further in solving our problems without radically rethinking how we were engaging social institutions.

That's when I seriously proposed what we might call group diplomacy. Our actions had to be expressed within some framework of rationality and sensitivity toward institutional processes. In the end, it all boiled down to our developing a group plan of action. When completed, the action plan was written, and rational, and it had the support of the group. In other words, the action plan was legitimate because it was fashioned through a political process.

When you look at those three characteristics of the action plan, you can see that we had reached a turning point. Earlier plans, such as *El Plan de Santa Bárbara*, which also was written as a rationalist document, have a more spontaneous quality to them, something akin to a theatrical production. They include much emotional venting. Remember your story of how some of you in social work confronted federal officials by showing them the picture of a gagged person? Earlier plans have that quality to them, which I thought was no longer functional.

Instead I advocated a more rational approach that included group planning, clarification of what we really wanted to achieve, and the designation of spokespersons who would negotiate with university officials. This approach was based on my understanding of interest groups as the key ingredient that drives the political process in the United States. American politics is driven by interest groups because that's what carries voting clout. Don't forget that the idea of voting is what subtends all the machinery of American politics. If you have ten votes and somebody else has only one vote, that puts you in a greater position of political power. A politician will pay far more attention to ten votes than to one vote. That is the fundamental practical rationality of our political system.

The Politics of Justification

RP: We as Chicanos didn't understand that basic point well enough in the early days. That's because we had come from a tradition where there was no effective suffrage so that it didn't matter how many votes you had. If you had 100 votes, the ruling party would have 101. If you had 1,000 votes, it had 1,001 votes. So you could never win with votes. What I mean is that in our political legacy there was a different way of exerting political power and influence.

So we had to transcend that legacy. We came to understand that it took collective action. But even then we did not know how to develop and undertake effective action. We did not understand in particular what society construed as legitimate action. We did not understand the distinction between official and unofficial actions or the nature of the bureaucratic organizations with which we had to deal. In short, we did not know how to justify ourselves, our actions, or our cause. That's because in the system with which we were most familiar there was no need to justify actions. All that was needed was to have the power to carry them out. If someone in power wanted something from the system, they simply took it. There was no accounting for it; no reason or justification had to be given.

The point is that the American political system is not organized that way. It is premised on the view that public actions must be justified in a public arena. Therefore, people in power have to account for and rationalize their actions. Thus, they at least have to make arguments in favor of the actions that they seek. In our case, we had no mechanisms to provide arguments to those people in power positions who could take action to benefit us. So we could not effectively orchestrate support for our agendas or demonstrate that we had political clout.

I saw all that as a serious problem. So my strategy was to develop in the group the social and political skills needed to take effective group action. We needed to reinvent our political techniques. We needed to master the new political rationality and to behave in a manner that was considered legitimate by those who might oppose us as well as by those who were our allies. Otherwise, our opposition would have no way of dealing with us. That is, we would have a fundamental lack of diplomacy, which would render us unable to communicate or deal with the society around us.

MM: We could not really be clear about what we wanted or we would ask for things in such an obtuse manner that practical people, those who are in power, were unable to respond to our concerns. It goes back to Barr's question about what it was that we wanted. When we told him that we wanted justice, he responded that he did not deal in justice, but he did deal in helping people get what they wanted. One needs a certain amount of practicality in approaching institutions; one has to make demands on which the institutions can deliver. Therein lies a little bit of conflict. The people who get the goodies are more often than not the people who do the advocating, and not necessarily those who need help the most.

Shaping a Group Agenda

RP: You have raised an important issue. How does the group's agenda get shaped? I have already suggested that group action involves a political process. It should also be a democratic process so that the group's behavior will be consistent with the larger social ideology. This way the group's behavior will already have one kind of legitimacy, i.e., ideological consistency with the larger society.

However, group agenda setting also requires able leadership, something that is incredibly difficult to find or even to cultivate. After many years of working with group action, I have concluded that the efficacy of group action is highly dependent upon leadership. I have always seen us as a people with high energy and high talent but we have had difficulty identifying and nurturing the kind of leadership that is needed for effective group action. With effective leadership everything seems to fall into place. Absent leadership, the entire paradigm of group action seems worthless to me. I mean, at best, leaderless group action is reduced to minor bureaucratic tinkering in a Kafkian kind of world.

MM: In the university there are only certain people who can exert leadership. In part it has to do with the circumstances surrounding people's lives. For example, it is more difficult for an assistant professor without tenure, or a staff person in student affairs, to exert leadership than a professor with tenure. Only certain people with the right set of circumstances and who have courage are able to push an agenda.

RP: Ten or twelve years ago we did not have those kinds of leadership resources in abundance. We had few senior faculty. So that was one of our problems. Another problem is that in the university as a whole, few people exert leadership. The university is a bureaucratic organization so that the exercise of leadership is constrained. You have to look in the highest levels of the organization before you can see leadership being exerted. And sometimes leadership is not exerted even there. That probably explains why when we finally got a group agenda going, we had to deal with the university president, rather than some pompous assistant dean or even dean who is looking after the next administrative job. But dealing directly with the president or the provost leads to weird distortions in terms of organizational dynamics, because normally you don't see an associate professor dealing directly with the president.

At any rate, over the years I became acutely conscious of the need to create leadership from the bottom up. So at the university my project was to stimulate the creation of leadership with and through the Chicano Faculty and Staff Association and through any other means that were available to me. It's as simple as that. I took this to be a five- to ten-year effort. I gave priority to leadership development because without it there was little hope of getting anything done as a group.

As far as I am concerned, you can hardly ever have too much good leadership. Yet leadership is such a difficult thing to define, to cultivate, and to exercise. But you need it if group action is to be effective. Leadership acts almost like an invisible ingredient that is required for successful group action. You can tell when you have proper leadership, and you can tell when you don't have it, but it is difficult to know how to get it. With good leadership you do not have to worry about establishing an agenda because effective leadership will create the right agenda for and with the group.

MM: In our discussion of university politics thus far, we make the assumption that institutions like the university are both rational and benevolent. We have cited many instances where clearly this is not the case. It seems to me that administrators and others in positions of power dissimulate when it comes to the power relationships between minorities and those in power and among minorities themselves as they pursue their self-interests. Administrators say, "If we do this for one group we will be expected to do it for all groups." This argument is used as a rationale for inaction, as a way to create a wedge between groups, and most importantly when efforts to serve one group are needed and legitimate, but there is an unwillingness to act for one reason or another. Minorities themselves interpret these efforts as favoritism. It is always a zero-sum game and always pits one group against another. Rarely do minorities consider the redistribution of existing resources as an option. This is why the strategy of the sixties seemed to work—it was a continuously expanding purse, and there seemingly was an ever-expanding economy. Institutional expansion became profitable for all—minorities, women, and the elite. The issue of minorities is approached primarily from a political perspective rather than from a sense of justice. The basic theme of university politics for administrators and professors alike is to view issues in terms of how they affect them as individuals and not on the impact that such issues have on other individuals or the institution. Often, the political pressures on administrators and on the institution are so intense that contradictory policies are allowed in the interest of maintaining "peace."

The Development of Leadership
RP: How does one go about creating scenarios in which the essential thing is to encourage and foster leadership? How does one develop the infrastructure of leadership? Along the way I learned that the best way to develop leadership is to put people in leadership positions. So you create leaders out of individuals by testing their leadership qualities. To do so you place them in leadership roles, even if the people are inexperienced, and then you help them to be successful. The last part is very important. Because if you put people in leadership roles and they founder and drown, you've lost it all and nothing is gained. So you must help them to experi-

ence success. Once they first experience success, and continue to do so, they get stronger and stronger and their leadership skills keep rising.

Organizations such as the CFSA provide opportunities to develop leadership. But because they are voluntary groups they are also very unstable. Moreover, nobody really wants to be at the head of the line in such a group. That's because in the dynamics of politics, the person at the head of the line is also a target. This may account for your observation that the ones who get the goodies are the ones who advocate. You see, they are also the targets, the ones who are willing to take the risks and also to exercise leadership.

So in order to create leadership, you have to overcome people's resistance to being at the head of the line. I also had to overcome the group's tendency to want to put me at the head of the line. Were I to place myself at the head of the line, I would be contradicting the most basic premise on leadership development that I am following: To put people in leadership positions in order to help them to develop higher leadership skills. It turns out also that leadership consumes everything. It is very difficult for a true leader to develop leadership in others and also to take the reins of leadership at the same time. Ask yourself, who followed Gandhi? Who followed Stalin? Whether you agree with them or not, these are examples of great leaders. It's very hard for great leaders to develop other great leaders because leadership consumes all the space around it. I understood that so the worst mistake for me with respect to my project of leadership development would have been to fill the space at the head of the line. If I had occupied the head of the line consistently, I might have developed great leadership skills myself, but I would have consumed all the leadership space around me and I would not have been able to develop leadership in others. So I would not have eased the scarcity of leadership for our cause.

MM: Maybe it would have been a more effective strategy if you had assumed the leadership positions. I have thought about that a lot.

RP: Success would have depended on having well-disciplined groups.

MM: Or if you have groups that you can control. You can only control people if you have power that goes beyond charisma.

RP: There's little or no real power in volunteer groups.

MM: That is the dilemma of leadership in such groups.

RP: Also, these groups typically are very undisciplined.

MM: Because they don't have formal structure and you can't control them through the usual means: incentives of money and status being the most obvious control mechanisms.

RP: And because you have little or no coercive power. Moreover, even if you have charisma, no one knows what is going on. Plus there is little or no wealth to spread around.

MM: Rarely is there any benefit. And altruism in a setting like the university goes against the existing university paradigm that is based on individualism, rationality, and the market.

RP: At the same time, there are any number of Chicano players who try to use the group as a vehicle to process their personal or small group agendas. That can create a tremendous amount of turmoil. That is one example of lack of discipline. Yet, it is within this chaos that one must try to develop leadership. So it can be quite a challenge.

MM: There are also legitimately contradictory agendas. What is good for the staff may not be good for the faculty and vice versa. What is good for assistant professors may not be good for the tenured professors. Take the distribution of merit money. If you make $70,000 a year as a full professor and an assistant professor makes $30,000, the university decides that the merit money will be distributed on a percentage basis. There is a significant difference between five percent of $70,000 and 5 percent of $30,000.

So circumstances can lead to legitimately different interests. Typically there are conflicts between the interests of the group versus the interests of the individual. Also, agendas can be legitimately different or it may be simply that there is only so much attention that can be given to anything. Therein lies the idea of agenda setting. Whose problems are going to receive attention first? Whose interests will be given attention at all?

The Dilemma of Leadership

RP: For me it was important to place individuals in positions of leadership because they needed to experience personally the dilemmas of leadership. One cannot experience the dilemmas of leadership without exercising leadership. One has to learn to make decisions and to handle the consequences, which can range from encomiums to having people throw stones at you. When people experience the exercise of leadership, it is very good for the group as a whole. Because when people step down from leadership responsibilities, they are better people for it. They are more disciplined in their group participation. Learning to become a leader also can help you to become a better follower when someone else is in charge.

MM: Because you are much more sympathetic. In other words, if you look at the people who are most critical they tend to be the people who never really assumed leadership or responsibilities. The more responsibilities you assume, the more appreciative you are of people who are in leadership positions.

RP: Leadership experiences also provide the opportunity to develop technical skills. For example, one discovers that there are generic problems related to group dynamics that have generic solutions.

MM: There are lots of little things that people don't think about, such as handling the group, meeting with officials, getting people to work on certain projects, and getting people to work together who have certain kinds of personality conflicts.

RP: Most people don't have structuring skills such as putting things in writing so that there is a history to the group and so that things can move rationally. The need for these skills is not very apparent to people who haven't had to exercise leadership.

So as I engaged my leadership development project, I used my energy to make sure that an organization such as CFSA would not go under as a result of the sheer chaos and conflict that is going on all the time. All along we would encourage people to take leadership roles in the group to gain experience and thereby become inoculated against many of the problems confronting such organizations. Moreover, we would be increasing the pool of leadership.

This also allowed me to share the many technical skills that I have acquired in the area of group action. In other words, I tried to create a "no-fail system" where people could have positive experiences in the exercise of leadership. That is very important. I wanted people to get to the head of the line and experience the thrill of success at getting something done as a group.

You have to remember, and this is very serious, that most people fail at getting what they want, whether they approach things individually or as a group. That's very important to understand. Most voluntary groups, because of the problems that we just talked about, are bound to experience failure because just about everything is stacked against their succeeding. Merely getting a group going, let alone doing something substantive with it, is quite challenging. When they do try something, they will probably not succeed. Once failure is experienced two or three times, taking further action becomes aversive. When failures build on each other, they kill the possibility for effective group action.

So besides promoting leadership development, rationality, and strategizing, I tried to get the group to learn that you focus your energy narrowly, what one of my old bosses called the difference between taking rifle shots and shotgunning. He was a man who believed in rifle shots. Many times all that people want to do is fire shotgun blasts all over the place to try to influence organizational processes when what is required is to take one or a few rifle shots. You shoot at one target at a time and use as little ammunition as possible.

While this may seem very pedestrian, almost as if we are missing the boat, it is actually quite crucial. You see, when a group comes together, many problems are put on the table. And it is very hard to make any sense out of the vast array of problems. So when someone says, "Let's do X," I try to make sure that X is a very significant little piece to a much larger strategic problem. So that when you take on problem X and then problems Y and Z, they build on each other and coherently address a much larger problem. At the same time, by taking on smaller problems, you maximize the chances of success. When you experience success in dealing with problem X, then problems Y and Z, pretty soon other people, including the opposition, start looking at you as a successful group, as a group that can do things. That kind of experience begins to build confidence in the group and its members.

Sometimes success can be as simple as getting the group to meet regularly. It is important to get someone to exert leadership, to pound the gavel and get things moving. Having the group experience success was a very important part of my strategy. Only by experiencing success will a group be willing to continue to act.

Chaos and the Uncontrollable

RP: So how did my leadership project turn out? That's an important question. One of the things that I learned over the years is that group processes are not really controllable. Who actually gets to the head of the line is critical for the group. Yet, there is really no rational process to determine who's going to head the group.

MM: It's a political and more or less democratic process. Sometimes there are elections and sometimes not because only one person is willing to take the leadership. Sometimes the president of the Chicano Faculty and Staff Association is in such terrible personal circumstances within the university that the president is incapable, even if he or she wanted to, of exerting effective leadership and pushing an agenda. The president is the victim of his or her own circumstances and the group is incapable of helping this person to transcend those circumstances. Then there are other situations when the president hits the ground running and everything converges, including help from legislators. Then many things get done that you never believed could have been done. It's not a rational process. It is political, affected by circumstances, and in many ways haphazard because it's uncontrollable.

RP: It is true that in spite of my efforts to overlay a sustained project of rationality, strategy, and tactics, the process is fundamentally chaotic. Under those circumstances you have to be very patient. You even have to be able to sit out a whole year if you know in the beginning of the year that nothing is going to happen because of who is at the head of the line. You don't let it bother you, or worse yet, call it quits and start another organization. You simply decide that this year you're going to do other things and wait it out. That's one of the important lessons that I have learned. It is also part of being a disciplined member of a group.

MM: But many people do not operate out of that paradigm. They do leave and set up their own groups. Then the various groups conspire against one another. It's all very chaotic.

RP: Some of that does go on, and it can't be helped. You just have to go along with it and whenever possible minimize it.

Revising the Action Plan

RP: One of the important things that came out of all this was that in 1984 we developed the university institutional plan for action. The action plan included twenty-five recommendations to the university from the CFSA. The action plan was prepared in such a way that the university could not just throw it out. In fact, the university reacted to many of the recommendations that we made.

MM: I think that it is important to note that the university responded in a positive fashion to the recommendations. I have mentioned this before. A high percentage of the recommendations had a positive response from the university.

RP: You have noted that. But let me tell you what concerns me about the action plan. The fact of the matter is that I put out those twenty-five recommendations out of my head before the group endorsed them. That's how the plan was created. The plan was part of my strategy to provide support to the group. Further, I was modeling for the group the rational approach as well as the use of strategy and tactics. I don't mean to say that the group just rubber-stamped my work. There was quite a bit of discussion. Nevertheless, I wrote the damn thing from beginning to end and modified it according to the input of the group. But basically it came out of my head. That's the first important point.

Four years later the mood of the group was to revise and update the action plan because obviously things are always changing. All eyes moved toward me to suggest that I revise the action plan. But I just looked right back at them. Remember that all along my project was to develop leadership and promote the rational paradigm. I simply smiled and said that I was not going to do it. Why? Because I expected the group to display some progress. I was not about to spend hours developing a group plan in which the group would play only a reactive role. I had a much better idea.

I said that the revised plan ought not to be as general as the original. If you look at the recommendations, they are very general: recruit more students, more faculty, and so on. These things you could pull out of any old plan that's been around for twenty years. I asked, how many people do we have in the university in faculty or staff positions? I was particularly interested in the staff and administrative positions, which I estimated at fifty to a hundred. I suggested that everyone in a faculty or staff position determine what needed to be done in his or her own position or department to promote the goals that the group was pursuing. What specific projects could be undertaken by each person and his or her department? I asked them to think creatively. They were to assume that they had the power and the money to carry out the projects that they felt were truly needed. In other words, they were to identify the projects that each one of them could undertake if resources were available that would solve the problems we were facing. The projects were to be carried out by the various units in which we had staff and each person would head the projects that they identified. I said that the collection of such projects would become our revised action plan.

Now, that seems to me like a very rational approach. Many of these people had complained bitterly about the many things that the university needed to do but had not done. So I simply suggested that we find out what it was that *we* could do, instead of the university in the abstract. Then we could work collectively to find the resources to do all the things that we wanted to do.

The Importance of Courage and Responsibility

RP: So what was the result? First I modeled the process myself. As director of the Hispanic Research Center I identified a list of projects that I thought the center could undertake. Then I invited everyone else to submit the list of projects that they and their respective units would be willing to undertake. What do you think happened?

MM: I don't know. That was a period in my academic life when I retreated. Over the past twenty years I have come in and out of the fights in the university. I get burned out, I revive and fight, and on it goes. What happened?

RP: Hardly anybody responded. Why? Why was it not possible to use this approach? What was going on? What does this tell us about the real nature of the organization?

MM: You're not talking about the nature of the organization. Now you're talking about the nature of the people in the organization. You did not request that the members do anything on behalf of the organization. You asked them to do something on behalf of themselves relative to their own particular units. This demands a totally different political stance. Remember that most of the people who work in the various university departments are isolated. They might be the only Chicano professor in the department or the only Chicano staff person in a particular unit. You're asking these people to operate in the context of their own units, not in the context of the Chicano Faculty and Staff Association. How are they going to do that? They were put in a very difficult position, one to which they were not accustomed. They have no idea what needs to be done.

RP: They knew what needed to be done because they kept complaining and saying that this or that needed to be done by the university.

MM: The issue is not so much what needs to be done but, more important, how it's to be done. Furthermore, these folks, who may not have had the experience of pushing an agenda, would be reluctant to get burned. You go through a great deal of turmoil when you alert the university to its injustices. It's a wicked process. You were asking these people to go through such turmoil in their units. Isn't this contradictory to your notions of leadership?

RP: No. They were cowards!

MM: Do you accept my observations? Think of what I just said.

RP: Yes, but what I heard you say is that they were cowards. I think most of them were cowards! I was testing their courage. I wanted them to stop the Mau-Mauing, the grandstanding, and the rubber-stamping. I wanted them to show their colors. If they really wanted an effective group, if they really abided by the lofty ideals of the group, why couldn't we become as effective as we could within the positions that we already controlled in the university? Remember that the whole idea was to develop a collective agenda where the group would be used to support individual action. They were not going to go at it alone.

MM: Well, doesn't my response account for this?

RP: You provided a possible rationale, but I'm telling you that they were cowards. Save for one or two, they did not come forward and say, "Look, I'd like to do this or that, but I don't know how to do it. Help me to design a project." No, they knew damn well what they were doing! They did not want to bring the ethnic group agenda that they had talked about and argued for into the formal organization. But, you see, that's exactly what we were all about as a group: Taking our agenda and connecting it to the organization. We had just spent four years trying to connect our agenda to the organization but in a very abstract way. Based on a lesson that I had learned many years before, I simply suggested that we connect to the organization in a concrete way: through each and every position that we already had in the organization.

MM: But I explained to you why that is not going to work.

RP: Why? Because they were not used to it? Because they didn't have the necessary skills? No, they didn't *want* to do it.

MM: My point is that you have been through these things. And you know how it is to get burned. My feeling is that maybe these people tried to connect directly before and they did get burned. Or maybe they didn't know how to do it. Or maybe they didn't want to do it.

RP: They didn't want to do it.

MM: But isn't that basically how everybody operates in the university? Well, there are some people who are astute enough, and who have the courage, to see what needs to be done and to go after it, for whatever reason. I agree with you that courage is a central virtue. It is courage that makes it possible to continue our struggle. It is also courage that gives us and others hope for a better life.

RP: The lack of courage means that most of the time our behavior is connected to a personal agenda. Individuals act because they may gain something personally. But I was not asking my colleagues not to gain something personally. I thought and expected that they would use the opportunity to say something like, "Well, what I need is another $50,000 and two staff positions to be able to recruit more effectively another 2,000 Chicano students." What's wrong with that? In fact, that is exactly the approach that I took in preparing the projects for the center. I said that we needed half a million dollars to set up an endowed chair and that we needed to hire an editor to do a journal. I put down what I thought we could and should do. If everyone else did the same, we would go as a group to the university and ask for the resources that we needed to carry out all of the projects. What was so unnerving about making that kind of a statement and putting a dollar figure to it? What was so difficult about saying it? They wouldn't even have to confront their bosses. We were supposed to be looking at programmatic needs. We were to describe what was programmatically justifiable based on our experience and that was doable within our respective units once we had written it out and estimated the need for resources.

MM: Maybe they didn't want to do it because it's too much work. Possibly they were afraid of doing it. There are many reasons. It also explains why we have been relatively unsuccessful in a lot of our political strategies.

RP: I believe that many of the groups that are successful do exactly what I suggested to the CFSA. Isn't that the ultimate meaning of networking, of group action that is also tied to individual agendas? It's the whole point of democratic politics. You tie your personal agenda to a public vehicle.

This is exactly the lesson that I was trying to get the group to learn as part of the exercise. I wanted them to see that there was an opportunity to take their personal agenda, in the sense that they might get more money, be more effective in their jobs, and so on, and leverage it through group action. But they didn't bite.

They didn't bite because they were cowardly. Cowardly not just in the sense of lack of fortitude, they were cowardly because if they had identified what could be done within their respective units, then they would have been personally accountable for fixing our problems. For me this is the real explanation for their behavior. When you make public what can be done, and if you get the resources to carry it out, then you, not the group or the university, are accountable. You are personally accountable because you came up with the idea, it's in your unit, and you implemented the project.

So my colleagues did not participate in the exercise because they did not want to be held personally accountable. They would rather stay perched high in the organization lamenting the fact that things apparently could not be improved. At the same time they wanted to be in an ethnic organization where they could Mau-Mau and say how badly things were going and how the university or the community wasn't doing anything about it. They were not willing to connect themselves personally to the problems or to take charge personally. They were not even willing to use effective group processes to bring political pressure to bear on the university and get it to respond appropriately to our needs.

So after ten or twelve years of my project to develop leadership, I have learned that what really makes things go is when a human being decides that it's important enough to do something and he or she is willing to say so publicly. And when he or she is willing to take the consequences for that public utterance. There aren't many people in this world who actually behave that way. So maybe that is what leadership is all about. That's why we tried to build the CFSA in the manner that I just described.

MM: I think to some extent what you say is true. It is important to remember that we exist within the university and it is in this fashion that we can understand our behavior. We obviously need to change ourselves but it will demand that we change the outside world, the world of the university as well. What is the ethos of the university environment? First, it is an environment of "entrepreneurs" who, because of their tenured status, do not have to take risks. In other words, they are people who feel that there are no consequences to their behavior so that there are some who violate the best interests of students and the institution. It is an environment where individual rights are paramount at the expense of justice. If, for example, there is unprofessional behavior on the part of faculty members toward one another, there is no way that other faculty members will interfere lest they become the targets. It is an environment where individuals see groups as a means for gaining individual advantages through collective agendas focused on taking the role of victims; and woe to those who dare to criticize any of the many interest groups for they will be accused of being sexist, racist, anti-Semitic, homophobic, ageist, and many other names that deter dialog. The discussions are left to extremists, thus driving underground the hostility among the many fragments that make up the university. Each of these groups believes in equal rights but only when it comes to members of their own group.

Over the years you and I have often talked about courage. I agree with you that courage is a central virtue. It is courage that makes it possible to continue our struggle. It is also courage that gives us and others hope for a better life. But what is courage?

I think that fundamentally courage is what propels human beings to act in a just manner. If we agree that justice is what tempers the extremes of freedom and equality, it is courage that makes it possible to do the right thing in spite of what others may think about our behavior. It is also courage that helps us change our circumstances when we see that we are trapped in situations that are not good for us or for those we love. Just like you "qualify" people, I think that I try to surround myself with people whom I can depend on and who, in turn, can depend on me. To the extent that we allow others to trample on us, or on those who are less fortunate than we are, to that extent we lack courage, and to that extent we lead meaningless lives.

Being a parent is about instilling in your children the idea that they can count on you. It is about protecting your children, and teaching them that they can depend on you under all circumstances. This understanding is what makes them strong human beings, and conversely what makes children weak is our inability to provide an environment where they feel safe.

When I read your book *The Leaning Ivory Tower*, I was struck by the anguish people have experienced trying to survive in the universities. The narratives reminded me of the difficulties Chicanos (and I suspect most academics) have in creating what Becker refers to as a "cultural hero system." It is obvious from reading your book that the university provides few opportunities for many Chicanos to reinforce their self-esteem and self-worth. If anything, the narratives show the lengths to which many academics go to deny others their due. It is as if the "other's" demise promotes their own self-worth. I don't know to what extent Chicanos are different from other academics in this regard. My guess is that we are not much different; that we operate in a similar fashion, but that we are merely unwelcome visitors to the university.

This is perhaps why we seem to lack courage. Why we seem to have an inability to assert our being in spite of what people might think or in spite of how people might want to punish us for claiming our self-worth. I feel that to the extent that we are denied this self-worth and to the extent that we fail to fight for it, we behave as cowards. It is this I believe that explains much of our behavior, for example trying to honor one another with awards that are not necessarily connected to honorable actions. But how do we acquire the courage necessary to promote a just life among one another? I will not pretend to know the answer to this question, but I will tell you that it is not a state of being, but a state of action. It is a continual struggle to remind ourselves and others that we need to act against unjust actions that are perpetrated against us and those around us.

Chapter 11

Epi(dia)logue

Reader Comments

Jaime Chahín: When you reflect on power and the university community, you mention Peter Skerry, but I also would include Robert Caro's *The Path to Power* or Christopher Matthews's *Hard Ball,* which describe how power is used and how coalitions are formed at different levels. To participate effectively in the public debate, we need to understand the systems and the coalitions that we need to cultivate. Janet Hagberg in her book *Real Power, Stages of Personal Power in Organizations* also outlines how we should transform the way we think about power and leadership in public institutions.

Your point about positioning ourselves within institutions to bring about change, rather than challenging them from the outside, is very well taken. However, you still need to have external pressure to ensure that an institution has an opportunity to compare and respond. The institution usually will select the lesser of two evils. Barbara Kellerman Burns in "Leadership: Multidisciplinary Perspectives" outlines the complex exchanges between leaders and followers and the question of causation.

In chapter 3 you provide an excellent analysis of the dynamics and complexities of the search process. This example clearly states that one needs to understand how the system works and the internal and external levers of influence. Your analysis significantly amplifies the booklet on search committees distributed by the American Council on Education.

The analysis of the power profile developed by the authors in several chapters is an example of a sophisticated and experienced administrator who learned from the *pinto* how to operate effectively within an organization. It is quite clear that one needs to understand the historical, psychological, political, philosophical, and organizational perspectives of an institution in order to bring about change. David A. Ramey in "Empowering Leaders" presents the thesis that strategic leadership requires a comprehensive assessment of human and financial resources.

The analysis of the lack of accountability for minority programs in higher education institutions is an example of our marginalized university communities who are by omission or commission excluded in the distribution of institutional resources and power. Effective programs require leadership, accountability, and positioning within the institutional structure. Perhaps the commission's lack of accountability is a reflection of the lack of a comprehensive commitment that results in piecemeal responses to significant institutional problems. The external political pressures that are described are clear examples of the dynamics of change and the complexity of the debate on issues that sometimes require multiple levels of pressure to effectively move an organization. Your analysis demonstrates the need for different levels of political involvement within and outside the university.

Your analysis of change from the bottom up in chapter 6 indicates that despite your organized mission and good intentions, the *group* was not able to significantly affect the distribution of resources. Thus, despite the fact that you engaged a group of Chicanos in a thoughtful, organized, and intellectual process, the results were not spectacular. Perhaps you did raise *conciencia* and fashion a *resolana*, but Alinsky and Cortes talk about change using incremental steps where small battles are the foundation for greater future change. Yet, I have observed that COPS (Communities Organized for Public Service) are effective in San Antonio not only because they are organized and informed, but also because they seize political opportunities when the organization is more susceptible to being tilted toward a more significant level. *Y no le suelten las riendas* (don't give control) as chair of the committee *a alguien* (to someone) who was not involved in the parade. *También, Roma no se conquistó en un día* (Also, Rome wasn't conquered in one day). José Ortega y Gassét in the "Mission of the University" also addresses the issue of what is the knowledge worth knowing and what is the function of the university.

The discussion of minority councils and proportional representation is a key issue. The problem is that most administrators have been socialized along Black and White issues in the development of an institutional strategy. When you include all groups, it is very difficult to achieve consensus when the various groups are at different levels of political involvement and sophistication. In the February 1975 takeover of the University of Michigan administration building, the Third World Coalition once inside the building ended up with five different sets of demands that were accepted by the president. The Chicanos had their own plan, because we never assumed that somebody was going to represent us. Again, politicians or community organizers are not so noble when they have the opportunity to seize the leadership to advocate their agenda. *Tomen los cuernos del toro y no los suelten* (Grab the bull by the horns and don't let go) until you accomplish your objective, but you must stay focused and have continuity.

Intellectual space, the complexities of personality issues, and the community requires finding the common denominator that will unify the collective efforts of everybody. Your analysis of the creation of the research center includes all the potential pitfalls in the development and integration of (ethnic) administrative programs. Your use of the Chicano legislators was paralleled by the administration's use of the same legislators to improve its discourse during the appropriations hearings of the university. It seems that what was a potential problem was used as political leverage with the Chicano legislators. At a major research university in Texas, when the Chicano professors requested additional funding for the Mexican American Studies Center, the funds were deducted from the general appropriations of the university. This has had negative political consequences for the center in the university community.

Your analysis of the selection of faculty for the center in collaboration with other departments substantiates the fact that we are a heterogeneous population with different levels of commitment and understanding of institutional issues. Even so, it is quite clear that the departmental criteria for promotion seem to be the faculty's main agenda and limit the faculty's vision of what they can do collectively or how the research center can be used as a resource for greater benefit. The issue of leadership requires the development of opportunities for both faculty and staff. Whether it's through committee or task force opportunities, the development of leadership skills is critical to the successful implementation of institutional plans. Commitment, courage, and focus are required to exercise leadership; when these are missing it is difficult to become an authentic leader, as Robert W. Terry notes in *Authentic Leadership: Courage in Action*. Furthermore, Charles Handy clearly states in the "Age of Unreason" that change requires courageous action and someone who is willing to think upside down to bring greater accountability; unfortunately, we do more dancing than real change in higher education.

I enjoyed reading your book. I commend you for your thoughtful case study of the dynamics of institutional change in a comprehensive university. It reminded me of the Hasenfeld study, "Human Organizations." I think that your critical analysis of the dynamics of change within an organizational structure will serve to guide other administrators and academicians who want to ensure the intellectual presence and development of Chicanos in the university community. As university scholars, both of you have integrated your personal knowledge, political experience, and organizational insights of the university to develop an excellent analysis of the dynamics of change, empowerment, and leadership.

Adalberto Aguirre: I like the format. It reminds me of Derrick Bell's conversations with Geneva. The use of narrative is an approach employed in critical race theory writings. The format draws the reader into the conversation. On the one hand, it creates a picture for the reader of the issues. On the other hand, it constrains the reader from asking questions that are under the surface.

There are a lot of issues covered in the various chapters. I believe that all of them have come together somehow to shape a context for Chicano faculty. The current criticism of affirmative action, for example, fits into a discussion of how Chicanos have gained from it. Should Chicanos follow the model used by Blacks? What are the costs of affirmative action to Chicanos? These are questions embedded in the conversation.

This leads to the following question: How does ASU compare and/or contrast with higher education institutions in the Southwest? Comparatively speaking, what has happened at ASU probably overshadows any other institution in the Southwest. Look at the fiasco with the Cesar Chávez Center at UCLA, the disestablishment of Chicano studies at UCSD, and so on. For what it's worth, the Hispanic Research Center is "something." A tighter focus on the building of the HRC at ASU would open a window for examining Chicano efforts at institution building: Why did it work at ASU and not at UCLA? Berkeley? Allusions are made to Berkeley but only as a point of origin, not as a point of departure.

I suspect that there are many themes you left undone in the conversation. One of these has to do with Chicano versus Latino identity. The 1990s have distanced Chicanos from higher education by bringing in Latinos. In the faculty ranks, one finds that Hispanics or Latinos, but not Chicanos, are the new entrants. How did this shift occur? Is it found at ASU? If it is, how is it dealt with? A look at this issue would be a significant contribution.

Don't be afraid. Remember, you refer to your colleagues as cowards in the last chapter. Don't let it end on a note of desperation. Why get desperate over something you never controlled? Higher education institutions are insuring that we will never control any part of their structure in the twenty-first century. Perhaps another discussion can focus on the lack of Chicano colleges and universities *à la* Black colleges and universities. Why for them and not for us? How have Chicanos been excluded from this process of institution formation (as opposed to institution building)?

As I read the book I was making notes, but I gave that up. There were too many, and I found myself rewriting stuff. I simply focused on two questions.

One, does this book add to our knowledge about Chicano faculty? It does. By focusing on ASU, it permits one to observe how negotiation, identity, agenda setting, and so on, operate from a Chicano perspective. At the same time, it permits one to observe how things can fail from a Chicano perspective.

Two, does the manuscript say anything about the Chicano experience? It does. One may not like it, but the Chicano experience in higher education has been one of multiple births, out of the same body but with competing parents. The twenty-first century will not bring together the Chicano experience. I suspect that diversity, mostly the fabricated version, will rob Chicanos of voice and identity. The book says, "Look at everything we did at ASU, yet we still have not altered the social fabric of the institution." In short, a few have gained from the efforts of many.

Bueno, there you have it. Your book may scare up some people, especially those Chicanos who have diversified themselves with the season. Don't worry about being politically correct. It's not our argument anyway. White people created it as a means of cleansing their guilt. Unfortunately we got caught in it because we believed that they really included us in their discussions. But, that's another story.

Rudolfo Chávez Chávez: The book is well conceived but I feel that some of the ideas need more dialogue, as well as the inclusion of insights from others who have helped you to redefine many of the issues. You should also appropriate critical ideas that have deeply influenced both of you as you have reconstructed your realities *a la nueva ola* (according to the new wave). Don't be afraid to illustrate to the reader the multifaceted connections to your ideas. I think that you have to somehow illustrate the complexity of your *mature* thought based on the genesis of your ideas. Also, I think that you have to somehow thread a consistent theme of how White-dominant academic hegemony is insidiously part of the dialogue. Somehow both of you have to make visible the invisible. Not for sour grapes purposes but to remind the reader of how hegemony is constructed.

José Náñez, Sr.: The book consists of a dialogue between two full professors with a strong and sustained history in the areas of Chicano higher education and politics within a university setting. What struck me initially about the book was that it is based on the oral history model not very common among academic writers today. The dialogue form is appealing, although I found it a bit awkward to begin reading the book.

The authors do a good job of telling the reader what happened, when, where, and why. They also relate who were the individuals involved and why (in the authors' opinion) the individuals reacted the way they did. This amounts to relating and analyzing a set of events and chastising other Chicanos for not having the insight, guts, or will to act for change within the university. (I offer that most of the problem with Chicanos in academia is the former. We lack the insight and/or skills to act in an informed, "rational" way.) Although there are smatterings of wisdom splattered in bits and pieces throughout the manuscript (suggestions for how Chicano academics can become empowered within their universities or departments), the issue is not addressed in a coherent manner. And although RP and MM have gained much knowledge concerning the Chicano experience within academia (through their own extensive experience in higher education and through their having engaged in the thought exercise that culminated in this important book), they do a poor job of telling the rest of us *pendejos(as)* how to go about creating an enlightened, empowered cadre of Chicano faculty and administrators in our respective universities. I suggest that RP and MM engage in a short focused discussion of where we go from here and what we must do to become the enlightened, empowered Chicanos that they would have us be. Perhaps there are no canned solutions, but the volume would be strengthened nonetheless by these two giants investing some mental energy on the issue.

Having said this, I feel that the book is timely given the current turmoil over the place of minorities in higher education. If Chicanos are to survive, let alone live, in the university, we need to take a long, hard look at our history within higher education. The book begins this process through a series of case studies. This book will be controversial if nothing else. If I were to describe it in one word, it would be "gutsy." It names names, points fingers, and tells it like it is (in the eyes of the authors). Many toes are stepped on.

In any case, dialogue such as that between RP and MM needs to be taken up. If we hope to gain power in numbers and leadership positions, someone is needed to initiate the hard process of Chicanos taking a self-critical view of the history of our failures and victories within academia. Within a university setting, only two "full bulls" with thick skin resulting from countless battle scars amassed over the years in the educational debate could undertake such a project.

I can foresee two possible outcomes resulting from the historical accounts related in this book: (1) It may backfire, resulting in retaliation toward the authors by some of the subjects of the discussion. (2) A preferred result would be using the case studies in the book to engage in an escalation of focused, heated, honest discussion among Chicanos(as) regarding where we should go from here and how we can get there.

Reynaldo Baca: The style is not appealing to me; but the truth you speak is most appealing. This may be totally personal. I'm a social scientist. I don't like novels; therefore, it is difficult for me to have an affinity with dialogue. I realize that this is a specific strategy; however, the style tends to hide your many messages and can leave the reader without hope. If I could repackage your book, I would exchange your dialogues for vignettes followed by parables. The rest of my comments will be free flowing, some directed at the entire book, especially its tone, and others to parts or sections of the book.

1. The book paints a bleak picture, one without hope. Certainly, it is not a time to be optimistic and, perhaps, during our last two decades in higher education, it was not a time to be optimistic. As I have been cautioned so many times, "be pessimistic and you'll live longer." However, is there any hope? Even slaves had hope. I don't feel that either of you has any hope. What will you pass on to the next generation of Chicanos and Chicanas that will give them hope for a better future? What parables of wisdom will you pass on to the chicanada? By Chicanos/as, I am referring to those Aztecas del Norte with a critical and class consciousness about their past, present, and future conditions. You have certainly covered the past and the present, but how will you shape the future for others? You have over two decades of experiences, so don't tell me you don't know. Risk being a prophet. What's beyond *El Quinto Sol* in higher education?

2. *The issue of fair play.* Twenty years ago I heard Chancellor Charles Young (UCLA) state that the university is not a democracy. This was said by a person who was the UC's strongest advocate for diversity and affirmative action; then again, he would not support a Chicano studies department (even though, I believe, UCLA has a Latin American Studies Department). Your first title (*No Fair Play*) reminds me of the time I went to the unemployment office and complained about fairness when I was reminded by one of the employees that this was an unemployment office not a career center. I don't know that this has to do with your book other than you were unaware of the rules of conduct. I also put to you the following paradox in response to issue of no fair play: What if there were fair play? Then, I ask, what would be the scenario for Chicanos and Chicanas in higher education? If our society, for example, were to truly espouse cultural pluralism, would Chicanos and Chicanas be better off or would we still have to guard against the tyranny of the dominant cultural group? It is as though you were postulating that if the play were fair, then *todo está* (everything is) fine! *No lo creo!* (I don't believe it!)

3. Early in the book you speak about change: "intent to change institutions of higher education in Arizona." It is not always clear throughout the book what you mean by change. To be part of the system? To have

the system accommodate a Chicano(a) intellectual agenda? To do both? I
agree with you that too many of our Azteca origin professors have been
unwilling to carve out a Chicano(a) intellectualism, but is it not OK to be
an Azteca-origin (AOP as opposed to EOP) professor of English renais-
sance literature (witness *el pobre* Richard Rodríguez who wasn't allowed to
be one, especially after he opened his mouth).

4. Chicano idealism! It sounds almost disdainful the way you portray
it at first. It is difficult to expect social justice from an institution that is not
predicated on democracy and that is a central political economic institution
in the reproduction of hegemony. Nonetheless, you still demand justice.
Why not? But you are correct in that Chicanos(as) were just another
political interest group situated at the university!

5. You bring up an interesting point on being a Chicano(a) professor
(I am not talking about the Azteca-origin folks on campus). Those who are
Chicanos(as) have more work to do. I remember my brief stay at U.C., Santa
Barbara. I was a Chicano professor in the department of sociology. At that
time there was one Chicano history professor, one Chicano education
professor, and one Chicano anthropology professor. There were ten
Chicano(a) professors in the Chicano Studies Department or the Chicano
research center. As a Chicano I realized that the composition of students in
my classes was substantially different than that of other professors. I had
a significant number of Chicanos and Chicanas, but I also had a significant
number of African Americans, all the Native Americans, gays, and femi-
nist-oriented women. The other professors had much more homogeneous
classes. I always felt that I should have had a reduced teaching load because
phenomenologically I had more classes to teach! And I recall a student's
question: "Is it better to have Chicano professors in the Chicano Studies
Department or is it better to have professors like you who teach with a
Chicano perspective?" Both answers are right. But I could have not been a
Chicano and avoided all of this. However, I agree with you (sometimes
more than I believed I would). If you go against the grain, should you not
expect this burden? Indeed, you are to be commended for wanting to set up
a Chicano Center for Critical Reflection so that Azteca-origin professors
would have the opportunity and infrastructure to cultivate a Chicano
intellectual life.

6. I am left somewhat puzzled: Idealism as a "reaction to . . .
oppression." If anything, Padilla, your life, as I have known it, was not only
the promotion of a Chicano intellectual life, but also one of liberating your
oppressor. Am I wrong? In fact, if I am right, then your book is missing this
element, that is, it is not directed at liberating Chicanos'(as') oppressors in
higher education.

7. The Chicanas you talk about also miss the point that it is their

responsibility to liberate the oppressor; not to reconstitute a Chicano's biography so that there is an implied affinity with the oppressor. I don't know what you can do with this comment. It is just one of my concerns.

8. Just what is the "Anglo way of life in the university"? I agree that only a few Chicanos carve out a Chicano intellectual or university life. But why does this paradigm stand so much in contrast to an Anglo way of university life? Is there a Jewish university life? I am certain that there is but does this engender a conflict with an Anglo way of university life? Is getting a Nobel Prize an Anglo way of university life? *Dígame* (Tell me). *¿Qué es esta pendejada de la vida gabacha?* (What is this silly thing about the Anglo way of life?)

9. The Black-White dynamic is a well-put point. You should elaborate on it. It is an issue that I must contend with when dealing with Blacks on campus. I am more likely to speak up on behalf of Blacks than are Blacks on the part of Chicanos(as). It is not only a Black-White issue, but one that does not allow Blacks to recognize other minorities.

10. I just want to add something that I have mentioned before. This happened at U.C. Berkeley. If memory serves me correctly, this was one year before you (Padilla) came to Berkeley. The following occurred. The university had granted over thirty faculty positions to the new Graduate School of Public Policy. When some of the Chicano students in the School of Education heard about this, a meeting was demanded with the dean of the Graduate School of Public Policy. We finally had a meeting. Several faculty from the new school were there. I remember Professor Martin Trow, a famous sociologist, coauthor of *Union Democracy* with S. Martin Lipset, and later the president of the academic senate. When responding as to whether there were any Chicanos(as) on the new faculty (or if they had considered appointing any Chicanos or Chicanas), I heard Professor Trow say the following in a low voice, "Who ever heard of a Chicano bridge?" Apparently Trow was saying that science is science is science! Science has no cultural context for Professor Trow. Public policy, therefore, has no cultural context. It is a science! Although I did not disagree entirely with Professor Trow, I did ask him if suspension bridges were Asian bridges. He did not appreciate my humor, but I responded that maybe those who are for a value-free science should consider, to take liberties with Cervantes, that there is a science that responds to necessity to spawn invention. Furthermore, a significant tradition in sociology was borrowed from the arts, not the sciences, that is, role, role set, role playing, presentation of self, reflexive self, and other dramaturgical metaphors. Then I got back to reality and asked a series of uninterrupted questions: Did you identify or attempt to identify senior level, competent, and brilliant public policy scholars who were also Chicanos(as) or women? If not, did you identify or attempt to

identify promising junior-level public policy scholars who are also Chicanos(as) or women? If not, will you identify, recruit, and support Chicano(as) or female graduate students who will eventually become an eligible pool of public policy scholars? Needless to say, I, a mere graduate student, was not deserving of a response.

11. I liked chapter 3 on university autonomy. It could be retitled, "The Lights Are On, But There's Nobody Home." You do, indeed, bring out the petty backstabbing so common at a university. You also bring out the irony of the career mobility factor, especially among chairpersons and higher-level administrators. Obviously, the line of action that an administrator cultivates is a line of action to open the next door, that is, dean to provost to vice president to university president to systemwide president/chancellor. What is endemic to administrative officeholders is that their actions are predicated on future appointments, even if they are not promoted. Nothing that they do in the present must upset their futures.

Likewise, minority issues, not only Chicano(a) issues, are viewed as local concerns when a university sees itself as discipline-oriented or internationally oriented (especially for the large research universities). Like administrators, professors, even those with tenure, may have a greater affinity with the discipline or with the profession (i.e., professional associations) and, therefore, are not socialized to view the local. It is an issue of local versus cosmopolitan perspectives. Yet, the local can be cosmopolitan. A social problem can be a social condition that has become politicized. Certainly, Chicano(a) issues can be discussed in terms of the political economy of the Southwest, of the interlocking relationship between Mexico and the United States, of an unequal relationship between Mexico and the United States that magnifies the unequal treatment that Azteca-origin people receive in the United States, and so forth.

12. You are correct when you say that denying a chair to a Chicano(a) is to deny a deanship, a provostship, and a presidency to a Chicano(a). Good point.

13. Was it a Chicano fight or not? Good point regarding your discussion on the selection of a dean in chapter 3.

14. I like the discussions, in chapters 3 and 5, of who runs the university. I liked your exposition on the university going to outside influentials; yet, they become upset when Chicanos(as) do the same. Then if we don't, we are asked who we represent. Next time ask them who they represent.

15. I like the idea of a statewide Chicano agenda for higher education that is discussed in chapter 6. It is a strategy similar to having constitutional protection rather than civil rights protection. Feminists were right in wanting a constitutional amendment. Protection under civil rights is not

sufficient. Similarly, it would have been better to say that Chicanos(as) were being discriminated against in school not because they were receiving an inferior or segregated education, but because they were receiving a *gabacho* education. If this logic had persisted, as was tried in Colorado, then we would have had a constitutional right for bilingual education rather than ostensibly having that right as an artifact of not discriminating on the basis of national origin. Similarly, it would have been prudent, although not winable, to declare immigrant rights in the case of undocumented children than to say that children cannot be held culpable for the crimes of their parents. But sometimes it is better to win on the wrong foundation than to be right and lose. Don't ask me why I said this. Your dialogical style of writing sometimes forces me into this style.

16. Good discussion in chapter 6 regarding Chicano demands versus the university's response on increasing the number of Chicano(a) students. But even more Chicano students is a complex problem. For example, if at UCLA admissions were based on socioeconomic background (assuming all other factors being equal), would the university have more Anglos and Asians, but fewer Chicanos(as) and African-Americans? Does this imply, with respect to the Chicano student population, that the pool has become larger and UCLA is skimming off the top rather than impacting the Chicano(a) community? Think about it!

17. Good discussion, also in chapter 6, on the social responsibilities of the university. Expand it. Show hope. Give the future Chicanos and Chicanas some parables of wisdom upon which to generate hope! You should think of the fruits of your labor being cultivated by others in the future. If you intend to see the results of your labor during your lifetime, then I hope you live well into the next century.

18. Your treatise on faculty not being rooted in the local community in chapter 5 is an interesting one and speaks of truth. Your conclusions and observations certainly have implications for the chicanada. But I have one comment to which I do not have an answer. When looking at data (raw) from the Ford Foundation-funded UCLA Mexican American Project done during the late 1960s, we (Joan Moore, Leo Grebbler, Ralph Guzman, and others) noted that "Mexican Americans" did not think of themselves as a national group (as compared to the responses given by Black Americans at that time). I still think this is true among most Chicanos, partially because *Mexicanos(as)* were incorporated differently in different sectors of the Southwest and elsewhere. Some were incorporated through political colonialism, cultural colonialism, and economic colonialism. Most were initial replacements for Chinese labor and most could come to the United States through a back-door policy. Others migrated along a combination of occupational/paisano networks so that *Michoacanos(as)* had particular

points of destination that probably did not overlap with the points of destination for *Zacatecanos*. And so forth. I believe that this contributed to a local orientation among *Aztecas en el norte* and therefore militates against the development of a national, international, and cosmopolitan perspective or affinity. If anything, today we need at minimum Western Hemispheric affinities and leaders with such affinities. Indeed, the university does not have a local orientation; but do the chicanada have a nonlocal orientation?

19. Your brief comments on leadership are important and should be elaborated. I remember recently a philosopher, I don't recall her name, saying that being a leader today is like being a shepherd with a "flock of cats." Truly, your own leadership sometimes reflects this issue. But you are still a leader. There are just more interest groups, even among Chicanos(as), for example, Chicana feminist, Chicano(a) Marxists, Chicano(a) "Richard Rodríguez types," first-generation Mexicano/Chicano students who do not have the legacy of the 1960s nor understand the struggle.

20. Expand the discussion on proportional representation. I agree with you; however, does the more "organized" group have an obligation to bring along those who are less organized? While I do remember Chicanos(as) being excluded by African Americans, I also remember African Americans advising me to organize politically. It may be that demanding proportional representation on the part of the university is a ploy to diffuse demands. You could turn that argument around and say that proportional representation should be based not only on the local demographics, but in direct proportion to the university's claim of being an international research institution. This would not leave much room for *gabachos*, would it?

Finally, you conclude with a section titled "The Importance of Courage and Responsibility." This is where you should start the book. Take off the gloves. Use your bare hands where the pain will be felt both ways.

Ernesto M. Bernal: This book provides the reader who will read beyond the first two pages a truly reflective and transcendent experience, one that is definitely not within the traditional academic publishing tradition; nonetheless it is an experience that is very rewarding for the insights that it provides and — perhaps more importantly — for the pauses that it engenders in the reader. As I read this extended dialogue, I found myself at times wanting to jump into the conversation.

Clearly, this book is about the Chicano presence in higher education in the United States, and is addressed primarily to Chicanos, whom the authors invite to participate in this special one-case study (albeit with many subcases within it) for the purpose of learning from the experience of the authors and trying to match this experience to their own, thereby generalizing the knowledge and therefore violating all of the rules of evidence that we first learned as undergraduates and to which we became inured as graduate students.

The book is a tour de force, one that engages us to attend to the one thousand and one issues that would require as many books or papers to portray scientifically. Perhaps this book, in the last analysis, is two Chicanos' contribution to the special intellectual tradition they would like to see us all cultivate; it is the seeding of the Chicano intellectual revolution in academia.

The early and now-emerging presence of Chicanos in higher education is described from highly personalized points of view. Because Chicanos truly have been strangers in academia in the United States, by and large educationally isolated from the intellectual traditions of Mexico, Latin America, and Spain, and because they have been made to struggle to survive in this arena, the dynamics of their presence in universities have evolved quickly and joltingly. The lessons that individual Chicanos have learned as a consequence have served either to remove them entirely from academia, to alienate them from other Chicanos, to acculturate them to the academic rigors imposed by non-Chicanos over many years in American higher education, or to establish Chicanos in a situation where they are simultaneously successful yet motivated to seek new avenues of expression, making unique contributions to the intellectual traditions of universities in the United States.

The authors convince the reader that academic institutions in the United States are in a state of drift precisely because too many leaders in these institutions are seeking other, higher, more prestigious jobs and are not willing to do the tough work of the job at hand so as not to create controversy that might reflect badly on their next bid for advancement. This institutional drift has probably worked to the detriment of Chicanos in higher education everywhere, especially the Chicanos who entered higher education in the middle 1960s to the middle 1970s who had themselves entered college in the late 1950s or early 1960s and remember the idealism of some of their old professors—albeit Anglo professors— who had come from the 1940s or before, professors who had mentored us through degree programs but who were not there to mentor us when we became new assistant professors, because they retired just as we came on the tenure track scene, leaving the field in higher education in the hands of second- and third- and fourth-generation gringo college graduates who know how to succeed without the idealistic commitments of their intellectual forebears. We Chicanos, on the other hand, believed our old Anglo mentors' rhetoric. But we had no previous generation of Chicano professors who could mentor us through the difficult times of discrimination and the depreciation of our teaching, scholarly efforts, and service where minorities were concerned.

Thus the authors focus on Chicano idealism; a whole chapter is given to it. For us, higher education represented the very antithesis of the oppression that we had experienced as youths. For some of us, this intellectual idealism augmented and fortified the idealism that comes with immigrant status. Even those of us who were not recently immigrated to the United States, such as the *manitos* from New Mexico or the earlier generations of Chicanos in the Southwest—who normally would be more pragmatic and more realistic and perhaps even more jaded in dealing with the world—were in many cases first-generation college students, which further added to our idealism. We were breaking new ground and we believed that the university—surely *The University* — was the place where fairness, goodness, and light could come together in a critical way to guide science, the arts, politics, and society in general. Those of us who pursued the academic life also pursued a vision about society, and it was only those of us who had to face the existential moment of deciding between a doctoral program and an academic career on the one hand, and expulsion to the netherworld of real jobs and real people on the other, who compromised this dream and rationalized it through the acculturational influences of formal institutions.

Finally, I find that for many Chicano academics their Catholic religious background has only served to sharpen their idealism and have them see their options in very moralistic terms. To paraphrase Samuel Beckett, *L'église catolique nous ha encoulé la gloire.* [La iglesia católica nos ha "enculado" el idealismo. The Catholic church has filled us with idealism.] This is the same pursuit of noble goals that has inspired Latinos throughout the Western Hemisphere in political, economic, educational, philosophical, and theological thought. Perhaps it is itself the precipitate of the Catholic-mestizo interaction.

A phenomenon that impacts the life of older Chicanos in higher education is their having taken "giant steps." Many of us Chicano professors, particularly those who got doctorates after having achieved bachelor's degrees as first-generation college Chicanos and who in many cases worked part of their way through school while trying to maintain decent grades in order to get to the next level of higher education, were not able to "round out" or perhaps "round off" some of our lack of formal culture. We have always been too busy getting on with the essentials of our studies and, later, with the practice of our profession, concerned with succeeding, moving ahead rapidly in definite directions, to take time to learn to appreciate intellectual leisure, as it were. Younger Chicanos do not suffer this deficiency as much, it seems to me. One of the results of Padilla and Montiel's new paradigmatic movement could be the exposure of committed Chicanos to other committed Chicanos who together represent many disciplinary points of view, from the performing arts to zoology, whose work could help liberalize our education. For just as John Henry Cardinal Newman saw the intellectual universe from its center, as it were, in his *Idea of the University*, perhaps there is within that universe a skein of interconnections among the disciplines through a Chicano theme.

The Hispanic Research Center and the Chicano Studies Department at Arizona State University are mentioned numerous times throughout the book. It is important to understand that both the Center and the Department were established expressly for the purpose of integrating many disciplinary points of view and were never intended to be isolated research and teaching ventures.

The authors also discuss the Arizona Association of Chicanos for Higher Education (AACHE) in what I consider to be a romanticized history if ever there was one! Perhaps their account of AACHE's activities in higher education is a small distortion to make otherwise valid points about AACHE's successes and failures. But I was an officer of AACHE for three consecutive years in the late 1980s, and I can state unambiguously that AACHE was never intended to serve as a new intellectual departure for Chicanos. Indeed, I do not believe that any organization such as AACHE can serve this purpose very well. The very name — AACHE — indicates an action group of Chicanos from all types of institutions of higher education, the type of organization that is designed to answer the bureaucrats' question, which figures prominently in this book, "What do you want?" What was and is needed to achieve the dream of a unique contribution is to integrate a variety of disciplinary bases per se — the kinds of things that are represented in the Hispanic Research Center and in Chicano Studies — not a statewide organization designed to achieve a measure of social and economic justice within higher education for Chicano faculty and staff. The intellectual agenda of which the authors speak certainly cannot be limited to just one state, whereas AACHE must perforce be limited to furthering the interests of its state membership.

If in fact the authors and many of their readers would like to sow the seeds of a new intellectual ferment among Chicanos — one explicitly designed to cultivate and establish a new intellectual tradition — then perhaps an interstate meeting of the minds of many Chicano activists and intellectuals needs to take place, a Chicano intellectual summit, as it were. We should seek funding for such a revolutionary effort. Strategically selected teachers could set a broad agenda with plenty of time for discussion. The meeting itself would require a lot of time from the participants — certainly a week or more — and probably would require yearly follow-up meetings as well, just like a national professional conference.

For Chicanos are not only diverse in terms of their intellectual disciplines but also in terms of their commitment to gringo versus Chicano and other "experimental" modes of thought. To this day, the most highly published Chicanos are the ones who have totally subscribed to the traditional modes of thought and writing in American higher education. They are, of course, concerned with their success in the eyes of the larger academic community, with their own hard-won leadership . . . and with their own self-importance. They would definitely not support the publication of Padilla and Montiel's book, based essentially, as it is, on a single institutional case. I wonder if they would participate — not attend, but participate — in a Chicano intellectual summit. It remains to be seen whether these prestigious Chicano scholars can be coaxed into trying something daring themselves and to see if they would be willing to allow more intellectually adventurous Chicanos to publish reasonable but nontraditional works in the journals that these established individuals control or influence. I would love to be proven wrong on this point!

Perhaps we need to think of establishing a new journal, one of great general interest, one that somehow goes beyond *Scientific American* and *Atlantic Monthly*. This journal may be called something like *Latino Intellectual*, one that would publish think pieces, examples of new ideas and perspectives, new poetry, drawings and paintings by Chicanos on the cutting edge, content that seeks to exemplify nongringo paradigms of thought.

Finally, the authors need to summarize the Chicano intellectual position somewhere. In the text numerous factors are mentioned, including value, soul, tolerance for diversity, *portándose como la gente* (a Chicano gentility), collegiality, humanist and humanitarian motives, and, most important a way of blending emotion and reason, enthusiasm and motivation with commitment and clear thought for the purpose of producing a deliberate, ethical set of actions that benefit an institution or society as a whole, a course in which individual persons find expression and fulfillment but do not feel a need to act selfishly or to promote themselves at the expense of others. These various elements need to be synthesized, if not by the authors then by the coming together of Chicano minds. Instead of idealizing intellectual thought as dispassionate, as in the gringo tradition, we might want to emphasize the importance of being rational in matters about which one feels very deeply, a Chicano primer on integrating the mind and the spirit.

Certainly *Debatable Diversity* is a book that challenges us to think about these matters in general, while examining our own actions and motives. It prompts us to reflect but it also prompts us to act in more collaborative ways to achieve what could be the crowning achievement for

Chicanos in American higher education: to stop institutional drift, to set universities upon a mission to lead intellectually, innovatively, and critically, and to rekindle the idealism within those of us who have chosen careers in higher education in a way that seeks not to imitate what has gone before but to emulate the deeper visions of the persons whom we learned to respect while we were still youths, while we were still new in the game. We must find ways to support one another politically, to promote our survival academically, while establishing new ways of integrating the knowledge that we have acquired for the purpose of finding new solutions to the nagging academic problems that have not been amenable to traditional paradigms of inquiry or action.

Coda: On Social Change

Miguel Montiel: We talk about changing ourselves and others because we are unhappy with *our* lives. Thinking about change, however, is easier than doing it. Why do we have difficulties changing our eating habits, our relationships with our family and friends, our study and work habits? Why are we lazy but don't do anything about it?

Change is difficult because we are not aware of our behaviors—we may think we are but we are not. We act in a mechanical fashion. We eat not what we should but what Ronald McDonald tells us; we relate to our husbands and wives (boyfriends and girlfriends) not with love and compassion, but with anger and jealousy because that is how we saw our parents interact; we fail to study and work with joy because we grew up in an environment where television dominated our lives; we are lazy (and bored) because we simply do not know how to live better.

It is not all our fault. All around us we see the forces that prevent us from living our own lives. Our thinking is dominated by our suffering (some resulting from our parents' suffering), by billboards and television with their vulgarity and pornography, by schools that operate with worn-out ideas, and by a society that does not care for us as individual human beings.

The other day I watched one of my friends on television talking about reforming the high schools. He talked about *schools* being out of touch with the times, about racism, about the insensitivity of teachers and administrators, about rich school districts getting more money than poor districts. These things are all true. He did not talk, however, about the idea of *personal* responsibility in changing ourselves and the world. Why?

His personal life has been a difficult one. He grew up very poor, and had difficulties learning in school. He has been married more than once, and his children have had to fend for themselves. Not unexpectedly, they have had many difficulties in their lives. His children, like their father, are also living mechanical lives.

The point of this story is not to denigrate him. I love and in many ways respect him. He is a good man dedicated to his community. Yet in many ways he lives mechanically, unaware of why he has not been able to change his present relationships that were formed by the past. He is no different than we are, and in some ways better than many of us.

Why is it that we criticize institutions for not changing when we do not know how to change ourselves? What is the connection between personal change and institutional change? We should remember that schools are composed of human beings like you and me, and if we are unable to change even minor things about ourselves, how can we expect to change our institutions? We need to lead happier lives, but we don't seem to know how to do it.

Raymond V. Padilla: You have touched on a number of key issues. To which I would add the following:

1. Paulo Freire has put your understanding in a broader context by arguing that men and women must learn that their vocation is to "become more human." This conclusion is based on Freire's notion that we are "incomplete beings." There are many reasons why we are incomplete, including the ones that you mentioned.

2. We fail to understand our ontological condition (being incomplete) because we are submerged within our culture, a culture that systematically tries to prevent us from thinking critically, from asking critical questions.

3. We can become more human through a collective project of critical action and reflection that includes dialogue.

4. Every man and woman has the innate capacity to gain critical consciousness about themselves and their situation, and to act critically and compassionately in their social world.

So we need to collectively engage in projects that will help us to become more human, and in the process to help alleviate the oppressive social conditions that envelop our society.

From my perspective, we as Chicanos have yet to discover a language and process of critique that can help us to become more human. All too often we reduce ourselves to praising everyone, including those who oppress us, or to venting our anger and frustration on whoever is around us. Too often we act as if our social institutions had not been ripped apart both in Mexico and in the United States. We are so hurt from this trauma that we can't even imagine that we are supposed to critique ourselves and society. And to make things better.

We also operate almost entirely out of self-interest. Our individual ambitions far outweigh our collective ideals. The utopian vision has lost out to the mundane business of achieving material success. We stop ourselves from demanding just treatment because we are afraid to lose even the scraps that have been thrown our way. We pay dearly for the smallest concessions and are afraid to risk what has been thrown our way for what is rightfully ours. We are thus submerged in a culture of spiritual and material poverty from which only we can extricate ourselves through pain and suffering and rebirth.

Glossary

bueno: all right.
chicanada: Chicanos collectively.
círculo de cultura: cultural circle; a dialogical group constituted to promote literacy and consciousness-raising following the ideas of Brazilian educator Paulo Freire.
conciencia: consciousness.
el grito: the cry for independence issued annually during the September 16 celebration of Mexican Independence.
el movimiento: the Chicano civil rights movement started during the 1960s.
la política: politics.
machista: adjective form of the Spanish word *macho (cf. machismo)*, which is used in the English language to mean an exaggerated sense of maleness.
Mau-Mau: expression from the sixties used to describe the actions of activists who were simply putting on a show; grandstanding.
mexicano: a Mexican.
Michoacano: a person from the Mexican state of Michoacán.
pendejo(a): simpleton.
personalismo: individual political activity within a hierarchical system of power.
pinto: an ex convict.
pobre: poor.
problemática: difficult situation.
resolana: a community space where public discourse occurs.
Zacatecano: a person from the Mexican state of Zacatecas.

References

Aguirre, A., Jr. (1995). The status of minority faculty in academe. *Equity & Excellence, 28*(1):63–68.

Aguirre, A., Jr., & Martinez, R. (1993). *Chicanos in higher education. ASHE–ERIC higher education report no. 3.* Washington, D.C.: George Washington University.

Aguirre, A., Jr., Hernández, A., & Martinez, R. (1994). Perceptions of the workplace: Focus on minority women faculty. *Initiatives, 56*(3), 41–50.

Aguirre, A., Jr., Martinez, R., & Hernández, A. (1993). Majority and minority faculty perceptions in academe. *Research in Higher Education, 34*(3), 371–385.

Alcalá-Zamora y Torres, N. (1980). *Nuevas reflexiones sobre las leyes de Indias* (*3a ed.*). Mexico: Editorial Porrua.

Alinsky, S. D. (1989). *Rules for radicals: A practical primer for realistic radicals.* New York: Vintage Books.

Aronowitz, S., & Giroux, H. (1991). *Postmodern education: Politics, culture, & social criticism.* Minneapolis: University of Minnesota Press.

Atencio, T. (1988). Resolana: A Chicano pathway to knowledge. Ernesto Galarza commemorative lecture. Stanford: Stanford University, Center for Chicano Research.

Becker, E. (1973). *The denial of death.* New York: Free Press.

Bennis, W. (1989). *Why leaders can't lead.* San Francisco: Jossey-Bass Publishers.

Bloom, A. (1987). *The closing of the American mind.* New York: Simon & Schuster.

Bok, D. (1982). *Beyond the ivory tower. Social responsibilities of the modern university.* Cambridge: Harvard University Press.

Bok, D. (1986). *Higher learning.* Cambridge: Harvard University Press.

Brown, D. (1990). Racism and race relations in the university. *Virginia Law Review, 76*(1), 295–335.

Brown, N. O. (1959). *Life against death: The psychoanalytic meaning of history.* New York: Viking Books.

Caro, R. (1982). *The years of Lyndon Johnson. Vol. 1: The path to power.* New York: Knopf.

Chaffee, E. E., & Sherr, L. AK. (1992). *Quality: Transforming postsecondary education. ASHE-ERIC higher education report no. 3.* Washington, D.C.: George Washington University.

Chicano Coordinating Council on Higher Education (1969). *El plan de Santa Bárbara.* Oakland, Calif.: La Causa Publications.

Clark, B. (1960). The "cooling-out" function in higher education. *American Journal of Sociology, 65,* 569–576.

Durant, W. (1961). *The story of philosophy: The lives and opinions of the greater philosophers.* New York: Washington Square Press.

Dye, T. R. (1976). *Policy analysis: What governments do, why they do it, and what difference it makes.* University: University of Alabama Press.

Fox, C. J., & Miller, H. T. (1995). *Postmodern public administration: Toward a discourse.* Thousand Oaks, Calif.: Sage Publications.

Freire, P. (1970a). *Pedagogy of the oppressed.* New York: The Seabury Press.

Freire, P. (1970b). *Cultural action for freedom.* Monograph Series No. 1. Cambridge: *Harvard Educational Review* and Center for the Study of Development and Social Change.

Freire, P. (1973). *Education for critical ccnsciousness.* New York: The Seabury Press.

Freire, P. (1985). *The politics of education.* South Hadley, Mass.: Bergin & Garvey Publishers, Inc.

Freire, P., & Macedo, D. P. (1995). A dialogue: Culture, language, and race. *Harvard Educational Review, 65*(3), 377–402.

García, Mario T. (1989). *Mexican Americans.* Yale Western Americana Series, 36. New Haven, Conn.: Yale University Press.

García Canclini, N. (1995). *Hybrid cultures: Strategies for entering and leaving modernity.* (Trans. C. L. Chippari and S. L. López). Minneapolis: University of Minnesota Press.

Goodman, P. (1964). *Compulsory mis-education and the community of scholars.* New York: Vintage Books.

Habermas, J. (1984). *The theory of communicative action.* (Trans. T. McCarthy,). Boston: Beacon Press.

Hagberg, J. (1984). *Real power; stages of personal power in organizations.* Minneapolis, Minn.: Winston Press.

Handy, C. (1990). *The age of unreason.* Boston: Harvard Business School Press.

Hanke, L. (1974). *All mankind is one: A study of the disputation between Bartolome de Las Casas and Juan Gines de Sepulveda in 1550 on the intellectual and religious capacity of the American Indians.* DeKalb: Northern Illinois University.

Harris, M. (1981). *Why nothing works: The anthropology of daily life.* New York: Simon & Schuster.

Harvey, J., & Immerwahr, J. (1995). *Goodwill and growing worry: Public perceptions of American higher education.* A Report for the American Council on Education. Washington, D.C.: American Council on Education.

Hasenfeld, Y. (1974). *Human service organizations: A book of readings.* Ann Arbor: University of Michigan Press.

Hawking, S. (1990). *A brief history of time from the big bang to black holes.* New York: Bantam Books.

Huber, R. M. (1992). *How professors play the cat guarding the cream: Why we're paying more and getting less in higher education.* Fairfax, Va.: George Mason University Press.

Hugh, T. (1995). *Conquest: Montezuma, Cortes, and the fall of old Mexico.* New York: Simon and Schuster.

Illich, I. (1970). *Deschooling society.* New York: Harper and Row.

Illich, I. (1973). *Tools for conviviality.* New York: Harper and Row.

Jencks, C., & Riesman, D. (1969). *The academic revolution.* Garden City, N.Y.: Doubleday Anchor.

Juhasz, J., & Martinez, R. (1996). Shared governance: Trusting faculty. Paper presented at the Trustee Conference of the American Governing Board, Chicago, April.

Keller, G. (1983). *Academic strategy: The management revolution in American higher education.* Baltimore: Johns Hopkins University Press.

Kellerman, Barbara. (1984). *Leadership: Multidisciplinary perspectives.* New Jersey: Prentice-Hall, Inc.

Kerr, C. (1963). *The uses of the university.* Cambridge: Harvard University Press.

Maranhão, T. (Ed.). (1990). *The interpretation of dialogue.* Chicago: University of Chicago Press.

Martinez, R., Hernández, A., & Aguirre, A., Jr. (1993/94). Latino faculty attitudes toward the workplace. *Journal of the Association of Mexican American Educators.* Special Theme Edition, pp. 45–52.

Mathews, C. (1988). *Hardball: How politics is played told by one who knows the game.* New York: Harper Perennial.

Mills, C. W. (1961). *The sociological imagination.* New York: Grove Press.

Montiel, M. (1970). The social science myth of the Mexican American family. *El Grito, 3*(4), 56–63.

Montiel, M., & Ortego y Gasca, F. (1992). Chicanos, community and change (pp. 49-66). In J. Erlich and F. Rivera (Eds.), *Community organizing in a diverse society*. Needham Heights, Mass.: Allyn and Bacon.

Montiel, M. (1970). The Chicano family: A review. *Social Work, 18*(2), 22–31.

Neiburg, H. L. (1970). *In the name of science*. (rev. ed.).Chicago: Quadrangle Books.

Newfield, C., & Strickland, R. (Eds.). (1995). *After political correctness: The humanities and society in the 1990s*. Boulder: Westview Press.

Newman, J. H. (1976). *The idea of a university*. Oxford: Claredon Press .

Newson, J. A. (1994). Subordinating democracy: The effects of fiscal retrenchment and university–business partnerships on knowledge creation and knowledge–dissemination in universities. *Higher Education, 27*(2), 141–161.

Nisbet, R. (1973). *The social philosophers: Community and conflict in western thought*. New York: Thomas Y. Crowell Co.

Olalquiaga, C. (1992). *Megalopolis: Contemporary cultural sensibilities*. Minneapolis: University of Minnesota Press.

Olivas, M. A. (Ed.). (1986). *Latino college students*. New York: Teachers College Press.

Ortega y Gassett, J. (1929–1933). *Obras completas. Tomo IV* (Sexta Edición). Madrid: Revista de Occidente.

Padilla, R. V. (1973a). A critique of Pittian history (pp. 65–106). In O. I. Romano-V. (Ed.), *Voices. Readings from El Grito 1967–1973*. Berkeley, Calif.: Quinto Sol Publications.

Padilla, R. V. (1973b). Apuntes para la documentación de la cultural chicana (pp. 117–160). In O. I. Romano-V. (Ed.), *Voices. Readings from El Grito 1967-1973*. Berkeley, Calif.: Quinto Sol Publications.

Padilla, R. V. (1975). *Chicano Studies at the University of California, Berkeley: En busca del campus y la comunidad*. Unpublished doctoral dissertation, University of California, Berkeley.

Padilla, R. V. (1987). Chicano studies revisited: Still in search of the campus and the community (Occasional papers series no. 6). El Paso: University of Texas at El Paso, Chicano Studies Program.

Padilla, R.V., & Montiel M. (Eds.) (1984). *Chicanos and the higher learning: An action plan for Chicano higher education in Arizona. Designed and approved by the Arizona Association of Chicanos for Higher Education*. Tucson: University of Arizona Mexican American Studies & Research Center.

Pelikan, J. (1992). *The idea of the university: A reexamination*. New Haven, Conn.: Yale University Press.

Pitt, L. (1966). *The decline of the Californios: A social history of the Spanish-speaking Californians, 1846–1890*. Berkeley: University of California Press.

Price, G. (1963). *The narrow pass: A study of Kierkegaard's concept of man*. London: McGraw-Hill Book Company.

Ramey, D. A. (1994). *Empowering leaders*. Missouri: Kansas City, Mo.: Sheed Ward.

Reich, C. A. (1970). *The greening of America*. New York: Random House.

Richardson, R. C., Jr., & Skinner, E. F. (1991). *Achieving quality and diversity: Universities in a mulicultural society*. New York: Macmillan Publishing Company.

Romano-V., O. I. (Ed.) (1973). *Voices: Readings from El Grito: A journal of contemporary Mexican American thought, 1967–1973*. Berkeley: Quinto Sol Publications.

Ross, L. E., & McMurray, H. L. (1996). Dual realities and structural challenges of African-American criminologists. *ACJS Today, 15*(I), 1,3,9.

Roszak, T. (1969). *The making of a counter culture. Reflections on the technocratic society and its youthful opposition*. Garden City, N.Y.: Doubleday & Co.

Servín, M. P. (1974). *An awakening minority: The Mexican Americans*. Beverly Hills: Glencoe Press.

Skerry, P. (1993). *Mexican Americans: The ambivalent minority*. New York: Free Press.

Solomon, R., & Solomon, J. (1993). *Up the university: Re-creating higher education in America*. New York: Addison-Wesley Publishing Co.

Steele, S. (1990). *The content of our character: A new vision of race in America*. New York: St. Martin's Press.

Terry, R. W. (1993). *Authentic leadership: Courage in action*. San Francisco: Jossey-Bass Publishers.

Thoreau, H. D. (1983). *Walden and civil disobedience*. New York: Penguin Books.

Tierney, W. G. (1997). Organizational socialization in higher education. *Journal of Higher Education, 68*(1), 1–16.

Tierney, W. G. (1988). Organizational culture in higher education. *Journal of Higher Education, 59*(1), 1–21.

Toffler, A., & Toffler, H. (1994). *Creating a new civilization: The politics of the third wave*. Atlanta, Ga.: Turner Publishing Co.

Tolstoy, Leo (1904). *War and peace* (Trans. C. B. Garnett). London: W. Heinemann.

Turner, B. S. (Ed.). (1990). *Theories of modernity and postmodernity*. Thousand Oaks, Calif.: Sage Publications.

Veblen, T. (1957). *The higher learning in America. A memorandum on the conduct of universities by business men*. New York: Hall and Wang.

Warren, R. L. (1972). *The community in America* (2nd ed.). Chicago: Rand McNally & Co.

WICHE Regional Policy Committee on Minorities in Higher Education. (1971). From minority to majority: Education and the future of the Southwest. Denver:

Western Interstate Commission on Higher Education.

Wood, M. (1992, November). Life studies. *The New York Review of Books, 39,* 7–11.

Wright, W. (1993). Higher innovation: universities in the nineties. Unpublished manuscript. University of Southern Colorado.

Index

community of scholars,
xxv, 2, 7, 180, 186, 189,
194, 197, 205
curriculum,
49, 68, 86, 125, 177
departments, xiii, 77, 155,
158, 170, 177, 181, 189,
196, 200, 239
efficiency, 7, 96, 143, 146
fragmentation, xxvi, xxix, 8,
65, 74, 76, 84, 96, 144, 235
governance, xviii, 30, 36, 169
institutional culture, xvi, 12, 25,
44, 51, 55, 58, 65, 81, 115,
159, 172, 201, 234
land grant, xiii, xxiv, 70
leadership,
xviii, 66, 78, 83, 91, 118, 153
mission, 89, 124, 249
planning,
7, 81, 122, 126, 131, 137, 229
politics, xvii, xxi, 1, 13, 28, 46,
50, 77, 93, 104, 142, 150, 171,
195, 209
resource allocation,
xvi, xvii, 28,
42, 55, 67, 80, 133, 142, 147,
159, 162, 187, 190, 193, 238
restructuring, xiv
searches, 24, 83, 136, 165, 173,
181, 183, 186, 196, 219
social responsibilities,
70, 142, 247
special interests, xvi, xix, xxv,
xxviii, 6, 28, 42, 54, 84, 119,
158, 226
student protests, 124, 150
students,
44, 64, 70, 88, 153, 210
University of Michigan, 73
unwed mothers, 48

V

Vietnam, xxvii, 125, 153
Vitoria, Francisco, 18
volunteerism, 164, 225, 227

W

War on Poverty, 25, 128
War with Mexico, 20
Warren, Morrison, 62, 78, 80
Washington, Alton, 135, 136, 139
Wayne State University, 123
welfare state, 147
Western Interstate Commision on
Higher Education (WICHE),
29
women, xiv, 6, 13, 25, 49, 56,
84, 110, 117, 129, 135, 171, 186,
204, 207, 218
Woods, John, 63

About the Authors

Miguel Montiel

Like many other minority academics of my generation, much of my career has been devoted to issues dealing with institution building, and attempting to resolve the many conflicts that these efforts have engendered. Arizona State University (ASU), like other institutions, struggles with the idea of building community. We live in a world where identifying, let alone achieving, a common purpose or "connectedness" among people is a difficult enterprise indeed.

I have taught at Arizona State University in the School of Social Work (1974-1985), the School of Public Affairs (1988-present), and the Honors College (1992); in the School of Social Welfare at the University of California at Berkeley (1972-1974); at the Universidad Autónoma de Guadalajara, Jalisco, México (Spring, 1982); and in 1987 I attended the Institute for Educational Management at Harvard University. In 1985, I served as Assistant Vice President for Academic Affairs at ASU where I had line authority for off-campus programs and served as Director of the Office of Minority Affairs. I was Co-chair of the Arizona Universities Committee on Minority Student Recruitment and Retention, Cofounder and Interim Director of the ASU Hispanic Research Center, and Co-director of Project PRIME—an outreach program for minority high school students. Currently I am serving on the committee that is overseeing the development of the newly created Department of Chicana/o Studies at ASU.

Over the years, as my commitment to minority issues has continued, I have become increasingly concerned about the acrimonious relationships arising among various interest groups on campus as they compete for recognition and resources. My primary concern is that these conflicts run counter to building a community of scholars. Over the course of my career,

I have come up with a negative portrayal of what is occurring in universities which I label "institutional exclusion". The reining paradigm of universities (meritocracy and intellectual purity) stands in stark contrast to their day-to-day practices. In our work we discovered a reluctance among university administrators to change existing routines. This reluctance, driven by career advancement considerations dependent on a national job market, resulted in administrators avoiding controversy and neglecting local concerns. Such behavior adversely impacts both universities (because it creates stagnation), and Chicanos and Native Americans who are viewed as unimportant and politically weak. University regents often are unable to see the contradictions that result from "institutional exclusion" because they over rely on university officials committed to the reining ideology and routines. A profound "outsider" critique is needed. This type of critique is located in what we refer to in this book as the "ethnic moment."

It is partly because of these negative perceptions that I have become involved in more inclusive and interactive activities, such as the development of the Campus Communities Project. In 1992, at the request of the university president, I became Director of the Campus Communities Project in the Honors College—a pilot program aimed at improving the campus climate for undergraduate students. In this capacity, I worked closely with the Office of Admissions, Residence Halls, and community agencies to arrange service learning opportunities for students. While acknowledging and celebrating diversity, the Campus Communities Project searched for a common purpose and "connectedness." The project, although fundamentally academic in nature, recognized that social interaction and experiential learning are an integral part of serious academic study. This project was the first step of an effort to "connect" not only students and faculty into a more effective university community but also with the wider community. Accordingly, students within the campus community studied literature of social reflection and participated in the formation of a campus community and in public service outside the university environment. A central assumption of this project was that communities are held together by a sense of duty and participation (and not only self-interest).

Outside of the university, I have worked with various public agencies at both the local and national levels. I have evaluated a volunteer program for the United States Information Agency that brought middle-management public sector workers from all over the world to work with agencies in various parts of the United States. I have headed an evaluation team to study the dropout problem in the Phoenix Union High School District. I am also evaluating a community gang prevention program for the City of Phoenix Head Start Division. I also was involved in an evaluation project conducted by the university and the City of Phoenix of the Community Partnership of Phoenix, a citywide substance abuse program funded by the Federal Government. I serve on the Maricopa County Community AIDS Partnership. Nationally, I have served as Chair of the Commission on Ethnic Minority Groups for the Council on Social Work Education, and on the Board of Directors of the National Center for Social Policy and Practice for the National Association of Social Workers. At present, I am working with the Superintendent of the Phoenix Union High School District (composed primarily of minorities usually at odds with one another) on a project that seeks to transform the district's orientation from an employee-centered to a student-centered organization.

Until the end of May 1995, I worked for the City of Phoenix as part of the university's loaned executive program. A colleague from ASU West and I conducted an assessment of the City's youth programs and participated in various projects sponsored by individual departments, including Parks, Recreation and Library, Human Services, and Fire. This experience has increased my awareness of the need for the academic community to keep in touch with the dramatic changes occurring in the public sector. It also has resulted in two articles that address the difficulties bureaucracies confront in collaboration. In one of our articles we examine the process of a failed collaboration involving a steering committee appointed to address the issue of youth at risk. We concluded that the Steering Committee failed fundamentally because the central players did not believe in the importance of collaboration in spite of the literature that tells us that the problems of youth are interrelated and that only planned, integrated interventions can work. This failure could be explained in technical terms: that is, because necessary structural arrangements were not established or because the group's rules were not clearly explained to the participants. In our judgment, however, the failure resulted primarily because most of the participants did not believe in the need for collaboration.

In the development of the courses I have taught on public policy issues, on minorities, "youth at risk," and welfare and education, it is clear that careful attention has to be paid to conflict among groups—racial and ethnic, men and women, and sexual identification all perceiving their environment as a zero-sum game. The changes occurring in society without clear paradigms for change have forced me to change my teaching approach to one that is more interactive, interdisciplinary, and focused on transformational change.

I think that a good way to continue and expand our dialogue is to examine the nature of our educational institutions and their impact on Chicanos and others. What is the ethos of the university environment? Is the university open to the types of changes needed to adapt to new circumstances? What changes do we have to undergo to make possible the kind of environment that we seem to be craving? I hope that our book will bring together people who are struggling with these same issues and help us to stop "talking past each other," which incidentally is the title of a paper I am writing on cultural diversity.

Raymond V. Padilla

My productions as an academic have been strongly influenced by family, cultural, and historical forces that have given shape and meaning to my work. As an immigrant to the United States, my childhood and youth were colored by the experience of dislocation and adaptation to a new and challenging environment. During my junior high and high school years, I became a member of the Sputnik generation when the national concern was for increased production of scientists, mathematicians, and engineers. I participated in various programs for the "academically talented" and thus enjoyed an enriched learning environment. I graduated as valedictorian of my high school class and everyone, including myself, expected me to become an electronic engineer.

I did start my college career as an engineer, but I attended a small liberal arts college that placed strong emphasis on the "great books" curriculum. As a result, my interest shifted to the humanities and the social sciences. Personal interest led me to study Spanish language and literature. During the two years that I spent in a small liberal arts college, I became thoroughly immersed in the classics and in the history of Western institutions and thought. However, my early interest in engineering and technology was never abandoned and is manifested today in my extensive use of computers and other advanced technologies in research and teaching.

Starting during the midsixties and lasting for about a decade, the United States went through a cultural revolution that was driven by the antiwar movement, the civil rights movement, and the youth movement that expressed itself in countercultural terms. As a participant in all of these social movements at a time of intellectual formation, my thinking, values, and commitments show this influence from the sixties. Following a two-year term in the Army during the Vietnam War, I completed my undergraduate degree in Spanish at the University of Michigan. At Michigan, my liberal arts education was completed, along with a thorough introduction to the world of serious scholarship. I took advantage of the enormously talented faculty of this great university and took courses from such distinguished scholars as Charles Gibson (Latin American history), Eric Wolfe (anthropology), and José Durand (Latin American literature); in addition, I took courses in various fields such as psychology, political science, economics, and sociology. These studies complemented my formal

major in Spanish language and literature where I studied with first rate
professors, such as Edward Glaser, Lawrence Kiddle, José Durand, Charles
Fraker, and others. At the end of my undergraduate degree, I was invited
to apply for graduate study in the Spanish department, but by then my
interests had shifted and I decided to pursue a career in a professional field
rather than a discipline. However, my strong preparation in Spanish
language, literature, and linguistics was to have a lasting influence in my
academic work.

I shifted to the field of education, with special emphasis in higher
education, and enrolled in a doctoral program at the University of California at Berkeley. Here I made a complete transition to the social sciences and
further developed my interest in serious scholarly work. However, I
applied all of my energy to improving the educational attainment of U.S.
Hispanics, Chicanos in particular. I soon realized that in order to pursue my
objectives I would have to gain a strong grounding in Chicano history and
culture, something that was not readily available at the time. This inclined
me to join the pioneering groups of Chicano scholars who were setting the
foundations for much of what today is recognized as Chicano scholarship.
My earliest intellectual productions appeared in *El Grito*, a journal that
made fundamental contributions to Chicano thought and scholarship. At
the same time, I realized that successful completion of my doctoral program would require total immersion in research methods and in the
overarching theories that drive inquiry. This led me to study with historians, sociologists, political scientists, anthropologists, psychologists, and
educators. Out of this experience, I became interested in qualitative research methods and in the critical assessment of the intellectual and
ideological frameworks within which research is typically conducted. A
strong and intellectually powerful institution, U.C. Berkeley was an almost
ideal place for me to develop fully as an academic under the tutelage of a
clinical psychologist (Paul Heist), a political scientist (Lyman Glenny), and
a teacher educator (James Stone), along with a small group of Chicano
professors, such as don Octavio Romano, and graduate students in various
fields, such as Reynaldo Baca, Miguel Montiel, and Nicolás Vaca.

At the completion of my graduate training, I realized that I was
committed to a career in higher education. At that time I set an unusual goal
for myself: to excel, over a lifetime, in the three fundamental activities of a
university—research, teaching, and administration. Had I been in a traditional discipline, this probably would have been an impractical goal. But
the field of higher education, where the university becomes both a workplace and a field setting, made it practical for me to pursue this goal. My
chosen field also made it possible for me to enrich my academic work with
Chicano projects of practical importance and to infuse the latter with

academic substance.

Throughout the mid-to-late seventies, after completing my doctorate, I accepted a series of appointments that usually put me face to face with very difficult and complex situations that required the analytic skills of a trained academic and the practicality of an engineer. In 1975 I learned a great deal about Chicano politics after spending a few months in a Chicano alternative university in Fresno, California. Later that same year, I joined the Michigan Department of Education as a higher education consultant and state coordinator for Latino education. There I learned some valuable lessons on how to implement highly theoretical and abstract ideas in a world that is full of practical limitations and political constraints. In short, I got a thorough introduction to the field of public policy and administration. In 1977 I was hired to direct the bilingual teacher training programs at Eastern Michigan University. There I found myself in a field that lacked strong scholarship and theoretical foundations, not unlike the experience I had already gone through with Chicano Studies. So I put my academic skills to work in shaping and advancing research and development in this field. My background in languages and research was essential to the success of this enterprise. My second wave of publications dates from this period. These publications focus on three distinct areas: (1) development of frameworks and paradigms to advance the field in general; (2) specific studies in policy analysis; and (3) technical papers dealing with specific issues in language and linguistics.

When I went to Arizona State University in 1982, my interest in bilingual education continued, but I also returned to my earlier scholarly interests in higher education and qualitative methodology. This was accompanied by a renewed interest in computers and in furthering research in Chicano Studies, one of the disciplinary foundations for the advancement of Chicano education. My publications of the last ten years reflect these multiple interests. In a way, the past decade represents a maturing of interests that were already evident during the previous decade: Chicano studies, bilingual education, higher education, multidisciplinary theoretical perspectives, and technical studies that reflect my interest in computers and linguistics. At the same time, I have been assiduously following my goal of excelling in the three major activities of an accomplished university person: research, teaching, and administration. By choice, the focus of this triad has been on issues of concern to Chicanos but with studious attention to the larger environment. The present volume brings critical analysis to bear on issues that were already raised in an earlier volume titled *The Leaning Ivory Tower: Latino Professors in American Universities* that was coedited by Rudolfo Chávez Chávez and me.